COUNTDOWN TO THE FUTURE

by

Barbara H. Martin

ISBN:0966805496

Cover design by
Selfpubbookcovers.com/Frina Art

Barbara's picture on back cover
By
Jessica Forinash

DEDICATED

To my friend Karin Berley

Chapter 1

"We interrupt our regular program with this important USN Headline News Alert. The Secretary of State, Herbert Downy, in a short statement to the press a few moments ago, has confirmed that Iran has declared war on the state of Israel. Due to the volatile and dangerous situation in the Middle East, he has issued a travel advisory for all US citizen for the entire region. All air traffic between the US and the Middle East has been suspended as of now. All non-essential personal in Israel and most of the Middle Eastern countries have been ordered to leave immediately via special military transportation. All other American citizens are urged to contact the State Department or the American Consulate in order to be evacuated immediately. Secretary Downey emphasized that it is entirely possible that any delay might make it impossible for the State Department to be of any assistance later, due to the possibility of nuclear war in the region.

When asked if the White House is seriously considering the possibility of a nuclear confrontation, the Secretary declined to answer and promised more information as soon as it becomes available.

Stay tuned as USN Headline News, as always, will bring you the latest updates as soon as we have them. This is Marsha Kendrick with USN Headline News."

Three Years earlier.

Thomas Peterson, MD entered the surgical suite with an uneasy feeling. It was as if he had been gone for three years when he looked around the gleaming, sterile environment with a mixture of awe and a certain feeling of nostalgia. What a difference a day makes! It had only been yesterday since he had walked the crowded streets of Jerusalem and watched the most famous trial and crucifixion in the history of the world.

There was a lump in his throat when he thought about his little girl Helena, his friend Lucius and the many people he encountered on his treacherous journey through ancient Israel. He would never see them again.

His heart took an extra beat when the picture of Yeshua appeared in his mind with crystal clarity. His warm, brown eyes and knowing, wonderful smile of unconditional love would always be with him. Yeshua's last words were seared into his mind as if etched in stone. "As the Father has sent me, I am sending you." And with that he breathed on him and said, "Receive the Holy Spirit." (John 20:21-22)

The words of the old man Jonah at the wedding at Cana appeared with equal power. "You are a stranger in this land and are filled with unbelief. And yet the Lord Jehovah shows me that you will see the Glory of His coming and be touched by Him in a special way. Turn from your doubts and prepare your heart for He will anoint you to take His message into a distant land and time."

The words of John the Baptist in the prison fortress of Machaerus were even more specific.

"You have seen the Meshiah, Thomas, I am sure of it. You have been sent by the God of Abraham, Isaac and Jacob to behold His Son and believe, for He will use you greatly in the far distant future. Do not resist Him, but repent for He has chosen you to serve Him in a different age."

How would he tell his family, his colleagues and especially his grandmother? They would mock him and Nana would be heartbroken that he left the Jewish faith to become a Christian.

Thomas suddenly realized everyone was looking at him with a strange look, because he was standing motionless, staring at nowhere in particular with a scalpel in his hand. He cleared his throat with an embarrassed little cough and held out his hand to the surgical nurse next to him.

"Scalpel, please."

She looked at him with obvious surprise.

"You already have it, Doctor."

"Of course, thank you Brenda."

With a certain amount of bewilderment, he noticed the absence of the adrenaline rush he usually felt as he guided the scalpel with steady, sure hands. He had no doubt he was still an excellent surgeon, but there was not the sense of accomplishment or pride connected with it that had been there only yesterday. A little smile crossed his face, hidden by the mask. He realized his priorities had changed dramatically since he accepted the Carpenter of Nazareth as his Meshiah during his dramatic dream.

"Brenda, you did a good job," he turned to the nurse when he was finished. "Thank you."

"I am surprised you noticed, Dr. Peterson," she said as they walked out of the surgical suite. "I have been assisting you for two years and you have never mentioned it before."

"I know and I am sorry." He looked at her with a warm smile. "It's time I do; don't you think?"

"What happened to you, Doctor? You are different; did you get religion?" She chuckled as she walked off without waiting for an answer.

It was late afternoon when his shiny, black BMW turned into the driveway of his large home surrounded by manicured landscaping in an upscale neighborhood. It was hard to imagine it had only been yesterday since he had come home to an empty house to find that his wife Melissa seemed to have forgotten his birthday. He had fixed himself a glass of wine and gone to sleep in his chair only to wake up in the market place of Nazareth in the year 27 A.D. Today, he still had difficulties separating the dream from reality and felt like he was in limbo between the past and the present. Nothing felt the same and he yearned for his life back then instead of living in the present. He had not shared his experience with anyone except Melissa.

As he got out of the car, he found himself wishing it was his horse-drawn carriage and shook his head in confusion. It had taken only an hour-long dream for his life to be turned upside down and shake everything he had ever believed in. He was still in shock over the appearance of the missing toe on his left foot when he woke up. It was a birth defect and its miraculous appearance proved beyond a shadow of a doubt, that what he had experienced was real. Still, it felt like the Twilight Zone.

"We are invited to your parents' house for dinner, honey. I guess they want to celebrate your birthday," Melissa said as she kissed him with great affection. "Are you going to share with them about what happened?"

He looked at his wife with a deep love he had not felt for several years. Their feelings for each other had returned when he returned and it was still a wonder to him.

"I don't know. It's all still so new to me. I was actually going to read the Bible tonight to see if the things I experienced are really in there."

"Trust me, from what you told me, they are. Every single one of them." Melissa smiled at him. "You are an eyewitness to what happened during Jesus' ministry here on this earth. I don't think I will ever get used to that." She looked at Thomas with sudden concern. "What do you think your parents are going to say?"

"I have some idea and that's why I dread telling them. I wouldn't blame them if they thought I have lost my mind; if it wasn't for my toe I would agree with them." He suddenly laughed. "Imagine, Yeshua wants me to use a toe to share about Him."

"I think this miracle is undeniable, especially for your parents. They will not be able to doubt your experience," Melissa said with conviction. "Let's face it, your father has the same birth defect and your mother definitely knows about both of you. So how can they not believe you?"

"You don't know my parents. They scoff at anything religious and take great pride in science to dispel faith of any kind," he answered as he got a glass of milk out of the fridge.

"And how in the world can they explain your toe with their precious science; answer me that?"

"I don't know, but trust me, they will manage." His voice took on a hint of confusion as he went on. "How am I supposed to explain it to them or to the rest of the world when I don't even understand it all? The great Chief of Thoracic Surgery at Philadelphia Mercy Hospital suddenly believes in God and miracles, because he went back to 27 A.D. and met Jesus, the Messiah." He looked at Melissa with a look of doubt. "Even I find that hard to believe; and I was there."

"The Lord will be there with you, Thomas. He will give you the words, don't you worry." Melissa hugged him and then kissed him on the cheek. "It will be alright, honey. You are not the one who has to convince people of what happened. All you have to do is share your experience and then let the Holy Spirit do the rest." She took his hand and led him to the couch in the living room.

"That is why God gave you the dream, so you can "go into all the world and preach the Gospel"."

"So you think Jesus wants me to be a preacher?" He cringed at the thought. "I have no intention of ever doing that."

"Then what do you think He wants you to do with what happened?" Melissa looked at him with astonishment and disappointment.

"I don't know. In a way I wish I was back there, because everyone believed what happened and didn't expect me to become religious." He leaned back with a sigh. "This is all too new and confusing and I really don't want to talk about it to anyone until I have gotten used to the whole idea of being a Christian." He looked at Melissa with pleading eyes. "Can you understand that?"

"I can, honey. The Lord will show you what to say and when to say it. If you don't want to go tonight, I will call and tell your parents we can't make it. It was short notice anyway."

"No, I somehow feel I haven't seen them in a long time." He smiled. "Like for three years maybe?"

"I will admit that sounds pretty crazy." She got up, "Let's get ready then."

Chapter 2

"Come on in you two." Thomas' mother was a petit woman in her mid-sixties with a short, stylish haircut which brought out her brown, intelligent eyes. Her tasteful make-up could not hide the signs of age, although, with her mauve lipstick matching her expensive silk blouse worn over equally expensive, black pants, she was still a beautiful woman. "It has been a long time since the two of you have come for dinner." She hugged Melissa with a fleeting hug and then kissed Thomas on the cheek in a distant sort of way. Sylvia Peterson was not a warm person. "Happy Birthday, Thomas," she added almost as an afterthought.

"Thank you, Mother, it is good to see you," Thomas said and walked passed her inside.

"Hi, Sylvia, how are you?" Melissa said with a forced smile as she followed Thomas. Her mother-in-law intimidated her to no end.

"Your father is waiting in the library, Thomas. Why don't you two join him there while I see that Collette handles things in the kitchen correctly."

Abraham Peterson, MD was a big man with a full shock of curly, white hair. His kind, brown eyes stood out in spite of thick eyebrows with a mustache to match. He was a man of substance with his tall, slender stature and the graceful, elegant way he carried himself.

"How good to see you, son. Happy Birthday." he said as he held Thomas with an affectionate hug. "I miss you, it's been too long." He turned to Melissa with equal warmth and gave her one of his bear hugs. "It's been even longer since I have seen you, girl. Where have you been keeping yourself?"

"Abraham, I am so glad to see you. I agree, it has been too long." She had liked her father-in-law from the start, in contrast to his wife Sylvia, whom she never managed to get close to in spite of a lot of effort on her part.

Collette, the housekeeper, brought in a beautifully arranged platter with crackers covered with cheese and shrimp salad surrounded by grapes.

"This will keep you and the Missus going till dinner, Thomas," she said in a beautiful southern drawl. Her face, red with her efforts in the kitchen, shone with delight as she pushed back a strand of unruly, red hair to match.

"Collette, you are the best," Thomas said as he reached for the food. "You look gorgeous as ever."

"And you are ever the charmer," she answered with a blush. "But I still like it, even if I know you are lying." She smiled at him with great affection. "Just remember, I wiped your nose and much more not that many years ago."

"Collette says she is going to retire. Life wouldn't be the same around here," Abraham said after she had gone back to the kitchen. "She is seventy now and we can't expect her to stay on much longer." He pointed to a leather couch with two matching chairs arranged in front of a fireplace surrounded on both sides by book shelves up to the ceiling.

"Sit down, kids, I have something I want to share with you." He pointed to the couch and then took a seat in a chair. "Your mother and I have been talking about this for a long time and agree it is time for me to retire."

"Dad, what are you going to do with yourself if you don't have your practice?" Thomas asked, worried. "Medicine is your life."

"I know, but life has a way of making you take notice of the signs of age, son. It is time your mother and I take some time and travel or do some of the things we've always wanted to do." He shifted in his seat. "This brings me to the real reason I wanted you to come tonight. I want you to take over my practice, Thomas. You are a skilled surgeon and I have every confidence you could do exceedingly well. Your skills are better than mine, especially considering my age. It is time I put down the scalpel and let you take over, what do you think?" He looked at Thomas with confident expectation.

Thomas cleared his throat and hesitated before he answered,

"Dad, I appreciate your confidence in me, but I am afraid I have other plans for my life. I don't know anything specific yet, all I know is that I am supposed to do something I have no idea how to do." His voice sounded shaky and he had a hard time looking at his father, knowing he didn't make any sense.

"What on earth are you talking about?" It was his mother. "How could you possibly turn down your fathers' generous gift after he has spent his life building up his practice so he can turn it over to you when the time comes. And the time is here, Thomas." She looked at him with a steely, hard expression. "How dare you think you can just walk away because you have some vague plans of your own." She sounded angry as she stepped next to her husband. "Say something, Abraham."

"You are my only son, Thomas, I have done all this for you," his father said with great sadness in his voice. "Would you mind telling us what it is you want to do?"

"I told you I don't know exactly what it is, Dad. All I know, I have no real choice but to do it," Thomas said in a faltering voice. "I am so sorry, but for now you will have to accept this as my choice."

"You are not making any sense, Thomas." His mother's voice was sharp and cold. "I expect you to come to your senses and do your duty as a good son. We are Jews and that means we take care of our parents and family before all else," she added.

"It's funny you should say that, Mother." Thomas was getting his bearing back. "You have never given our Jewish heritage a lot of thought as long as I can remember. If it wasn't for Nana, I would know nothing about being a Jew.

"While we are not as fanatic as Nana, both your father and I know who we are and where we come from and we expect you to do the same."

"Don't worry, I have every intention of doing just that. As a matter of fact, I plan to move to Israel and live there and share with my people about Yeshua, the Meshiah who came two thousand years ago to die on the cross for my people. I will also tell them that He rose from the dead just like the Christians believe, in order to make it possible for all of us to spend eternity with Him." Thomas leaned back into the couch with a deep sigh, afraid to look at his parents.

A stunned silence filled the room. Finally, his mother spoke, barely able to restrain her anger.

"Have you gone completely mad?" And then she turned to Melissa. "This is your doing. You finally managed to influence our son to become a Christian. How dare you! I never wanted you to marry him, but as long as you left him alone with your ridiculous religion I didn't say anything." She looked at Melissa with open hostility. "How dare you!"

"Mother, Melissa didn't say anything to me," Thomas interrupted before she could go on. "I had a dream yesterday in which I was transported to the market place of Nazareth in ancient Israel to the year 27 A.D. and walked the land for three years. There I met the Carpenter from Nazareth who showed me that He is the Messiah." Thomas bent over to remove his left shoe and sock and held his bare foot up for his parents to see. "Here, to show you the dream was real, I now have five toes on my foot. Look, Yeshua gave me my missing toe."

Abraham and Sylvia leaned over to have a closer look, still too stunned to say anything.

"Did you have surgery somewhere without telling us?" his mother finally managed to say. "How else is this possible."

"Check it, Father and tell me if that looks like a toe was surgically added," Thomas said. "You are a surgeon, you ought to know." He held his foot up to his father.

Abraham reached for his glasses in his breast pocket and leaned over to look at it for a long time.

"My God, Thomas, this is remarkable. Whoever did this is a genius. I can see no scars of any kind. Is this the doctor you are going to work with instead of taking over my practice?"

"Father, for heaven's sake, look closer. There are no scars, no signs that anyone added a toe! I am telling you, I was healed by Jesus in my dream and this is the sign that what I experienced was real." Thomas was almost shouting.

"I am sorry, son, what you are saying is ludicrous on so many levels, it defies the imagination."

"Will you believe me if I get your friend Mark Reider to examine my foot and confirm that my additional toe was not surgically added?"

"There is no way you will embarrass us by involving our friends in this, Thomas." It was his mother. "I will not allow it under any circumstances! It would make us the laughing stock of the medical community."

"I have to agree with your mother, Thomas," Abraham said with sadness in his voice. "You seem to have gone through an emotional trauma that has produced hallucinations. I can ask a very good psychiatrist in Chicago to treat you. They have made tremendous advances in the field in the last few years."

"Father, I am not delusional and neither did I have a psychotic brake." He was shouting. "All you have to do is accept that I now have five toes instead of four like you; and without surgery. Why would that be so hard to accept? There is no way you can deny that there are no scars or any other signs that it was added by a surgeon, can you?"

"Abraham, I will not allow you to embarrass us among our social circle by going along with this ridiculous story," Sylvia said in a steely voice. She turned to Thomas. "Under the circumstances, I must ask you and your wife to leave. This is simply too upsetting for your father and I. I can't even imagine what it will do to Nana when she hears you have become a Christian."

On the way out, Abraham looked at Thomas with profound sadness mixed with confusion.

"Remember, Thomas, I love you," he said in a low voice so his wife could not hear him. "Your mother didn't mean it. She'll come around, you'll see."

Abraham stood in the door, suddenly looking very old as his eyes followed their car down the driveway.

"I told you they wouldn't believe me or accept what happened to my foot," Thomas said into the silence on the way home.

"I was surprised to hear you say that we will move to Israel and preach to the Jews. Were you going to tell me about that any time soon?" Melissa sounded hurt.

"I had no idea until I heard myself say it. I am just as surprised as you are and have no idea where that came from." Thomas looked at her confused.

"I am sure the Holy Spirit had something to do with it." She smiled at him. "It sounds exciting to me. When are we leaving?"

"This is crazy. I wouldn't even know where to go or what to do." He shook his head. "I can't just fly to Israel and walk the streets and start preaching, I will get arrested."

"God will make a way if you really mean it about obeying Him. And if you are, then He will have to bring it about. We will just have to wait and see when and how He is going to do it." Melissa sounded confident.

"This is no way to do business, if you ask me," Thomas said. "It reminds me of when I talked to His disciples. They seemed a bunch of uneducated, simple men totally unsuited for the job of spreading the Gospel."

"But they did, didn't they?" Melissa answered with a grin. "Just think what He can do with a smart man like you, Dr. Peterson."

"I didn't sound so smart with my parents, did I? Even with a real miracle as proof, they still didn't believe me and disowned me just like I knew they would." He sounded frustrated and sad at the same time. "I think my dad would have tried at least, but I guess Mom wouldn't allow it. She has always run his life for as long as I can remember."

"If you ask me, they sounded more scared than anything else," Melissa said. "Think about it, you threatened everything they have believed for seventy some years; and then you rejected them when they wanted you to take over their life's work. You will admit, that's pretty upsetting. Give it time, they'll come around." She touched his arm in a loving gesture. "I know they love you and are proud of what you have accomplished. Can you blame them if they are upset that you are willing to throw it all away for a religion they hate? Think about it, only yesterday you would have agreed with them without hesitation."

Chapter 3

In the weeks that followed, Thomas spent many hours after work reading the New Testament and there, to his astonishment, he found every one of the incidents he had experienced in his dream. It was a strange, yet exhilarated feeling to read the full account of Jesus' ministry written by his friend Lucius in the book of Luke and Acts. He wished he could tell him what a special purpose he fulfilled for countless of millions of people over the centuries. Yet to Thomas he would always be his friend Lucius, who stood by him throughout the many trials during the three years he spent with him.

"When I was with Lucius he never mentioned a man names Theophilus," he said to Melissa. "I wonder why?"

"Maybe he didn't know him yet when you were there," she said. "Just like he didn't know the apostle Paul at that time."

"I cannot tell you how strange it is to have been there and then read about it in the Bible. It is like Lucius wrote a diary for me and God saved it for two thousand years for me to read it."

They were on the road to the outskirts of the City to see his grandmother. He was extremely nervous considering the way his parents had reacted to his story.

"What if she disowns me as well," he said to Melissa. "It would make me feel worse than it did when Mom and Dad asked us to leave." He sighed deeply. "I love Nana. She has been the one who loved me the way my mother never did."

"I don't think she will ever disown you, honey. She may not like what you tell her, but she would never reject you. She may even be convinced by the toe on your foot that you are speaking the truth." Melissa sounded so sure. He wished he was.

"I wonder if my parents told her about it," he said as they drove up to the front of the high-rise condominium in an upscale, new area of Philadelphia. "I can't make up my mind if that would be good or bad," he added.

"Good to see you, Dr. and Mrs. Peterson. Your grandmother is doing fine; I just saw her in the lobby this morning." The doorman tipped his hat with big smile.

Thank you, Ben," Melissa answered with friendly nod. "You keep up with the place, don't you?"

"That I do ma'am; it's part of my job."

Thomas felt nervous as they rode up to the 17th floor in the plush, quiet elevator.

Lord, don't let me lose my Nana, please. He took a deep breath as he knocked on her door.

"Tommy, my boy, how good to see you. I have been worried about you." She smiled as he put his arms around her.

"Nana, it's so good to see you." Thomas looked at her with great affection. "I love you."

"I love you, too, Tommy." She was a tall woman with silver-grey hair and intense blue eyes. Her face was a profusion of wrinkles which radiated kindness and warmth as she looked at Melissa. "How good to see you, dear. You look happy. I haven't seen that on you in a while." She waved for both of them to follow her into the spacious living room and pointed to a couch facing a large window overlooking the skyline of Philadelphia in the distance. "Let me fix you a cup of coffee and then you must taste the lemon cake I baked just for you two. I know it's your favorite, Tommy."

"Nana, we have come to tell you a story," Thomas said after they had finished eating. "Please, promise me you will listen and not think that I am crazy or had a psychotic episode like Dad tried to tell me."

"Your mother mentioned that you had some kind of a nervous breakdown, but wouldn't go into details. That's why I called you and asked you to come and see me. I am worried about you. What was she talking about?"

"You know how Mom is, Nana. I am perfectly fine and there is nothing wrong with me." Thomas took her hand and held it for a moment. "It is hard for me to talk to her sometimes."

"She is a force to be reckoned with I suppose when she disagrees with you, I know. Abraham has always had his hands full with her. I told him from the start she would not be easy to handle when he told your Papa he wanted to marry her; but he was smitten with her." She looked out the window as her thoughts wandered into the past. "She was a beauty, there was no denying it."

"Nana, Melissa and I have come to tell you something very important and I want you to promise me you will listen to what I have to say without interruption."

"Of course I will, Tommy. If it is important to you, I will listen." Her smile reminded him of his father. The older he got, the more he looked like her.

It took quite a while until he finished sharing about his dream and his newfound faith in Jesus. He ended up by telling her about his plans to go to Israel. His grandmother sat motionless, her strong, slender hands folded in her lap.

"I am not surprised your mother thinks you are having a nervous breakdown, Tommy. Although I don't agree with her, I am totally shocked at what you are telling me. However, I am convinced you are telling the truth as you see it. You have always been a man of science and not given to wild emotions or telling lies. But this, I must say is a bit hard to swallow."

"Do you believe me, Nana?" He held his breath.

"You are asking me to throw away my heritage and faith as a Jew and believe that this Jesus, who I believe to be a heretic, is my Messiah." She looked at Thomas with profound sadness. "I can't do that, because it would go against everything I have strongly believed in all my life."

"Nana, I understand and would never have told you about this except for this." He bent over and slowly took his shoe and sock off of his left foot and held it out to her. "This Jesus, whom I believe to be our Jewish Messiah, gave me my fifth toe. Look, Nana."

She leaned forward with a look of astonishment.

"Thomas, you have five toes on your foot! How can that be?" She stared at his foot. "I was there when your father was born and when you were born. Both of you have only four toes on your left foot." She looked at Thomas. "This cannot be, what happened?"

"Nana, I went to sleep like I told you before after I came home from work one day and when I woke up after an hour, my left foot had five toes on it. Jesus did that to let me and others know that my dream was real and He is the Messiah just like the Christians say He is."

There was silence in the room as his grandmother tried to comprehend what she was seeing and hearing. Finally, she asked,

"Tell me again what you saw in your dream, Tommy?"

"I was transported to the market place in Nazareth in Galilee in the year 27 A.D. and lived there for the next three years. While there I found out what a prideful, arrogant man I really was when I met the Carpenter called Yeshua. In spite of my disbelief in Him and my terrible failings in every way with those around me, He loved me with a wonderful, deep love and healed me of leprosy when I was dying. Before I woke up from my dream, He filled me with His Holy Spirit and told me to go and tell His people that He came for them and to accept Him as their Meshiah, because time is short."

Nana looked at Thomas with a mixture of astonishment and doubt.

"Are you telling me this Jesus is who the Christians say He is, the long awaited One of the Jews?"

"Yes, Nana, how can you or I doubt it when you look at my foot?"

She looked at Melissa with an almost pleading look and said, "You knew this all the time, didn't you?"

"Yes Nana, I did. He is the Son of God, sent into the world to save us from our sin. It is explained in the book of John in the New Testament with these words,

"God so loved the world that he gave his one and only Son that whoever believes in him shall not perish, but have everlasting life." (John 3:16)

"Nana, I saw the miracles He did and the love He had for those who crucified Him," Thomas said, leaning toward her. "I also saw Him after He rose from the dead and walked among us. Nana, He is alive today and wants you to accept Him into your heart as your Messiah. Do you want to do that?"

She looked at Thomas with astonishment mixed with sorrow and said,

"He came two thousand years ago and my people missed Him and killed the One Yahweh sent as He promised in Isaiah. I know the Torah and have read the scriptures about the One who will set my people free." She continued as tears streamed down her face, "Now thank the God of Abraham, Isaak and Jacob for letting me live long enough to know my Meshiah." Slowly, a radiant smile made her eyes light up and she leaned toward Thomas. "Blessed are you, Thomas, for having been chosen to go to my people Israel to show them their Redeemer." She motioned for him to come closer. He knelt before her as she laid her hands on his head and continued in a clear, authoritative voice. "The God of Abraham, Isaak and Jacob gives you His anointing and will open doors for you to go in His Name and tell our people about their Meshiah Yeshua. Go, Thomas and do not be afraid. Go and fulfill the purpose for which He has raised you up; and He will be with you till the end."

Her voice and manner reminded Thomas of Jonah, his slave Abraham and John the Baptist; and he realized God was prophesying through his Nana in the same way.

"Does that mean you believe in Him?" Thomas looked up at her beaming face. "I do, Tommy, I do. Maybe you, Melissa can help me understand more and explain what is written in the Christian Bible."

"Your Torah is a part of it, Nana as well as the accounts of the life of Jesus in the four Gospels. The rest of the New Testament was written by different writers who explain further how the Lord wants us to live according to the words of His Son Jesus." Melissa knelt beside Thomas and looked up at the old woman. "Would you give me your blessing as well so I can go with my husband to the land of Israel and take the Good News to those who will listen?"

Nana put her hands on Melissa's head and said in that same tone, "You shall be by his side and together you will fulfill the purpose Yahweh has for you. The journey will not be easy and many trials await you, but God will be with you, never fear."

Thomas and Melissa remained sitting at Nana's feet after she was finished praying.

"Maybe you can go to a Bible study with me on Thursdays every week. Gloria is a good teacher and can answer the many questions you must have," Melissa said, looking up at her.

"That sounds great, I can't wait." Nana sounded excited.

"What are you going to tell the congregation at your synagogue, Nana?" Thomas asked her, sipping his coffee. "What do you think they are going to say?"

"I am going to tell them nothing for a while until I know and understand more of this. I will continue to go there and listen with new understanding when they read out of the Torah." She took a deep breath. "I still can't believe that an old woman like me would have such favor with the Lord that He would take notice of me and let me know the Redeemer of Israel." She leaned back in her chair with a happy sigh.

Chapter 4

The room grew silent the moment Thomas walked in. Everyone tried hard not to look at him as he took his seat at the head of the table. *They know. Oh God!* He pretended not to notice as he opened the folder in front of him.

"Good Morning," he finally said and looked up and cringed when he saw their looks of curiosity mixed with a benign feeling of pity. The great Dr. Peterson got religion! These were most of the surgeons in his department of Thoracic Surgery. He counted ten of them. Some were interns, some residents and three attending. Mark Kosack was the only one who was a Fellow and his archrival, the one who had been extremely upset when Thomas was made the youngest Chief of his department ever at the large Philadelphia Mercy Hospital. He noticed a sarcastic smile on Kosack's face as he continued with the routine meeting on this Monday morning.

"We have a full schedule this week and I want to go over every one of the surgeries. You have your assignments. Make sure you check carefully if you have the intern you want. I would like to ask that you remember that this is a teaching hospital. That means you teach instead of discussing other people's business." He raised himself up in his seat as he stared at the group of men and women in front of him. He noticed some of the doctors staring down at their paperwork, avoiding his looks.

"I can't blame them with the news of you becoming the latest miracle worker, Thomas." It was Mark Kosack. "We are all wondering if what we hear is true about you being a time traveler who makes toes miraculously appear."

There was snickering around the table. Thomas had no idea what to say and wondered if he should ignore the remark. There was no doubt he had become the talk of the hospital and realized, he would have to address the issue sooner or later. He took a deep breath before he spoke.

"No matter what I say about this subject, I have no doubt it will be met with ridicule and sarcasm; so I will stick to the only fact that is indisputable." His voice got stronger and more confident as he went on. "Some of you know that I have a left foot with only four toes. There can be no doubt it was an inherited birth defect from my father. It bothered me a great deal as a kid and in High School, even in college." He cleared his throat and then bent over and took off his left shoe and sock and held it out for everyone to see. "I am sure you all realize what a great surgeon I am, but even I, nor anyone else, can do this without leaving a scar or any other signs of surgery." He looked at them with an open, friendly smile. "You be the judge. It is true, that I have become a Christian, because I did have an encounter with Jesus in a very miraculous way." He leaned back in his chair after he had put his shoe and sock back on and continued. "It is up to you what you want to do with what I have told you. I am a man of science and yet nothing in science can explain what happened to me. All I can say is, I had four toes one day and an hour later, after a vivid dream, I now have five." His voice had a sudden softness about it they had never heard in him and realized that something had changed him.

"I would like to hear more about this, Thomas," Kelly Anderson, a third year resident said into the stunned silence.

"I would, too," another said.

"So now everyone is going to get religion around here, is that it?" Mark Kosack said with a loud, angry voice. "I don't care what you say, Peterson, this whole thing is ludicrous and has no place in this hospital. I think you should give up your day job and become a preacher or something." He got up and walked out and slammed the door behind him.

"For those who want to find out more details, get with me and we can meet after hours. Mark is right, this is not the place." Thomas closed his folder and got up from his seat. "Let's get going. We have a lot of surgeries to do today." Without waiting for an answer, he walked out.

"Dr. Peterson, may I talk to you for a minute?" The voice belonged to a man standing in the hallway, holding a mop. "My name is Mikail Rochenko. I would like to talk to you when you have a minute." The man spoke with a heavy Russian accent.

"What can I do for you, Mikail," Thomas said. "I don't have long, I'm on my way to surgery."

"I am sorry to bother you, but the Lord told me to speak with you."

Thomas stood very still.

"What is it you want to talk to me about?" He held his breath.

"God told me you are going to the land of Israel very soon and will need someone who speaks Hebrew," he said in a quiet voice.

"You're kidding, right?" Thomas knew instantly this was from the Lord.

"I am a Russian Jew who was raised speaking Hebrew, Sir. I came to this country two years ago, because I knew I would be needed for something important. I never knew what it was until today when I saw you walking down the hall toward me." He looked at Thomas with sudden doubt. "If I am wrong, please tell me and I will not bother you again." He started to walk away when Thomas stopped him.

"I am absolutely certain that the Lord sent you. Please, give me your phone number and I will call you as soon as I can." Thomas took a sheet of paper out of his folder. "Write it down right here and wait for may call."

It was late afternoon before Thomas finished with his last surgery. Conversation during the procedures was kept to a minimum, since no one knew what to say to a doctor who claimed he talked to Jesus two thousand years ago and got a new toe in the bargain. The hospital was buzzing with the news and the more often the story was told, the more bizarre it became. Thomas felt like he was in the eye of a hurricane, since no one dared to approach him with the subject. He had a lot of time to think about Mikail Rochenko, the man with the broom, as he performed his surgeries. Thomas was not surprised Yeshua would use a member of the cleaning crew to help him, given the down and outers who served Him during His ministry. Once again, he felt like he was in limbo between the past and the presence. *What would Lucius think if he could see me in this gleaming, sterile, modern environment?* He smiled under his mask when he realized, his friend became one of the most famous writers of the New Testament, which was a lot more important than being a mere surgeon among thousands. He had a long way to go to get rid of his pride.

"We have been un-invited from the Garden Party at Dr. Mendelson's, Thomas," Melissa told him after he got home.

"What do you mean un-invited?"

"Mary Mendelson called me and made it clear, since they were Jews, it would be inappropriate to have us in their home, causing trouble with our newfound anti-Semitic religion."

"Well, after what I've heard around the hospital today, I doubt we have any friends left. We seem to have become outcasts. Why am I not surprised?" he added with a sigh. "This is a new world we live in and we better get used to it." He took Melissa and held her close. "It's just you and me, kid, what do you say?"

"This is the 21st Century, I'm astounded there is so much bigotry left when we want to be so enlightened," she answered with a sad little smile.

"Not much has changed since the time of Jesus, has it?" He chuckled. "We think our society is so open- minded until you are a Jew or a Christian. Anti-Jewish sentiment is on the rise in the US and in much of Europe these days, while in spite of what ISIS does, the Muslim religion is on the increase everywhere. For the life of me, I don't get it. The Western world is turning a blind eye on their past with WWII and refuses to see the bleak prospect if Sharia law takes over our free societies in the present." There was anger in his voice. "They thought they had problems with the Romans in ancient times, this is every bit as bad." He sounded angry.

Melissa walked over behind him and put her arms around his shoulders. "It looks like you have your job cut out for you, honey. It won't be easy to preach the Gospel to a world that has gone mad. But at the same time, Jesus is the only answer, because the world has run out of solutions."

"That reminds me, I have to call a man named Mikail Rochenko." He took out the piece of paper in his breast pocket and dialed the number. "Mikail, this is Dr. Peterson. Is there any way we can get together? You are welcome to come to my home, I want my wife to hear what you have to say." He held his hand over the phone and whispered," Melissa, is it ok if this man comes for dinner tonight?"

She nodded with a big question mark on her face.

"Mikail, why don't you come for dinner at seven and we will discuss what you told me." He nodded his head. "That sounds great. Let me give you the address and then we see you here at seven."

Mikail Rochenko arrived promptly at seven, dressed in what Thomas assumed was his best suit. He was a man in his mid-thirties with dark, curly brown hair. His prominent nose gave away his Jewish heritage. Intelligent brown eyes dominated his clean-shaven face. He was a small man, slender, with a friendly demeanor.

"Come on in, Mikail," Thomas said with a wave of his hand. "Dinner is just about ready," he added and led the way to the dining room. "Can I offer you a drink?"

"No thank you, Sir, I'm fine. It is an honor to be here." He acted nervous and out of place.

"This is my wife Melissa. She is a fine cook and I know you will like her famous fried lemon pepper chicken with baked potatoes and green beans."

"Welcome, Mikail, it is good to meet you. I am excited to hear what you have to share with us," Melissa said with a friendly smile as she put the food on the table. "Please have a seat right there." She pointed to a chair and they all sat down.

"Mikail, I am intrigued by what you told me at the hospital," Thomas said half way through the meal. Please tell us a little about yourself first and then we want to hear what you think the Lord is saying to you."

"Dr. Peterson, I would have never dreamed of speaking to you if the Lord had not wanted me to. Please forgive me if I was forward, but I knew I had to do it." He wiped his mouth with the napkin and went on. "I was born in Russia to Jewish parents who made me speak only Hebrew at home. They told me from childhood that I would have a special purpose for knowing that language, but never said why exactly. I am certain they did not have any idea." He looked at Thomas. "I still don't know why; all I know is that I had to talk to you about it." He smiled at Thomas and went on, "Five years ago the police came to our house and arrested my parents. I was not at home and found them gone when I returned. The neighbors told me what happened. My father had been a Rabbi until he accepted Jesus the year before. He was barred from the Synagogue and shunned by all our family and friends. When he started to speak openly about his faith in the streets of our city, he was threatened several times by the authorities to stop or be arrested. I did not accept his belief at first, but when I listened to my father as he explained the prophesies about the Messiah in the Torah, I joined him in his ministry when my job allowed it." He had finished his meal, but since no one made any move to leave the table, he continued with his story.

"Eventually, my father was set free and started his own church. The authorities did not bother with us for several years and the church grew. I gave up my job and helped him take care of the parishioners. Eventually, he became the only pastor in the area and we traveled to four other communities to meet once a week with the Christians there. It was on one of those trips, when he had taken my mother with him instead of me, a gang of the local Mafia stopped his car, killed them both and stole the vehicle. I never really found out any details, since the authorities were afraid of the powerful gangs. I knew one of their members from school, and he secretly informed me, that they planned to kill me as well, since I was urging the police to do something." He took a sip of water and went on.

"One night I looked out of the window and saw several motorcycles in front of my apartment building. I knew they had come for me. I had prepared a backpack for just this eventuality, filled with my legal documents and other necessities. Since it was summertime, I escaped out the back of the building and hiked across to the Finnish border and asked for asylum. They let me in and after a year, I was allowed to come to this country, where I found a job at Mercy Hospital as a janitor."

"What was your job before you gave it up?" Thomas asked.

"I was a lab technician in the large hospital of my city."

"That is quite a story, Mikail," Thomas said. "Why do you think the Lord had you talk to me today?"

"I don't know, Dr. Peterson. All I know is that when I saw you, the Lord wanted me to tell you that I speak Hebrew. I do not know why; but it must be important or you would not have invited me to your home." He smiled a shy little smile. "I also heard the story about your dream in the meantime and how you walked with Jesus and He gave you a toe when you woke up."

"I think everybody has heard about that." Melissa said as she put a bowl of fruit salad on the table.

"Would you like to go to Israel with us, Mikail?" Thomas asked. "Before you answer, there is a chance they might arrest you there for preaching the Gospel, the same way they did to your parents in Russia."

"When are we leaving, Dr. Peterson?"

Chapter 5

"Dr. Peterson, this is Mr. Cranston's secretary. The Administrator wants to see you in his office when you are done with your last procedure for today."

He had expected the call for several weeks. This was it; he knew he would be asked to resign as Chief of Thoracic Surgery or even give up his medical privileges altogether at Mercy Hospital. It was inevitable. Any doctor who insisted on telling people he walked with Jesus in the year 27 A.D. and was healed of a birth defect, could not expect to be allowed to practice surgery at a prestigious hospital like Mercy. Rumors of a nervous breakdown, hallucinations brought on by a brain tumor, and drug withdrawals were spreading like wildfire. Patients were starting to cancel their surgeries or demand to be treated by another doctor in ever increasing numbers.

"Mr. Cranston will see you now, Dr. Peterson," the secretary said as soon as he entered the office.

"Thank you, Mary," Thomas answered with a smile as she held the door open for him.

"Close the door, Mary and hold all my calls." Jason Cranston was an imposing man in his fifties with almost no hair. His face was set in a grim smile as he waved for Thomas to sit down. He looked at him with a mixture of compassion, anger and confusion. "Before I tell you what the majority of the board wants me to do, I would like to hear from you what is going on in your life. You have been an excellent surgeon all these years. What has happened to you that you wish to throw away your career with religious ramblings of a disturbing nature we on the Hospital board can no longer afford to ignore." He leaned back in his chair and sighed. "Please, try to explain it to me, Doctor."

"Mr. Cranston, I appreciate you giving me a chance to tell you what happened to me; not that it will make it any easier on you or me. "There is one thing I wish to say before all else. I am not delusional; neither did I have a nervous breakdown or suffer from hallucination. I don't have a brain tumor either. As a matter of fact, there is nothing physically or mentally wrong with me." He looked at the man across from him with a crooked little smile. "Like the crazy man in the asylum, I tell you I am perfectly healthy and normal. Nobody believed him either."

"Then what for heaven's sake are you doing, man?"

"I am not really doing anything other than I have become a Christian. The last I heard, that is not yet illegal in this country; and you certainly do not have the right to fire me because of it."

"No one said anything about firing you, Dr. Peterson. However, we do have the right to ask you to resign your position as Chief of your department if your religion interferes with the performance of your duty as a surgeon."

"Have I in any way made mistakes during my surgeries or put my patients in danger?"

"No, you haven't as far as I know."

"Then what is it you and the board object to?" His voice remained calm and steady in spite of rising anger inside.

"There are these rumors and accusations filling the hospital of strange talk on your part of having traveled back in time and meeting Jesus personally." He leaned forward as he added, "You will admit that is what you are saying, isn't it? As you can imagine, this kind of talk seems delusional to say the least."

"I do agree with you and I am sorry. I had no intentions to share with anyone about this, but the hospital grapevine works well as usual and embellished it to the point of no return."

"What really happened then, could you tell me?" Jason Cranston suddenly sounded curious.

"It is very simple, Sir. I fell asleep one day after I came home from work and had a dream. In this dream I spent three years in ancient Israel and experienced things that were so real, I still have a hard time separating them from reality. During these three years I was confronted with the real me, which I found out was not the great person I thought I was. My journey coincided with the time Jesus walked the land and I met Him and watched Him get crucified, die on the cross and rise again. It was then I decided He was my Messiah and I accepted Him into my life. When I woke up, only one hour had passed." He shifted in his seat and bent down to take his shoes and socks off. "I am sure it is in my medical records that I was born with only four toes on my left foot, just like my father. Yet I now have five toes on both feet, which proves my dream was real. Mr. Cranston, I cannot explain how it happened, all I know is, it did. As a surgeon, I know it has to be miraculous, since there are no scars and no signs the toe has not always been there." He walked around the desk until he stood before the hospital administrator, barefoot. "Look carefully, I now have five toes on both feet."

Jason Cranston stared at his feet and then at Thomas.

"My lord, this is incredible. I know about this hereditary condition from your father. We used to laugh about it from time to time." He raised up and looked at Thomas with total confusion. "I don't know what to say. What am I going to tell the board? I can't very well fire you for having experienced a real miracle, can I?"

"But you are going to anyway, aren't you, Mr. Cranston," Thomas said in a gentle tone. "Let me ask you a personal question, Sir. Do you go to church every Sunday?"

"Yes, I do."

"How then can you not accept that the Jesus you pray to and believe in is not able to do this?"

Jason Cranston looked at Thomas with surprise and then sadness.

"I don't know, I never thought about it that way."

"Do you not realize, if you fire me, you will be guilty of persecuting a man who was touched by this same Jesus you say you believe is the Son of God, who came to die for your sins. If that was me, I don't think I would want to be responsible for that kind of action and still go to church every Sunday." Thomas smiled at him with a warm, loving smile. "Don't worry, I will forgive you and so will Jesus. It is you who will always have to live with the guilt." He watched Jason Cranston shrink in his seat and added, "You remind me of a man named Pontius Pilate, who told me he knew Jesus was innocent. I also told him, that in spite of it he would have Him killed anyway. He had that same look on his face you do right now. There is one difference, he did not realize who Jesus was, you do." Thomas bent down, picked up his shoes and socks and quietly walked out of the office, still on his bare feet.

Chapter 6

He went into the doctor's lounge and sat down on one of the comfortable couches, a coffee in hand. It was two days after the meeting with Cranston and he had not heard anything back from the administrator.

"I would really like to talk to you about your experience, Dr. Peterson."

Thomas looked up and was surprised to see one of the orthopedic surgeons.

"I am Robert Durham from Ortho. You have become a famous man in this hospital Dr. Peterson." He smiled at Thomas with a friendly smile. "I can only imagine what you must be going through."

"I'm sorry, I can't say that I want to chat about it, Dr. Durham. I really wish people would find something else to talk about." Thomas took a sip of his coffee and picked up a magazine on the side table and pretended to read.

"I can certainly understand why you are tired of the furor this has caused," Robert Durham said as he sat down in a chair across from Thomas. He was a man of medium height, slightly overweight, in his late forties with reddish hair and piercing blue eyes. "I am not asking out of sheer curiosity, nor do I doubt what you have experienced." He stroked his closely cropped, reddish beard as he went on. "I am an Irish Catholic and believe in miracles. Not only the ones from centuries ago as experienced by the saints my church tells me about, but rather the modern day interventions of God, which cannot be explained with science. I also believe I would like to be a part of what Jesus wants you to do, no matter what or where that is." He leaned toward Thomas with an intense look. "You see, I am convinced we live in the end times and God needs workers for the last great revival to come."

Thomas looked up from his magazine and put down his cup, "Then you don't think I'm a lunatic?"

"On the contrary, you are one of those fortunate people who have been personally invited by the Lord to work in His Kingdom.

Where that will lead you, I do not know, although He may have already told you." Robert Durham added with a grin. "Has He?"

"He has, Doctor. I am to go to Israel and share with His people and mine what I saw and heard in my dream." Thomas had a slight hesitation in his voice as he went on. "I have no idea how I am going to do that, but neither do I have any doubt He will show me when the time is right."

Of that I have no doubt," Dr. Durham said with a mysterious smile.

Before Thomas could answer, his cell phone rang. It was Mr. Cranston's office.

"I would love to talk to you some more, Doctor," he said as he got up. "But I think I'm about to get fired."

"May I meet with you again, Dr. Peterson? Here is my card; call me. I think I know how." He handed Thomas his business card. "I really need to talk to you."

Mr. Cranston is ready to see you, Dr. Peterson," the receptionist said in a professional tone. "Please go right in."

Jason Cranston got up from behind his desk and held out his hand.

"It is good to see you, Dr. Peterson; have a seat." He seemed tense. "I talked to the Board of Directors and told them what you related to me." He cleared his throat. "It was a unanimous decision. They want you to resign as Chief of Thoracic Surgery. Mark Kosack will take your place." He looked at Thomas with a look of sadness. "I guess I am just like Pontius Pilate after all. But I did insist that they will not take your hospital privileges; that much I could do for you. There were voices who wanted you gone to save the reputation of the hospital, but I convinced them otherwise."

"And avoid a lawsuit for religious discrimination, isn't that right, Mr. Cranston?" Thomas said with a crooked little smile. "Don't worry, I am not going to sue you or anyone else. It simply wouldn't be the Christian thing to do." He got up from his chair and looked down at Jason Cranston with pity. "I have no problem with losing my position as Chief and will continue to do my best as a surgeon for as long as I remain," he said in a calm voice. "It is you I feel sorry for, because this hospital has given in to political correctness with their decision and you went along with it. It seems to be the thing to do these days." He said with resignation and turned to go, when the administrator stopped him.

"Dr. Peterson, I don't know how to say this, but I believe the story you told me. All my life I have gone to church and yet I have never really believed in God. I can tell that you do and I would like to have that kind of faith." He looked down on his desk and took a deep breath before he looked at Thomas. "Could I come and talk to you after work sometime and ask you about Jesus and your dream?" He was near tears. "The things you said about Pontius Pilate made me realize what a hypocrite I am. I cringe at the thought of having been a part of this by not standing up for you in that meeting. You are right, I did it out of expediency and fear after I listened to our legal advisor. I based my decision on that more than listening to my conscience, thinking the proposed compromise would get me off the hook."

"So what is the point in telling me, Mr. Cranston?"

"Your forgiving attitude and kindness, Doctor. I have known you for some years and have never seen you act in this manner before. Something clearly happened to you that has changed you; and I want to know what it is."

"It is exactly what I told you the other day. I met Jesus in a dream and after an arduous journey of self-discovery, I found out that I am not such a nice person or can ever be good without His help. I have since read the New Testament and found all the things I experienced are in there. Not only that, He is alive and still heals us today, just as He did back then." Thomas walked back and stood in front of the desk and held out his hand to Jason Cranston. "You are welcome to come to my house this Saturday and talk to me for as long as you wish. My wife Melissa can probably tell you more about my new faith than I can since she has been a devout Christian for a long time."

"I may just do that, Doctor. Could I bring my wife? She is just as interested as I am." He let out a deep sigh of relief.

"Please call me Thomas, Mr. Cranston," Thomas said and put out his hand.

"I'm Jason, JC to my friends."

"I just met another doctor who believes me and is interested in talking to me. I will give him a call and see if he and his wife can join us."

"That sounds wonderful to me. Let's have an old-fashioned prayer meeting," he said with a broad grin. "I can't wait."

Before Thomas could answer, his cell phone rang. It was the head nurse on the surgical wing.

"Dr. Peterson, could you come and talk to your patient, Mrs. Landers. She refuses to let you operate on her unless she talks to you first. She is in room 301." The nurse sounded like she was upset.

"I will be right there," he said. "Got to go, JC. I will see you and your wife Saturday then. Melissa will call you with the time."

This would be unpleasant. Another patient had fallen victim to the rumor mill. He noticed the staff avoiding eye contact with him when he grabbed the chart at the nursing station on the third floor. Without a word he proceeded to room 301 and took a deep breath before entering.

"Mrs. Landers, how are you? Ready for the procedure tomorrow?"

"Dr. Peterson, I overheard the nurses talking last night when they thought I was asleep and I didn't like what they had to say about you. I have no intention being operated on by a surgeon who is having a nervous breakdown." She sounded agitated and close to tears. "I am really scared after what they said."

"Mrs. Landers, look at me, do I look like someone who is not in control of his faculties?" He gave her a big smile.

"I can't say that you do, but why are they saying those things," Doctor?" She had calmed down some. "They must have a reason to talk about you like that."

"I don't mind telling you. You see, I am Jewish and have become a Christian in a pretty dramatic way." He looked at her with calm assurance. "What they are really in an uproar about is the fact that Jesus healed me of a birth defect." He pointed to his left foot and explained what happened.

"You haven't turned into one of those evangelical fanatics, have you?" She was skeptical.

"Mrs. Landers, I don't even know what that means, so I guess I am not one of them." He smiled at her as he looked up from the chart. "You are doing good and I see no reason why I should be less of a good surgeon now that I am a Christian than when I was Jewish, what do you say?"

"I guess it'll be alright." She looked at him with a stern expression. "You need to tell your nurses to stop gossiping in the patients' rooms. We are not idiots, you know."

"I could not agree with you more, ma'am. Rest assured, I will definitely do something about it." He shook her hand and said with a friendly smile, "I will see you first thing in the morning in surgery. Get a good night's rest and relax, I will give it my best to do a good job."

He checked the schedule when he returned to the nurses' station. When he couldn't find it, he walked up to Rhonda, the head nurse.

"I need to speak with you, Rhonda, now."

"Yes, Doctor, what can I do for you?" She sounded nervous. "Who was on duty last night in room 301?"

"That would be Katie and Helen," she said without hesitation, like she had already spoken to them.

"Rhonda, if you were waiting to have major surgery, would you like to hear from the nurses that your surgeon is probably having a nervous breakdown?"

"No, Sir. I am sorry it happened. I have already reprimanded them."

"That's not good enough. It is time that you as the head nurse make sure those under you act in a more professional way than this. We are all here for the patients, not for the gossip." He tried hard to keep his anger under control. "There is one more thing, I have been relieved of being Chief of Thoracic surgery. Dr. Kosack will take over starting tomorrow. Please make sure you give him your best, the way you have given to me for the past two years, until now. Also, make sure you tell your nurses and thank them for me." Before she could answer, he turned around and walked to the elevator.

"Dr. Peterson, wait a minute!" It was Rhonda. "I want to apologize for the way we have acted. I am very sorry about all this. You have been a great boss and we will miss you."

"Of course I forgive you. Remember, I talked to Jesus and He told me I had to," he added with a big grin.

She looked at him, surprised. "You know what, I really believe you did, Dr. Peterson. You are different somehow."

Chapter 7

The next day was Friday and Mark Kosack was officially introduced as the new Chief of Staff. As Thomas was told much later, Jason Cranston gave a short speech in which he praised the fine job Thomas had done. He actually took longer to compliment him than welcoming the new Chief. There was muted applause when he finally presented Mark Kosack as the new boss. Thomas was glad that he could not make it to the small ceremony because of an emergency surgery. When he got back to the floor, no one mentioned the meeting to him.

Thomas had called Mikail, JC and Bob to set up a time to meet at his house tomorrow. Melissa had agreed to fix a nice lunch for everyone. He even called Nana to be there, since she was now a Christian and supportive of his plans. Thomas was anxious to hear what Bob Durham wanted to share. I sounded intriguing.

"Peterson, how the mighty have fallen!" It was Mark Kosack. "How does it feel to be a nobody, Thomas?" he said in a sarcastic tone. "Excuse me, let me phrase that in the way your Messiah would say it, "the first shall be last".

"Congratulations, Mark. I hope you have a successful run as chief. If I can be of any help with the transition, don't hesitate to ask." There was an embarrassed silence at the nurses' station. "The job should've been mine from the beginning, Thomas old boy. I don't understand what took them so long to see the light." He looked around with a grin. "Ah, I forgot, you're the one who sees lights and watches folks walk on water. I bet you had no trouble doing it in your dream, did you?"

Thomas smiled and reached for a set of charts and said with a chuckle, "Funny you should say that; every time I tried to walk on water in my dream I got wet, no matter how hard I tried." There was laughter and he watched some of the staff looking at him in a much friendlier way.

He was still glad when the first day after his demotion was over and he could get his bearing over the weekend. It would not be easy. His old pride made him cringe on the inside, but he tried hard to remain friendly and kind towards everyone, in spite of the awkwardness of the situation. Several times he had to refer the staff to Mark Kosack, who made sure to let him know he was in charge now. Just when Thomas was sure he couldn't take it anymore, he thought about Yeshua hanging on the cross, listening to the soldiers mocking Him. With perfect clarity he heard the Master ask the Father to forgive them for they did not understand what they were doing. If the Lord could still love those who killed Him, then he, Thomas should have no problem dealing with Mark Kosack's remarks. It helped him to remain calm and even kind in return, to everyone's astonishment.

When he came home he hugged Melissa for a long time. It felt good to finally be in friendly territory. She understood what he had been going through and held on to him with fervor until he felt the tension and stress leave him. When they finally sat together on the couch with a cool glass of iced tea, she smiled at him with compassion and said,

"Tell me about your day, Sweetheart. It was hard, wasn't it? I have been praying for you all day."

"It was, but let's not talk about that. I have invited a whole bunch of people over for lunch tomorrow. I hope you're not mad. They want to hear more about what happened to me and about Yeshua." He looked at her questioningly.

"I suppose I better get used to this as part of your ministry. Who is coming, Preacher?" She asked with a broad smile.

Mikail was the first to arrive the next day. Once again, he wore his best suit and looked extremely nervous when Thomas met him at the door.

"Welcome, Mikail, it is good to see you again," he said and shook his hand.

"I am honored to be invited to your house again, Doctor," he said as he followed Thomas to the living room.

"Mikail, we are all serving Yeshua and that makes us brothers. My name is Thomas," he said with a big smile.

"That will take some getting used to," the little man answered, fumbling with his tie.

"You can take that thing off, Mikail," Thomas said. "This is going to be very informal. "I want you to feel comfortable if we are going to travel together, don't you think?"

The doorbell rang and Thomas left to greet Bob Durham and JC and their two wives.

"Please, come in and welcome to my home, ladies and gentlemen," Thomas said in a cheerful tone. "Melissa and I are glad you could make it. Mrs. Cranston, we have met you at hospital functions; you may remember us, "he said as Melissa walked up to them.

"Of course I remember both of you and can't wait to get to know you better. Please call me Pat." She shook their hands with a broad smile. "It is good to see you both again." She was a middle-aged woman, stout in the middle, but with an infectious smile. Her blue eyes, surrounded by a circle of not so fine lines, sparkled with delight. "You have no idea how excited we both are to be able to talk to you about what happened, Dr. Peterson."

"Thomas will do just fine, Pat," he answered and then turned toward Bob Durham and his wife.

"And this must be your lovely wife, Bob," Thomas said as he shook her hand. "I have seen you in a crowd at the hospital, but never had the pleasure of talking to you."

"This is Claudia and, just like Jason and Pat, we can't wait for you to share what happened." She was a tall woman, young looking for her age with a toned body due to daily exercise. Her long, black hair was matched by dark, intelligent eyes. Her light make-up enhanced her high cheekbones and flawless skin. She reminded Thomas of the Roman woman Claudia in his dream. He met her when he treated her slave for a broken arm, which proved to Lucius that he was indeed an accomplished physician.

"You remind me of a woman in my dream and her name was Claudia as well," he said.

"That is exciting, Thomas. I bet she was a much better person than I could ever be," she said, slightly flustered.

"On the contrary, she was a heathen Roman lady who owned slaves."

"Oh dear, that sounds terrible." She pretended to be upset.

"No, no, Claudia, I am talking about her looks. She was very beautiful." He said, totally embarrassed.

"You better quit while you're ahead, sweetheart," Melissa said, laughing. "It is wonderful to meet you, Claudia. Thomas still has trouble separating the past from the present. You will have to get used to that. Please everybody, come in and make yourselves comfortable. Lunch will be ready in a minute."

It was at that time, Nana arrived with her usual cheerful smile.

"I'm sorry I'm late," she said without going into any more detail.

Before long, having finished a delicious meal, they sat in the living room, waiting for Thomas to share the dramatic story of his journey into ancient Israel.

"You did say you were an atheist and knew nothing about the Bible?" Claudia asked when he was done.

"I had never read the New Testament and barely knew the Torah, if it hadn't been for Nana to teach me some things of my Jewish heritage when I was boy. It was definitely not enough to make me a biblical expert on the ancient writings or the prophesies that dealt with the Messiah to come."

"And yet you learned all that in your dream?" Bob asked with astonishment. "I am intrigued that you heard everybody speaking in English and yet you knew they actually spoke in Hebrew, Greek, Aramaic or Latin."

"It made things a lot easier than it will when I go back this time." He turned to Mikail. "That is why the Lord sent Mikail. He speaks fluent Hebrew. Please, share with us how that came about, Mikail."

"My parents were Russian Jews and would only allow me to speak Hebrew at home. From what my father told me, the Lord instructed him to teach me the language, because He would have need of me one day. And I believe that day has come." He smiled a shy smile as he looked around. "I am to go with Thomas and Melissa as a translator when the time comes."

"It looks to me the Lord is slowly arranging for everything so that you can go," Bob said, turning to Thomas, "and I am here to show you who will make that possible."

"Because I sure don't," Thomas said. "Tell us, Bob, what is it?"

"I am involved with a Christian organization called "Shalom Outreach". It is based out of Chicago and its mission is to reach Israel for Christ. The organization is not very large and not widely known, but it has made inroads into Israel by having obtained official status to send representatives into the country. We are not allowed to openly proselytize. However, sending a physician over there who wants to treat the poor would be something we would love to have. And I believe, Thomas you are it!" He was so excited, he nearly spilled his drink. "This is unbelievable the Lord has sent you for that purpose; to do what you did in your dream. Only this time it is for real."

Thomas looked at him with a smile and then at Melissa.

"Are you ready to pack, honey?"

"I am," she said quietly.

"And so am I," Mikail said with awe in his voice. "I have no doubt the Lord has arranged this since I was a boy." He was nearly in tears. "I cannot believe He would pick me to go out into all the world for Him."

They sat in stunned silence until JC spoke up.

"I always thought there had to be more to Christianity than what I heard in church all my life." He turned to his wife and then to Thomas. "I don't know what it takes to become a follower of Jesus other than belonging to a church, but whatever it is, I want to do it. How about you, Claudia, what do you think?"

"I agree, we have played church long enough," she answered, looking at Thomas expectantly.

"This is where Melissa comes in," he said, "she is the one who knows how to lead someone to the Lord."

"Before I pray with them, Thomas, why don't you share what you said to Yeshua before you were healed of leprosy," she said.

"I hope I remember everything," he said and bowed his head. "Master, I am a wretched, sinful man and You have known all along what was in my heart, yet I would not listen. Please forgive my pride, my arrogance and the horrible crimes I have committed. I am not worthy of anything but death and eternal punishment. But I know You love me, You always have and told me You have come for the lost. I am lost and blind and crippled and deserve to be punished for what I have done. Forgive me, Lord. You said You died for my sins on the cross so that I may live. I give you my life, my body and my mind to do with as you wish. You are my Meshiah and I take you into my heart from this day forward."

"That is called the prayer of salvation," Melissa said. "There is no formula which says this is the only way to pray, but it contains everything we need to tell the Lord if we want to turn our life over to Him," She turned to Thomas. "Why don't you say it again and all of us repeat it after you? She looked around the circle. If you are serious about giving your life to Jesus and believe what you are saying, according to the Bible, you are saved."

"This calls for a celebration," she said after Thomas was done. "This is your first altar call, Preacher," she added with a broad grin. "You are doing good." She turned to JC and Claudia. "Welcome to the Kingdom of God. You are now followers of the Yeshua Meshiah as Thomas calls Him." She went over and hugged them both and then turned to Bob. "I would like to ask you to say a prayer of thanks and directions over Thomas, as well as Mikail and myself. I have a feeling we are going to need it."

"I would be honored," he said.

Chapter 8

"This is USN Breaking News. I am Marsha Kendrick. Japan is on high alert over North Korea's plan to launch a ballistic missile within the next two weeks. US satellite images have confirmed the missile is capable of carrying a nuclear warhead.

In defense, Japan has stationed patriot missiles along its border with North Korea. According to a government spokesman in Tokyo, North Korea is in direct violation of several international treaties it has signed with the UN Security Council in the past.

What is particularly worrying to the US Defense Department, according to Kyle Berger, a high ranking spokesperson, is the fact that North Korea has a second missile program which cannot be monitored by satellite. Therefore, our government has no idea how advanced their technology is toward nuclear capability to reach the United States at this time. What we do know is, there has been increased activity in the production of uranium in the last few months, according to Berger.

Stay tuned for more information. I am Marsha Kendrick, USN Headline News."

Thomas turned the radio off. He hated to listen to the news and had an uneasy feeling of dark clouds engulfing the world. Where would it all end? Melissa tried to tell him about the end times, but he did not understand a thing when he read Revelations and dismissed it for now. Maybe, when he knew more about the scriptures, he could try to listen to some of the teachings she was involved with.

It was late afternoon. It had been a long day with three surgeries, who proved to be more difficult than he expected. He was on his way to see his parents. He sighed, trying to decide whether the world situation was more difficult than facing his mother. She didn't say what this was all about, but had made it clear she did not want Melissa to come along.

His father answered the door and led him into the study.

"What's up, Dad? Is anything wrong?"

Abraham sat down with a deep sigh and pointed to the couch.

"Sit down, son. Nothing is wrong with us, but plenty seems to be wrong with you. We hear terrible things from the hospital and your mother is devastated that you lost your position as Chief." He looked at Thomas with great concern and continued. "Apparently, you have continued with your ridiculous religious claims and it has cost you your job. Mother and I are terribly upset about it."

"Dad, it's alright. I am doing just fine. As a matter of fact, there is a lot less paperwork for me to do and I can concentrate more on what I like best – doing surgery." Thomas tried to sound calm and confident as he looked at his father with a reassuring smile.

Until his mother walked in.

"You cannot tell us you don't mind being demoted and ridiculed by the entire medical community?" she said in an ice-cold tone. "We have not been invited to any functions or parties since this happened; and even Mark Reider, your father's best friend, has stayed away." She stared at him, trying to control her fierce anger.

"That's not all, son," Abraham said, "your Nana has informed us that she believes you and is praising God for accepting Jesus as her Messiah. In other words, she has become a Christian."

"I know, Dad," was all Thomas managed to say. "Is there anything else you want to talk to me about? Because if there isn't, then I must tell you that I get enough of this kind of doubt and accusation at the hospital." He stood up. "I have no intentions to listen to your anger and disappointment toward me and neither will I change my mind. It looks to me, Mother, you worry more about your ruined social life than me." He turned to his father.

"I don't know what your concerns are, Dad, but it isn't about me, that's for sure. I am a Christian now and that's that. I have nothing more to say about the subject." He looked at his parents with deep hurt as he started for the door. "As a matter of fact, if you want to spend some time with me before Melissa and I are leaving for Israel, you better hurry." He looked at his mother with sadness. "But then again, the sooner I'm gone, the sooner you can get back to your friends."

"Wait!" his father said as he got up from his chair. "What do you mean, you are going to Israel? For how long and what are you going to do there?" He was almost shouting.

"I have signed up with an organization called Shalom Outreach. They are sending Melissa and me to Israel, where I will be treating the poor and telling them about Jesus."

"Are you insane?" his mother screamed. "I will not allow it!"

"I do not recall having asked for your permission, Mother. There is nothing you can do to stop me." He looked at his parents before he walked out and suddenly realized, they both looked old, confused and heartbroken.

His anger vanished and he took his mother into his arms. "I love you, Mom. Don't be sad for me, I am doing what I want to do."

She was sobbing uncontrollably. "You are my only son and I can't stand the thought of losing you."

"You won't lose me; I will always love you, no matter what." He reached for a tissue and gently dried her tears. "I know you don't understand any of this Mom, but that does not take away that I am still your son, doing something I was meant to do." He held her at arm's length. "Can you accept that?"

She looked at him and for the first time in his life, he saw his mother helpless and vulnerable.

"I have no choice, Tommy, because I love you." She wiped her eyes. "I know I don't say it often enough, but I do."

Thomas hugged her again and looked over her shoulder at his father. Their eyes locked and he knew things would be alright between them.

Chapter 9

"Dr. Peterson, my name is Marcia Menendez. I am the Director of Shalom Outreach. After speaking with Dr. Durham, I cannot tell you how excited we are that you and your wife are considering joining our organization as a medical missionary to Israel."

"How nice to hear from you, Ms. Menendez." Thomas cleared his throat. "Let's not get ahead of ourselves until my wife and I have had time to look into your organization first. I can't say that I have ever heard of it before and must tell you that I have a lot of questions about your mission statement, funding and operations, among others."

"Of course, Doctor, I understand completely. That is why I have been authorized by our Board of Directors to invite you and your wife to come to Chicago and 'look us over' so to speak. We will pay for your airfare and put you up for one or two nights in our modest quarters designed for traveling missionaries. Just name the date and we will arrange everything."

"I must tell you that my contract with Mercy Hospital doesn't run out until June of this year. That is four months from now."

"That sounds perfect, since it would take that long to get your work visa and the other legal documents necessary for you to be allowed to practice medicine in Israel. In the meantime, I will send you any information you might want about our small organization, including financial backers, mission statement and the three locations of our ministry in Israel. With your help we would love to start an outreach post in Haifa, but that is something for the future."

"There is one question I have, Ms. Menendez, does any of them include a medical facility?" Thomas asked.

"It does not; that's where you come in, Dr. Peterson. But I'm afraid we are getting ahead of ourselves. Why don't you come and talk to the Board and then we see what happens?"

That was two weeks ago.

"Are you nervous, honey?" Melissa asked as she leaned over to him in the narrow seat on the airplane.

"I am. What if this is not what we are supposed to do? It is after all a very small organization with modest resources and uncertain funding," Thomas said with doubt in his voice. "Think about it, this whole idea is based on a dream. Do you realize we would have to give up our way of life, our income, our friends and everything we have valued all our lives if we do this?"

Melissa reached over and took his hand.

"I do realize it and it is ok. You don't have to decide until the Lord shows you and gives you confirmation. All we are doing right now is taking a look. No one says we have to commit to anything while we are there."

"You are right." He breathed a sigh of relief. "Everything seemed easier in my dream. There I gained a lot of money, here I'm losing everything." He smiled at her with a weak, little smile.

"You haven't lost me, sweetheart," she said, "we are in this together, remember?"

I hope He lets me know what to do. Thomas shifted in his seat and then leaned back with a deep sigh. He closed his eyes, giving in to the soothing, steady hum of the engines. After a while he looked at the man next to him. He was startled. Where was Melissa? He stared at the old man, dressed in a long, brown robe over a white tunic, his long, curly beard hanging down to his chest.

"You are Jonah, the old man in my dream at the wedding of Cana," Thomas said, astonished. "What are you doing here?"

"I am an angel, sent by God to remind you of the message He gave you back then. You are a stranger in this land and are filled with doubt and unbelief. And yet the Lord Yeshua wants you to know that you will see the Glory of His coming and be touched by Him in a special way. Turn from your doubts and prepare your heart for He has anointed you to take His message to His people Israel."

"Does that mean I am supposed to go with Shalom…?" Before Thomas could finished the sentence, the old man was gone. He opened his eyes and saw Melissa sitting there, reading a book.

"You fell asleep for a little while, didn't you?" she said. "We are getting ready to land in Chicago, honey."

Thomas' heart was racing. He remembered the old man well and the fervor in which he had spoken to him then. This time he had been much more calm, but his voice still had that touch of warning in it. Thomas stared at Melissa with a bewildered look. Did this mean he was supposed to be a part of this ministry? He felt the old familiar feeling of frustration rising inside him. Why did the Lord have to talk to him in riddles again? As usual, His words only made perfect sense after the fact. Thomas stared straight ahead. He didn't feel like telling Melissa what happened until after they had taken a closer look at the organization.

"I am Richard Hanson with Shalom Outreach. Welcome to Chicago." He was a tall man with thin, blond hair, matching his lanky frame. His blue eyes had a sparkle in them as he reached out to shake Thomas' hand. "You must be Dr. Peterson." He turned to Melissa and shook her hand as well. "You have no idea how excited we are that you have agreed to come and look us over. While we are a small organization, the Lord has given us favor so far, but all of a sudden, they are only interested if we can send a physician and open a clinic for the poor." He stopped abruptly. "Listen to me rambling on. Please, follow me, someone is waiting with a car after we get your luggage."

It took almost an hour through heavy traffic until they reached the modest office building on the outskirts of the city. A heavy-set, middle-aged woman greeted them at the door. She was definitely of Latin-American descent with her smooth, olive skin and dark eyes covered by even darker, thick hair held back by a large, brown comb.

"I am Marcia Menendez, welcome to Shalom Outreach, Dr. and Mrs. Peterson. You have no idea how delighted we are you are here. Please come with me to the boardroom. The entire staff is waiting to greet you."

Thomas was taken in by her friendly, open demeanor and decided she would be someone he could work with.

"Thank you, Ms. Menendez, Melissa and I are glad to be here," he said as they walked down the hall.

There were five people sitting around a large, oblong table. It filled almost the entire room, with barely enough space for the chairs.

"May I introduce our local staff to you, Dr. and Mrs. Peterson," Marcia Menendez said. "This is our Chairman of the Board, Rev. Charles Brockmeier," she said, pointing to an elderly man at the head of the table. "He is the senior pastor of New Harvest Church here in Chicago." He was a man in his late sixties with thick, wavy, white hair, tall, and with a muscular built. His grey eyes exuded a keen intelligence, softened by a kind smile.

"Next to Pastor Brockmeier is Marvin Keller, our computer expert. He keeps us in touch with our staff in Israel via the internet." He was a shy young man with short, unruly, curly hair. "And this is Marjory Hellman, our very capable secretary. That is her official title, but in reality, she is the soul of this place and keeps us all in line." In her late fifties, the stout, short woman had a face filled with the most delightful tiny, little wrinkles as she smiled at Thomas and Melissa. Her blue eyes were lost behind a set of thick glasses. "You have met Richard, he is the man of many talents who never tires fixing everything around here and is there when we need help of any kind."

She turned to Thomas and Melissa and pointed to two chairs next to Pastor Brockmeier. "Have a seat; and if you are not too tired, we would like to explain how our organization works and answer any questions you might have."

"Before we get started, I would like to make very sure that Melissa and I have not made up our mind to work with Shalom Outreach," Thomas said. "It is strictly an informational visit on our part. Until I talked to Dr. Durham, I had never heard of Shalom Outreach. But then, I have not heard about any Christian missionary organization of any kind since I was an avowed atheist until three months ago. This is all new to me and to be honest, I am not very comfortable talking to people who know much more about Christianity than I do." He turned to Melissa. "My wife is the seasoned Christian; I am only a novice at best."

"Dr. Durham has told us your story how you came to accept Christ in your dream," Rev. Brockmeier said. "We are all fascinated by it and can't wait for you to tell us more."

"I have experienced a solid wall of ridicule, scoffing and general opposition at my hospital and I am quite reluctant to talk about it to people I don't know. Even my parents wanted to disown me at first and still don't believe a word of it. Not only that, the hospital has taken away my position as Chief of Thoracic Surgery because of my new belief. The only reason they did not fire me, they were afraid I would sue them on grounds of religious discrimination."

"Dr. Durham has told us all about that and we are truly sorry," Marcia Menendez said. "I can assure you, your story has caused great excitement and rejoicing among us. We believe your dream and know the Lord has sent you to us, because we have been praying for a physician just like you to join our team." She leaned forward, her eyes fixed intently on Thomas. "You are not only a Messianic Jew, but you are also a surgeon. That is exactly what we need to be allowed to stay in either Israel or Palestine at the moment. You can see how important it is for this organization for you to be a part of it," she added almost in a whisper.

There was a sudden silence around the table.

"I am sorry, Dr. Peterson, I am getting ahead of myself. Please forgive my presumption. I know you have not made up your mind and I understand that. But we truly feel that you could be the perfect person the Lord wants to use if you decide to join Shalom Outreach." Marcia looked around the room, embarrassed; and then, a sudden smile crossed her face. "I guess there is no denying we want you, Dr. Peterson, is there?"

Thomas looked at her with a grin.

"I guess there isn't. Please, everybody, call me Thomas. I have a lot of questions, but the main one is, does your organization have any kind of medical facility anywhere?"

"No, we don't," Rev. Brockmeier said. "We have the promise of funding for one, but can't go forward, because we don't have a doctor. You can see why we are so anxious about you coming on board."

"There is a man named Mikail Rochenko at the hospital," Thomas said. "He is a trained laboratory technician and wants to go with me. He is also a Messianic Jew." He pointed to Melissa. "My wife is a registered surgical nurse. It looks like we have a full clinical staff without even trying."

"Praise the Lord," Marcia whispered into the silence.

Chapter 10

Thomas took one last look out of the back of the taxi before the house disappeared from view. It was as if he saw for the first time how beautiful it was. For some reason he had a strong feeling he might never see it again.

It had been a heart-wrenching good-by yesterday at his parents' house. Especially his mother seemed to have aged overnight as she held his hand, trying to keep her emotions in check.

"You will visit, Mother, now that Dad is retiring. Just think, you two will get to see Israel, the land of our heritage. Nana will probably want to come with you, won't you, Nana?" Thomas tried to sound cheerful, but to no avail. Nana looked at him with deep sadness.

"I am too old to fly around the world, Tommy. You two will just have to come back and visit as often as you can."

"Nana, don't be silly, you are in good health and there is no reason why I can't take you on a tour to Jerusalem to see the sights you always wanted to see." Thomas leaned over and held her hands. "I remember them all from my dream and can describe them to you the way they looked two thousand years ago."

"Thomas, are you ever going to give up talking about this silly dream?" He heard a hint of the familiar sharp tone in Sylvia's voice. "I thought we had decided not to talk about that anymore."

"Mother, I don't think I can ever *not* talk about the event that changed my life, but I will try, how is that?" He smiled at her and squeezed her hand. "One day you will understand."

"Son, your mother and I are planning to visit you when you are settled in. I will be busy closing down my practice for the next six months. Until then we'll keep in touch with Skype."

Thomas sighed as the taxi sped to the airport. This was harder than he had imagined. The feeling of finality overwhelmed him. It made no sense to him. After all, Israel was not the end of the world, yet he was sure somehow he would never see Philadelphia or the United States again. He wondered if Melissa felt the same way, but didn't say anything. There was no need to add to her anxiety. It had been just as hard to say good-by to her family, although, there was a certain excitement of seeing their daughter and her husband being sent by God as missionaries. He took her hand and squeezed it and smiled.

"This is it, sweetheart. It was easier in my dream."

"No instant travel this time, hey?" She smiled at him. "Are you nervous?"

"You can say that. I know it's crazy, but I am expecting Lucius and Helena to be there to greet us and take us to my villa. Octavia will be getting the house ready and have the cook prepare my favorite meals. What I miss the most is that I won't run into the Carpenter from Nazareth. I feel lost somehow that none of them will be there." He looked at Melissa. "I didn't tell you. On the way to Chicago on the plane I saw Jonah, the old man from the wedding at Cana. He was sitting in your seat right next to me in his brown robe with a white tunic. When I asked him what he was doing here, he told me he was an angel sent by God to remind me of the prophesy he gave me back then."

"You are kidding," Melissa said with awe in her voice.

"It was at the same time I was wondering if all this was real and if I was doing the right thing going with Shalom Outreach."

"Was he upset with you for doubting?" Melissa asked.

"No, I can't say that he was, but he was very stern." Thomas tried to remember. "It was a very short encounter and before I could ask him anymore questions, he was gone."

"How come you didn't tell me about that before?"

"I don't know. I guess I was a little embarrassed because of my doubts and fears about all this. After all that's happened, you would think I would have more faith," he added with a sigh.

"Is here anything else you haven't told me?" She looked at him with a frown.

"Well, there is, actually. I have the strangest feeling we are never going to come back to the US."

"That's funny, I feel the same way," Melissa said, astounded. "I wonder what it means?"

"I don't know, but it makes it much clearer to me how drastic this thing is we are doing."

“Are you having second thoughts?” Thomas asked.

“No, not at all. After what you have been through, this is the Lord’s doing and we will experience miracles and astounding things we cannot even imagine, you will see.” Melissa sounded excited.

“I wish I had your faith,” Thomas said wistfully. “Why didn’t He let you have the dream; you seem to be much better equipped to handle all this.”

“The Lord knows what He is doing, honey, don’t you worry.”

They had arrived at the airport.

Mikail Rochenko was waiting for them at the gate for their flight to Boston and from there with El Al Israel Airlines to Tel Aviv. He looked excited.

“Hey, Mikail, how long have you been here waiting?” Thomas asked. “I thought we were early.”

“I got here an hour ago, Dr. Peterson. I couldn’t stand to wait any longer.” He was dressed in jeans with a T-shirt and a jacket., a carry-on bag slung over his one shoulder.

“Please, Mikail, call me Thomas and this is Melissa. We are going to be working as a team in the days ahead and hopefully will become good friends. We are all in this together.”

“It is hard for me to do that, but if you insist, I will try.” He smiled his shy little smile and sat back down. “The flight is on time. I was worried we might miss our connection to Israel.”

“You haven’t flown often, have you?” Melissa asked.

“No, I haven’t. The only time I have been on a plane was when I came over to this country and I can’t say that I liked it very much.”

“It will be a long flight from Boston to Tel Aviv, Mikail. Altogether it will take about sixteen hours to get where we are going,” she added. “By the time we arrive, you will be a seasoned traveler. Besides, since we are on the Lord’s mission, nothing bad will happen to us. He has work for us to do in Israel and will give His angels charge over us.”

“That’s true, Mrs., ah Melissa,” Mikail said. “I am glad you said that, it makes me feel much better.”

It was a long sixteen hours and by the time they landed at Ben Gurion International Airport in Tel Aviv, they were exhausted. It took another hour to get through customs and wading through the special permits and entry papers, since they did not come as tourists, but medical personnel with Shalom Outreach. In a special office, they were met by a government official who was accompanied by Caleb Weinstein, the director of Shalom Outreach in Haifa.

"Welcome, Dr. and Mrs. Peterson. And you must be Mikail Rochenko? I am here to help you with the paperwork and any questions this gentleman from the Israeli government might have."

He was a young man in his late thirties with sandy colored, curly hair hanging down over his ears. Baggy, light brown pants hung loosely on his lanky, tall frame. And an even more baggy t-shirt could have used ironing, but one had the impression Caleb Weinstein had never ironed anything in his life. He presented a picture of total sloppiness until his boyish smile lit up his bright blue eyes in a remarkably warm and kind way.

Thomas decided, there could not possibly be anyone who could ever dislike this young man as he shook his hand.

"We are grateful you are here. Please call me Thomas and this is my wife Melissa and Mikail."

"Everyone can't wait to meet you guys. We are ready to start the clinic as soon as you say the word," Caleb answered and then turned to the man from the government. "This is Dr. Peterson, a well-known American surgeon who will be in charge of the new clinic to be opened by Shalom Outreach near Haifa." He opened a large, brown shoulder bag and produced a thick stack of documents, which he handed over to the stocky, bald man behind the desk. Nothing was said for a long time as they watched him shuffle slowly through them.

"Everything seems to be in order," the man finally said and looked at Thomas. "I do have one question. Why would a rich, American doctor want to come to Israel to treat the poor?"

"Because I am Jewish," Thomas said without hesitation.

The man looked at him quizzically and started to say something, but then decided otherwise. "Since I can't find anything wrong, good luck with your work here. I am sure there are plenty of people who can use your services."

"Thank you, Sir," Caleb said before Thomas could answer. "We appreciate your kindness." He was speaking Hebrew now.

Thomas could tell he did not want him to say anymore. Like everywhere else in the world, it never pays to aggravate a government type, especially if they are inclined to agree with you, he thought.

"You do seem to know how to handle the legalities very well," Thomas said to Caleb after they left the office. They were on their way from Lod, the city where the airport is located, to Haifa, about 12 miles along a modern highway.

"This was unusually easy. The Lord must be with you. I have never met any of these government types who did not find at least one thing to argue about," Caleb said with a good-natured grin. "Let's hope this is a sign for how it is going to go in the future with the clinic. Things are done a little differently here than in the good old USA," he added. "We are going to a small house where our ministry is located. You will be staying on the premises. They are modest, but clean."

Thomas had an almost eerie feeling as their car entered the highway. He was back in the land of Israel and nothing looked like it did as he remembered it. He felt like a total stranger, lost in a strange land the way he had at the beginning of his dream. Would he ever adjust to this modern place like he had to the ancient land he had come to love? How he had wished then for reality, almost as much as he yearned to be back in the dream now. The only thing the same in both places, was not being in control. He found himself wishing to run into at least one familiar person, but especially Lucius and his little girl Helena. *Yeshua, it would be nice to see Your wonderful, knowing smile again.*

He sighed, apprehension and fear filling his heart as he watched Haifa come into view. It looked like a big city with a modern skyline and busy roads. He laughed on the inside. He had actually looked for Lucius to wait for him outside the airport, sitting on the wooden cart, drawn by Igora, the little donkey and suddenly felt homesick to the point of pain. There seemed to be no connection in his heart to this modern, sterile environment. *Yeshua, are You sure this is what You want me to do?*

Chapter 11

He woke up the next morning, disoriented and his body ached from the hard mattress. At least that was the same as in the dream. Melissa stirred next to him. He looked around the tiny room that would serve as their quarters for a while. The double bed took up most of the space and left little room for a tiny table with two wooden chairs on each side. In the left corner, shielded by a dark, brown curtain reaching all the way to the floor, was a small kitchen sink and an even smaller stove with two burners. A toaster and a coffee pot were the only two items on the counter.

"Are you awake, honey?" Melissa asked as she looked over to him.

"I am admiring the palatial accommodations," he answered with a grin. "This is the true meaning of down-sizing."

"We better get used to it, because I have the distinct feeling we are not going to live in the lap of luxury from now on." She snuggled up to him and laid her head on his chest. "I don't mind, as long as I am with you."

There was a rap on the door.

"It's Caleb, are you guys awake?" He stood with a plate of jelly donuts and two steaming cups of coffee. "I thought you might like some breakfast. The rest of us have already eaten."

"What time is it?" Thomas asked.

"It is eleven o'clock. It will take you a couple of days to get used to the time change. I will introduce you to the others when you are ready to join us in the meeting room down the hall. They can't wait to meet you."

Thomas looked at the people staring at him with excitement and expectancy as he and Melissa entered the room. They were squeezed around an old, scratched up, narrow, table with none of the chairs matching. For an instant he remembered the hospital board room in Philadelphia with its gleaming, polished surface and comfortable, cushioned leather chairs, until he thought of the simple surroundings in Nazareth and Cana when he first arrived in his dream; and for some reason he felt himself relax.

Dr. and Mrs. Peterson, I am Eric Foster, the head of Shalom Outreach's three missions we have in Israel. Welcome to Haifa." He was a middle-aged man with short, grey hair and a mustache to match. His piercing, pale blue eyes were softened by a set of friendly wrinkles when he smiled. "I'm from Hendersonville in North Carolina and have been with the ministry since its inception nearly seven years ago. My mother was Jewish and my father was a Baptist preacher." He shook their hand with a firm grip. "All of us are looking forward to working with you and Mikail."

Thomas looked around and spotted the Russian at the end of the table.

"Melissa and I are excited and eager to get started. Please call me Thomas," he said, "and this is my wife Melissa. That goes for everyone. We are in this together, working for the Lord."

"That sounds wonderful, Thomas," Eric said. "Allow me to introduce the rest of the gang." He pointed to a tiny woman next to him. "This is Meta Lieberman. She is our resident local who speaks fluent Hebrew and English. Meta is from New York. Her parents are Jewish and disowned her when she became a Christian. It was then she decided to immigrate to Israel. Her heart is on fire to take the Gospel to her people."

Meta was a wisp of a girl in her early twenties with dark, curly hair and warm, brown eyes. Her facial features were definitely Jewish. She wore no make-up, but with her olive complexion didn't need any. She wore a loose-fitting, long, multi-colored dress and sandals. Thomas sensed a touch of reservation in her smile as if she was not going to trust him until he proved himself.

"Next to Meta is Karl Westhoff. He is our technical guru and talks to computers in a language all his own," Eric continued.

Karl was a big guy in every way. Thomas imagined he must weigh at least two-hundred and fifty pounds and all of it muscle. In his thirties, with brown hair and rough facial features, Karl looked more like a boxer than a missionary.

"Don't believe everything these clowns say, Doc," he said with a broad grin. I can make these machines sing if I want to. They're all jealous they don't speak computereeze."

A chuckle went around the room.

"As you can see, Karl is in a league of his own," Eric said and then pointed to a tall, awkward looking woman in her forties. "This is Leona Caldwell, our secretary and all-around wonder woman. There is nothing she can't find out, get done or make magically appear of whatever we need.

Leona had one of those faces where nothing matched. Her features seemed to have been put together from left-overs. Her nose was too big, her eyes tiny and set too far apart. Her auburn hair hung down to her shoulders in thin, spindly strings, held away from her face with a plastic half-ring. Her shapeless figure was hidden by an even more shapeless dress, which had seen better days. As she smiled at Thomas, she showed a set of powerful teeth, crooked and with a slight overbite. And yet, there was such a sweet spirit in her eyes as she looked at him, he immediately forgot how homely she was.

"And here we have Petra Petrovnowich, our Russian Jewish immigrant to Israel," Eric went on. "Petra has only been here for two years and is in charge of the kitchen and the household. She keeps us all well fed." He looked at Thomas and Melissa with a smile. "So I would advise you, if you want to eat, be nice to Petra. She will also supply you with personal items you need like toothpaste, soap and the likes and sees to it your clothes get washed. We look on her as our resident Mamutchka."

Petra was a woman in her late fifties with a ruddy complexion and thick, gray hair, wildly arranged in no particular style. Her tiny blue eyes sparkled as she smiled at him. Her hands were rough from a life of hard work back in Russia and her rotund figure was covered by a simple, blue dress with an old-fashioned apron over it. She presented thc perfect picture of a typical Russian peasant and Thomas liked her immediately.

"That means you can talk in your language," he said, turning to Mikael.

"I have already become acquainted with Petra. We are actually from the same region in the North," Mikail said with a bright smile.

"That's wonderful," Eric said. "We know who gets the best food from now on," he added with a grin and turned to a little man further down at the table. "This is Paul Ryan. He is the man who will be instrumental in helping you set up the clinic. Not only does he hold the purse strings, but he stays in touch with the donors and those who are interested in this ministry by informing them through a newsletter and other correspondence of what is going on." He turned to Thomas. "You need to get with Paul and let him know what it is you need for the clinic in the way of technical equipment and medical supplies."

Thomas smiled at Paul and nodded. He knew the type, efficient, short on words, but long on getting things done. In his forties, his black hair was getting sparse with a touch of grey at the temples. Thomas figured him to be of Italian descent, although his temperament didn't seem to match with his rather severe demeanor as he looked at him.

"Paul hails from San Diego and came to us a year ago with his wife Theresa, sitting next to him. She is in charge of the spiritual side of this team and leads a Bible study and services on Sunday. She also helps with ministering to those who are interested in becoming a Christian in the community and has a team of local volunteers proclaiming the Gospel in the streets of Haifa and the surrounding areas. All of us are expected to join her on Sundays and are required to take her training classes from time to time to brush up on how to lead people to the Lord."

Theresa was taller than her husband, a striking woman in her forties, with long, blond hair and blue eyes. She could be a model, Thomas thought as he noticed her simple, yet stylish outfit. It stood out in contrast to everyone else's drab clothes. She radiated an easy confidence with her warm and ready smile when she looked at Thomas.

"You are going to have to share your dream with us, Thomas," she said. Her clear voice didn't leave any doubt he would. "I will arrange a prayer meeting for Friday evening after work for you to tell us what happened."

"I would be glad to," Thomas answered, knowing he had been ordered rather than asked. He smiled, because she reminded him of Octavia, the woman in charge of the slaves in his household, just a lot prettier.

"Lastly, I want you to meet three local volunteers who work with us on different days. All of them are Messianic Jews and have dedicated their lives to this ministry by spreading the Gospel to their people. They are Sarai Rosen and Esther and Miriam, her two daughters. Sarai is the wife of a high ranking official in the Haifa city government. He husband is not a Christian, but allows them to be a part of this ministry. Esther goes to the University of Haifa in Mt. Carmel and is studying pre-med, while Miriam is still in High School. I am certain Esther would love to volunteer in your clinic when it is established. She has been extremely excited to be able to learn under a famous American surgeon."

"I don't know about the famous, but the part about the surgeon is certainly true." Thomas looked at the young woman with a smile. "I would love to have you on my team."

Like her sister, she had long, black hair and dark, brown eyes in an oval face. They almost looked like twins, if it wasn't for the age difference. Both were of slender built and average height and didn't look at all like their mother, Sarai. She was quite tall and held herself with grace and elegance, like a woman used to moving among the leadership of the city.

"This concludes our team. Once again, I can't tell you how excited we are to have you three on board," Eric said as he looked at Thomas, Melissa and Mikail. "Like Theresa mentioned, we will meet on Friday evening so you can tell us about yourselves and how you came to know the Lord. From what little we know, we feel He sent you to us in a very special way; and that means He has a great purpose that is going to be much more than just a medical clinic. God is more interested in our spiritual well-being and will use your presence here in other areas as well, I am sure of it."

Thomas looked around the table. A feeling of apprehension came over him. Everyone looked so much more qualified to talk about Christianity than he did. He would just have to stick to the medical part and let the others handle the spiritual aspect of this mission. He still didn't understand why Yeshua would have picked him and not Melissa or some of these others, but as usual, he didn't know why the Master did what He did half the time. Maybe that was what faith was, never knowing what God was doing until it was time to do it. At least that part felt familiar.

"Thomas, do you have any questions?" Eric asked.

"You mean, what am I doing here and how am I going to do it?" He smiled as he looked around the table. "I sincerely hope you don't think I am this spiritual giant, just because I had a dream and walked with Yeshua. I never really knew what I was doing then, nor do I know what I'm supposed to do now, other than practice medicine. But then, that is how it all started, isn't it? I will be the doctor for the poor. That part I have no trouble handling; it is knowing how to tell strangers what happened to me, is difficult for me. I just don't know enough about Christianity to have all the answers." He looked around and shrugged his shoulder in a helpless gesture.

"And you honestly think we have all the answers?" Caleb asked with his boyish smile. "None of us has walked with the Lord and talked to Him. That pretty well makes you the expert, wouldn't you say?"

"In that case, I can state unequivocally, it will be the blind leading the blind." Thomas leaned back in his chair. "This reminds me of the time I met the disciples for the first time. They looked like a bunch of simple men, uneducated and some even doubting and questioning if Yeshua was the Meshiah. I wondered then as I do now, how in the world He managed to use them and still get anything done. But, like Melissa pointed out to me, look at what He accomplished with them."

"Are you saying, there is hope for us?" Eric said with a chuckle.

"I'm sorry, that is not what I meant," Thomas said, embarrassed. "I'm sorry, I was talking about me."

"You are probably more right than you think," Theresa said. "There is no one here who is qualified to work in the Kingdom. The only reason we do it, because Jesus appointed us. That is the only qualification necessary, Thomas."

"He definitely did that, although I still don't understand why he would choose me for a job I am not trained to do," he added.

"You call walking in ancient Israel during the time of Jesus, meeting Him, talking to Him and being an eyewitness to His ministry, trial, death and resurrection not having been trained?" Theresa laughed. "That is more training than anyone I know has ever had, wouldn't you say?"

"If you put it that way, I guess I have to agree with you. However, you forget the part, that for most of those three years I was not exactly the perfect person, even by modern standards. Wait till I share the things I did, and maybe you will think differently about me."

"I can tell you one thing I am sure about, Thomas, if you were good enough for the Lord to save you and appear to you in a dream and tell you to take His message to Israel, you are certainly good enough for us here at Shalom Outreach."

She looked around the table as everyone nodded in agreement and added, "Now that that is settled, we can get started doing what the Lord has commissioned all of us to do, take His message to the people of Israel. And you, Thomas will be the one to lead the way.

He cringed. *Oh God.*

Chapter 12

He stood alone, the disk of the sun touched the skyline of Haifa with a red glow that spread an eerie light across the sky. It matched his feelings of discouragement, depression and doubt.

Everything had gone wrong since he had come here a month ago. The permit for the clinic was denied with no reason given, his license to practice medicine suddenly withheld, and the rental agreement to the house of Shalom Outreach was revoked for minor infractions by an inspector of the city of Haifa. All Sarai could tell them, after she asked her husband, that a new member of the city council was opposed to any kind of Christian presence after he found out Sarai and her daughters were involved with Shalom Outreach. Sarai's husband decided not to allow his wife or daughters to associate with the ministry any longer. While this official could not force Shalom Outreach to leave the area, he had enough influence to hinder, delay and undermine all efforts to establish a clinic. They would have to move by the end of the year and find a new place. And that, Thomas was told, was pretty well impossible in Israel as overcrowded as it was.

Where are you, Yeshua? I feel like a stranger in this land and nothing makes sense. You told me to come here, how is it You are silent? I have no idea what to do or where to go. Everything we have tried has failed and I wish I could go back home. These people look to me to lead them. What a joke! I have no idea what to do, now that I am here. All I know is to be a doctor, but I have no clinic and no place to put one. Everything *we have tried has failed, the authorities are against us and even Eric and Caleb have run out of options. Unless you give us directions, there is nothing for me to do here. I WANT TO GO HOME!*

He stood, his shoulders slumped in a picture of defeat. *I have given up everything for You, Lord. I told you I was not made to be a preacher. I am and always will only be a surgeon, nothing more, but I can't even do that here. I warned you, Lord, you picked the wrong man for this job. Just let me go home, please.*

There was no answer as he watched the darkness swallow the last fading rays of the red glow in the sky. He sighed and turned to go back into the house.

That's when he saw the man in the shadows. He was unusually tall and dressed in the clothes of ancient times. In spite of the darkness, Thomas could see his face clearly as he stepped toward Thomas. It was Lucius!

"So that you may know I am sent by God, I come in the likeness of your friend. I am an angel sent to tell you that Yeshua has not forsaken you, but will give you favor in the days to come. "The people to whom He is sending you are obstinate and stubborn. Say to them, 'This is what the Sovereign Lord says.' And whether they listen or fail to listen – for they are a rebellious house – they will know that a prophet has been among them. And you, son of man, do not be afraid of them or their words." (Ezekiel 2:4-5)

Thomas' heart pounded as he listened. He felt such fear he nearly fainted. This was not a dream! This was 21st century reality and yet, here he was, talking to an angel.

"What does Yeshua want me to do?" he wanted to ask, but the angel had gone. He fell to his knees, unable to speak. All he knew, he was not alone, Yeshua was with him. He didn't know how long he had knelt, when he felt Melissa's hand on his shoulder.

"Are you ok, honey?" She knew instantly that something had happened as soon as he looked up at her. "You heard from the Lord, didn't you?"

"I did." He was unsteady when he got up and had to lean on Melissa's arm as they walked back into the house.

"What did He say?"

"It was an angel with the face of Lucius. You have no idea what it means to me to see my old friend again, even if it wasn't exactly him. Yeshua is so good, He knew I was desperate to see a familiar face." He smiled at her. "Things will be alright in spite of what it looks like. The Lord is in control and His purpose will be fulfilled in spite of what anyone says." There was a new hope in his voice.

Another two weeks went by and except for Thomas, everyone was discouraged. When he told them about the angel and what he said, they had been excited at first, but then, doubt took over when nothing happened. Even Theresa had a hard time going among the people of Haifa and was now taking Meta to go with her since Thomas and Melissa turned her down and spent a lot of time in their room instead, studying the scriptures and praying for guidance. Thomas felt it was important to familiarize himself with the Bible in order to talk to others about it and was convinced he was still woefully ignorant in all things Christian.

"I feel I have a personal relationship with Yeshua, but know nothing of theology," he told Theresa when she urged him to come with her.

"Don't you understand, that is what all Christians should be like, Thomas?" she asked him, frustrated. "You have what most of the rest of us are striving for."

But he declined.

Eric had gone back to Jerusalem and then Tel Aviv to oversee the other two ministry sites.

One morning, sitting around the breakfast table, Thomas looked at Caleb.

"I would like to go to Capernaum and Tiberias and see if I can remember anything from my dream. I understand Capernaum is no longer there except for some ruins, but I am sure I can make out where Lucius and I had our medical practice. Would you mind taking us there tomorrow in the van?"

"That sounds like an excellent idea. It will get us out of this depressing inactivity. I have room for six people. Whoever wants to go, let me know now."

Three hands went up. Theresa, Mikail and Meta.

"That is great," Thomas said. "Mikail, you can translate for us, while Meta can explain some of the details of the ruins and the different towns along the way. I wonder if I will be able to recognize anything?" he added.

A feeling of awe and excitement filled him as the car turned onto the highway to Tiberias. Haifa is situated almost straight across from the ancient city, connected by modern highways. Thomas sat up front with Caleb. He looked intensely for any landmarks familiar to him on the way, but the landscape was dotted with fields and orchards just like it had been in ancient times.

He remembered Tiberias well and cringed at the thought of the lascivious life style he had been a part of there. King Herod's court, as well as wealthy Romans and Greeks had flocked to the bath's and houses of entertainment, where gossip about Cesar Tiberius and Herod's court at Sepphoris were the favorite entertainment of the spoiled upper class. Thomas strained to see if he could spot any familiar sites when they entered the northern part of the city, but found only ruins and lone standing walls. Although, the familiar brown hills on one side of Tiberius and the Sea of Galilee were the same as he strolled through the ancient ruins. He could not find even one familiar spot as he wandered among the low, remaining stone walls, where splendid buildings had once stood. He was actually glad when Caleb suggested it was time to leave to go north to Capernaum, or Kfar Nahum, as it is still called. His heart pounded as they drove north on Hwy 90 along the shore of the Sea of Galilee. From the distance, Thomas could see the mountain range on the other side, exactly the way it had been and felt transported back in time. It was not until now that he found out, this was the lowest fresh water lake in the world. He closed his eyes and visualized how he had traveled this stretch so many times in his carriage, going from his villa to Capernaum to visit his patients.

"Do you think we could go and see if there is any sign left of my villa?" he asked as they were speeding along.

"Sweetheart, I don't think it will be there, since it never was, except in your dream," Melissa said and took his hand. "I know this must be very real to you," she added and touched his shoulder with her hand. "Maybe you will recognize something when we get to Capernaum.

He sat in silence as they approached the ruins of the small place he had called home. His heart raced as Caleb drove closer to where the town had been carefully excavated not that many years ago.

Caleb looked at Thomas.

"Do you recognize anything?" He pointed to a modern, octagon-shaped building by the sea. "This is supposed to be the spot where Peter's house was located."

“That is not where it was,” Thomas said with certainty. It was further down that way,” he said and pointed to a spot on the lakeshore.

“How about the ruins of the Synagogue?” Caleb asked. “Let’s walk through it and see if they look familiar.” He stopped on the main road and parked the van in a spot designated for tourists. “We will have to walk over there if we want to get a closer look.”

Thomas slowly walked up to the ruins, with a row of thick columns right down the middle, leading up to a solid wall at the end. He was stunned.

“I remember these columns,” he whispered. “Yeshua stood right here when he came out of the synagogue the day He healed Esther, my slave woman,” he said and pointed to the first one with awe in his voice. “I remember the crowds enjoying Him chastising the Pharisee for not wanting to heal her on the Shabbat.” He ran out to the road in front of the ruins and pointed to a certain place on the dirt road. “I drove on this very ground with my horse-drawn carriage to bring Esther, bent over and in terrible pain. In this spot I argued with the leader of the synagogue whether to let her in or not.” Thomas began to shake as he looked around. “I have been here, I have seen the Master, it was real!” He began to shake and sank to the ground. “I am not worthy, but I talked to Yeshua right here.” He pointed to the spot as his shoulders shook and he began to sob. “I was here and so was He.”

Melissa sat down next to him in the dirt and took his hand. “I believe you, sweetheart.”

The others stood in silence, filled with awe and a certain amount of fear, realizing they stood in the same spot as the Son of God had stood two thousand years ago. No one spoke for a long time until Thomas slowly got up and looked over the excavation site of the remnants of what was once Capernaum.

“I listened to Yeshua talking one day. I was in my carriage to visit a patient. He stood and looked out over the general direction of Capernaum and some other towns in the region. I clearly remember how sad He sounded when he spoke as He said,

“And you, Capernaum, will you be lifted up to the skies? No, you will go down to the depths. If the miracles that were performed in you had been performed in Sodom, it would have remained to this day. But I tell you that it will be more bearable for Sodom on the day of judgment." (Matthew 11:23-24)

"I didn't hear what He said before that, but I have read since then He included Korazin and Bethsaida." Thomas, his voice, thick with emotion, continued, "His words came true. Buried in the depth for nearly two thousand years, this town was finally unearthed, broken and useless, never to be built up again." Thomas looked at the others as if waking up from a dream and said with sudden certainty, "It doesn't matter what things look like right now. The Lord will open doors and fulfill what He has told me to do, to take His message to His people Israel." He turned to the others with a solemn look. "Do not tell what you have heard me say, because someone will build a ridiculous shrine on this spot if they find out. Whether any of this is real or not, Yeshua let me know He is in control and will be with this ministry, no matter what hindrances men will devise against it." He smiled at them with a new-found confidence. "We will see the Glory of God and be part of the harvest of the end-times to come."

Chapter 13

It was three weeks later, on a hot, sweltering day, when a visitor knocked on the door of Shalom Outreach. Thomas watched him approach from the window. The man seemed in his mid-thirties, dressed in jeans and a white t-shirt with white sneakers to match. He was definitely of Arab descent, with a slender built and a short, cropped beard. Thomas couldn't see much of his face since he wore a baseball cap pulled deep over his eyes. What was odd, he carried an expensive leather briefcase in contrast to his casual clothes.

"What can I do for you?" Caleb asked, as he opened the door a small way, looking at the visitor with suspicion.

"I am Fouad Nabeth from Tel Aviv. I have come to talk to a man named Dr. Thomas Peterson from America," he said in a hushed tone. "Could you please let me in before someone sees me?"

Reluctantly, Caleb opened the door just wide enough to allow the man to enter.

"What do you want with Dr. Peterson, Sir?" he asked with reservation in his voice. "We are a Christian mission and wish to live in peace with our neighbors."

Thomas stepped out of his room.

"I am Dr. Peterson, what is it you want with me?"

The strange visitor stretched out his hand and said in fluent English with just a slight Arabic accent, "I am so very pleased to meet you, Doctor. What I have come to discuss will take a little while. Would it be ok if I sat down and talk to you? I assure you, I mean you or this ministry no harm.

"This is the man you need to speak with," Thomas said and pointed to Caleb. He is in charge of this mission."

"That would be perfectly acceptable, Sir," the young man said with a smile. "As a matter of fact, what I have come to say will affect everyone here, not just Dr. Peterson." He had a polished mannerism that spoke of a good upbringing and wealth.

"Please follow me to the boardroom, Mr. Nabeth," Caleb said.

"Wait," Thomas said, "I insist that my wife be present as well. Allow me to get her and we will meet you there." He turned around to get Melissa before anyone could object.

Soon they sat at the table across from the visitor.

"What is it you have come to talk to me about, Mr. Nabeth?" Thomas asked, curious.

"Please call me Fouad, Dr. Peterson."

Thomas did not offer the same in return, but looked at the young man with a certain amount of caution.

"We are waiting," he finally said.

"Of course, Doctor. Like I said, I am Fouad Nabeth and I am here to offer you a building for a clinic in Tiberias. It is large enough to house this ministry as well."

"Why would you do that, Mr. Nabeth," Caleb asked, his voice filled with suspicion. "You are obviously a Muslim. Why would you want to help a Christian organization?"

"I am a Muslim, Sir. Not only that, my father is Mohamed Nabeth."

"*The* Mohamed Yusuf Nabeth?" Caleb asked, his voice filled with astonishment and fear. "That makes it even more unlikely for you to do something like this." He looked at Thomas. "I am sorry, but I don't trust this man."

"Who is Mohamed Yusuf Nabeth?" Thomas asked.

"He is one of the wealthiest diamond dealers in Haifa and maybe in the Middle East; and no friend to Christians."

Thomas looked at Fouad.

"That is true, Dr. Peterson. As a matter of fact, my father hates them."

"Then what are you doing here offering us a house for this ministry?" Caleb cut in before Thomas could say anything.

"Thomas, you don't know the animosity that exists between Muslims and Christians. He turned to the visitor. "You are putting us all in danger by coming here. Your father is suspected of being a part of the Muslim Brotherhood and some say, even ISIS, better known as the Islamic State."

It was the first time Thomas saw Caleb upset to the point of frantic.

“Those are merely rumors, Sir. My father maybe many things, but he is not a terrorist, Dr. Peterson, I assure you,” he said emphatically.

“That may or may not be true, Mr. Nabeth, we cannot take a chance,” Caleb answered instead. “Besides, why would you want to help us if you are a Muslim?”

“That is what I have come to talk to you about, if you will give me a chance.” The man sounded urgent. “I don’t understand any of it, all I know, I am here to offer you a house in Tiberias for your clinic, Dr. Peterson.”

“Dr. Peterson does not make those decisions, I do,” Caleb said in a sharp tone. “If you cannot address me, then I must ask you to leave.”

“Caleb, let’s listen to what he has to say,” Melissa said in a gentle tone. “This could be the answer we have all been waiting for.”

“It could also be the end of Shalom Outreach if this is a trap.” Thomas could tell Caleb was trying his best to get his fear under control. “You guys have no idea what these people are capable of when it comes to religious matters,” he added.

“Wouldn’t it be amazing if the Lord used our enemies to help us?” Melissa added, looking at Caleb with a smile. “It would not be the first time. Let’s at least listen to what he has to say.”

Caleb looked at her and then at Fouad Nabeth.

“I suppose, since he is here, it can’t do any more harm than it already has. The damage was done when I let him into the house.” He looked at Melissa and Thomas with resignation and turned to the man. “You might as well tell us what it is that makes you want to help us.”

Fouad Nabeth took a deep breath as if trying to find the words.

“Some weeks ago, I was looking out over the Sea of Galilee in Tiberias on the terrace of my villa. Having been brought up in a wealthy home, you might think it strange, but I have always felt there has been a call on my life to serve Allah in a special way. Unlike my three brothers, I never indulged in their seedy lifestyle or the many excesses of the privileged. Instead, I studied the Koran extensively and then attended a University in the US and got a degree in business. I wanted to be a good son to my father and join his business when the time came, Allah willing.

While in the US, I met a girl and fell in love. Since she was not a Muslim or from my country, my father forbid me to marry her and called me back to Tel Aviv to take a job in his enterprise. I obeyed him, because that is what Allah expects of me, but I have been unhappy ever since. A surprising thing happened to me when I returned. Having been exposed to other faiths and listening to the press reports about the many terrorist attacks all over the world, the Muslim religion suddenly seemed unyielding and stuck in the Middle Ages. To my astonishment, I began to see Allah as a harsh, cold god and wondered what drove so many young Muslim extremists to violence and hatred on such a wide scale.

One day, by chance, I picked up a copy of the New Testament left by one of my servants, hidden behind a shelf in the kitchen when I was looking for a snack in the late evening. Curious, I started reading it. To my surprise, I discovered that this prophet Jesus was different. While Allah wants us to kill our enemies, Jesus wants us to love them. While Allah demands sacrifices, Jesus gave Himself to be a sacrifice. I was stunned to find that the God of the Christians is different from all others in that He not only *has* love, He says He *is* love. That is a concept I had never heard of, and it intrigued me. As I read more, it shook my Muslim faith to the core, and I began to doubt what I knew about Allah. Yet out of fear, I decided to stop reading, because if my family knew of my doubts, but especially my interest in the Christian faith, my life would be in danger. I had no doubt, I would definitely lose my inheritance and be cast out by my father. This prospect frightened me to such an extent, I joined the lavish lifestyle of my brothers instead to help me forget.

That was three years ago. Since then, I was made a partner in my father's business and have become a wealthy man in my own rights. But no matter how successful I have become, I am unable to forget about this Jesus of the Christians, no matter how many times I have cried out to Allah to show me that he is the one god."

"What does all this have to do with our ministry, Mr. Nabeth," Caleb asked.

"I am coming to that, if you will allow me to continue, Sir," he answered.

Caleb nodded for him to go on.

Fouad Nabeth shifted uneasy in his chair and looked at Thomas with an almost pleading look.

"I have no idea how to explain what I am about to tell you, other than it happened exactly this way. Like I said in the beginning, I was sitting on the terrace of my villa in Tiberias early one morning, when a tall man, dressed in a brilliant white garment suddenly stood before me. I was startled and reached to call for my security guards, when he said, 'Do not be afraid, the Lord God of Abraham, Isaak and Jacob has sent me to tell you that He has heard your cry for the truth. He wants you to know that you are to go to Haifa, to the Shalom Outreach Mission and ask for an American by the name of Dr. Thomas Peterson. You are to give him your building on the outskirts of Tiberias to use for His purpose. In return, you will find out what you must do to inherit the Kingdom of God."

"Before I could ask what all this means, the man vanished before my eyes." Fouad looked at Thomas with pleading eyes. "Please, Sir, do you know what this means?"

"I do," Thomas said with awe in his voice. "It must have been at the same time, several weeks ago, I stood outside one evening and cried out to Yeshua to let me go home, since everywhere I looked, nothing was happening and I realized I had made a mistake to come here. That was when an angel appeared to me and told me God's purpose would be fulfilled." Thomas looked to Caleb and said, "I never told you about that, because I was embarrassed. Everyone looked to me to lead this ministry, yet I had no idea what to do or where to go and knew I was a failure."

Into the stunned silence, Caleb finally managed to say,

"You are indeed sent by God, Fouad. I hope you realize what this means for you. Your life will be in great danger if you agree to accept Jesus into your heart. Are you willing to lose it all for gaining the truth you have been searching for?"

"Since I don't know what that truth is, I cannot answer you until Dr. Peterson tells me." He looked expectantly at Thomas. "Will you tell me like that man told me you would?"

"I will be glad to, but it is a long story. You see, I was an atheist, so sure of my own goodness without the need for any god," Thomas said and proceeded to tell Fouad Nabeth about his dream.

"It was more than a dream, wasn't it?" Fouad Nabeth finally asked when Thomas was finished.

"It was, Fouad."

"Does that mean Allah is not real?"

"There is only one God and He is the God of Abraham, Isaak and Jacob. He is also the One who sent His Son to die for your sins. I found out, that on my own I cannot ever be good enough to enter the Kingdom of heaven. Even if I do good works every day, it will never be enough to earn the key to enter. Only by accepting the sacrifice of Yeshua and worshiping Him as the Meshiah will you be allowed to spend eternity with Him. His gift is there for everyone, but you must receive it into your heart. Are you willing to do that?" Thomas asked.

"Does that mean I have to renounce Allah in order to accept this Yeshua?" Fouad asked with a tremor in his voice.

"Yes, you do, my friend," Caleb said. "Nobody can serve two masters, he will love the one and hate the other, Jesus said. But it is your decision, no one can make it for you" he added.

There was silence until Fouad finally spoke,

"I will lose everything if I do this and my family finds out, even my life."

"Trust the Lord," Melissa said and took his hand. "Since He has chosen you to help us, don't you think He is capable of protecting you? Our God is bigger than any other god or any person, even your father. Put your life into His hands and He will be with you, no matter what comes."

"What must I do?" He asked, looking at Thomas with a mixture of fear and hope.

"Tell Yeshua that you are a sinner." Thomas answered with a smile. "We all are. And then give Him your life to do with as He wishes. Tell Him in your own words what is on your heart and what you have decided. We will listen and agree with you."

The young man looked down on his hands for a long time and then bowed his head,

"You sent an angel to me, because You want me to follow You. All my life I have prayed to Allah, but now I believe that You are the one and true God. I also believe that you sent your Son Yeshua to die for me, because you love me. Allah never did that. You tell me to love my enemies, Allah never asked that of me, but wants me to kill them. I don't even know what name to call You, but I will find out. All I know is that You are the God of the Jews and the God of the Christians, and there is no other. I renounce Allah and accept You, Yeshua. You are more than a prophet, more than a man, You are the Meshiah and I put my trust in You. Take my life and do with it as You wish and allow me to serve You for the rest of my life, however short that might be."

He was crying, whether out of faith or fear, Thomas did not know.

Chapter 14

After Fouad left, there was a feeling of excitement mixed with apprehension and even fear among the team members. The realization that the rich son of an even richer prominent member of the Muslim community had chosen to join them secretly was both exhilarating and dangerous. It wasn't that they didn't trust him, but how could they possibly buy a building he owned in Tiberius without his family knowing about it. Fouad had told them to wait until he could get things lined up.

After a few days, Thomas, Caleb and Eric met with him in a small café just outside of Tel Aviv, where he told them how this could be done. They sat in the corner, each with a cup of coffee and a piece of cake, partially hidden from the rest of the tables.

"I have figured out how to do it," Fouad said with a bright smile. They immediately noticed a change in him as he shared with them about his clandestine plan.

"Shalom Outreach will have to buy the building outright for a certain amount," he started.

"We don't have that kind of money," Caleb said before he could go on.

"I know that, Caleb," Fouad said and put his hand on Caleb's arm. "Take it easy and hear me out. I have transferred the funds into an account in the US belonging to a wealthy businessman who is also a supporter of your ministry. It will be done under the guise of consulting fees. He in turn will transfer it to Shalom Outreach and they will then be able to buy my building without anyone being the wiser."

He leaned back with a triumphant smile.

"Neither my father nor anyone else will ever find out as long as no one here tells. I hope I can count on your discretion. As a matter of fact, there is no need for anyone but the people at this table and the leadership in Chicago to know about it."

"You are as wise as a serpent and as gentle as a dove, Fouad," Caleb said. "I am impressed.

"I have been reading the Bible as often as I can find a private moment," Fouad said. "I have even shared a little with a girl my father has chosen for me. She confided in me that she heard about Christianity from one of her maids. I have to be careful since I don't know how serious she is about this. We are just getting to know each other. Both, my father and her parents would be mortified if they knew we even talked about this. I have no intention to lose another woman because of Allah. This time I will be careful and trust the Lord to talk to her when the time is right," he said. "Maybe the two of us are destined to serve Him after we are married."

The day finally arrived when they drove to Tiberias to sign the paperwork for the building. Eric, Caleb, Thomas and Melissa walked up to the four-story building in the center of town with apprehension. Fouad's office was on the second floor. They had decided they would act as if they did not know each other to avoid any suspicion. He was there with two of his lawyers and greeted them in a formal way.

"It is nice to finally meet you, Mr. Foster," he said and shook Eric's hand.

"I want you to meet my associates, Mr. Nabeth," Eric said and pointed to the others. "This is Caleb Weinstein, and Dr. Peterson and his wife Melissa. We are all glad to meet you."

"These are my legal advisors, Mahmud Assad and Faruk Haddath," Fouad said and pointed to the two men with him. "They will handle all the legalities and have you sign the appropriate papers."

It took quite a while until the sale was finalized and Fouad dismissed the lawyers.

"Now we can talk," he said as they sat down in the group of comfortable chairs to the side of his desk. "The building is yours and I am excited to see what the Lord is going to do with it."

"Did you have any trouble with your father selling it to Shalom Outreach?" Eric asked.

"There were some raised eyebrows when he found out I sold property to a Christian Mission, but when I told them about the good price I got for it, he calmed down. I guess money trumps religious objections," he chuckled. "I will help with the renovations to make it suitable for a clinic, but it will also have to be done in secret," he added.

"There is no way we can ever thank you enough for what you have done, Fouad," Eric said. "Believe me, we all realize the danger you subject yourself to in doing this. May the Lord richly bless you in ways we never could."

"I have talked with my fiancé some more. She seems to be open to the Christian faith, but I will have to wait until she is my wife before I can share my new faith with her. Under our law she has no right to question me then, and has to go along with whatever I tell her."

"Do you really feel you have the right to do that?" Melissa asked. "I mean; do you still agree with that sort of thing now that you are a Christian?"

"I didn't agree with it before I became one, but in this case, it is a good thing for my safety." He looked at Melissa with a boyish grin," Don't you worry, I will treat her nice, the way you and Yeshua would want me to."

Melissa turned crimson. "I didn't mean it that way."

"Yes, she did," Thomas laughed. "She only looks meek and mild, on the inside she is a tiger."

"Thomas!" She punched him on the arm. "You are terrible."

"In order to keep my cover, I must ask you to leave now," Fouad said and got up. "It would look suspicious if I sat and talked to Christians longer than necessary. I will make a way to meet with you and learn more about the faith. I can't say that I would stay a rich man doing business like this on a regular basis, but looking at it from an eternal point of view, I think I came out the winner here." He laughed as he shook hands with everyone. "Take care, until we meet again and may Yeshua be with you."

"We are the proud owner of a clinic in the making," Caleb said on the way back to the car. "I can't believe I almost threw the man out, if it hadn't been for you two." He looked at Thomas and Melissa. "Isn't it amazing what the Lord can accomplish in spite of me," he chuckled good-naturedly.

"That goes for me, too," Thomas said. "Just think, I was begging the Lord to let me go home not too long ago. And here He is, allowing me to go back to Galilee, where I treated the poor two thousand years ago. You will admit, that is exciting." He looked at the others. "I wouldn't even mind if I still had my carriage and two sleek horses to get around in. What would top it off would be seeing Yeshua up on a hill between Tiberias and Capernaum, preaching to the crowds. It was amazing how His voice carried without a microphone. I wondered about that many times." He looked out as they drove down the highway amidst fields of grain and orchards on each side. "This hasn't changed much, not until you get into the cities. They don't look like anything from back then and make me feel like a stranger."

"Your dream must have been more than real, Thomas," Caleb said. "It is amazing how you remember it the way it really was and not the way it could have been. I will never forget when we got to the ruins of the synagogue in Kfar Nahum, how you knew where Jesus stood. It definitely makes it more than a dream, since you had never been there before. The whole thing is absolutely fantastic."

"Everything about my life is fantastic since I met Yeshua," Thomas said. "And the real work has just begun," he added.

It took six weeks to renovate the building to make it suitable for a clinic and an office building. The funds for the work appeared regularly from Chicago and no one ever asked where they came from. The shipment with the medical equipment and the medicine needed to treat the patients arrived one afternoon in two large trucks. Thomas and Melissa, as well as Mikail worked for three days to get it set up and put in order.

On a hot day, toward the end of the summer, the clinic doors opened to a large crowd of on-lookers. Word had gotten around that an American surgeon would operate on people, even if they didn't have any money. Several local women had been hired as nurses' helpers and Mikail found one young man who was proficient enough to perform simple tests in the laboratory.

It was not Mercy Hospital in Philadelphia, but it was good. Thomas looked around with a feeling of satisfaction. *Lucius would be proud.* Meta and Mikail were standing by to translate for the Hebrew speaking patients, if necessary. They were still looking for someone who spoke English and Arabic, but had found that many understood enough English to make do without.

The first patient was a woman with a little girl in her arms. Thomas couldn't tell how old she was, because she wore a heavy, black shroud covering all but her eyes. Melissa led her right in to see Thomas, because the little girl was burning up, yet listless and unresponsive.

"Her appendix burst, Melissa. I have to operate right away," Thomas said as soon as he examined her. I hope it is not too late. Make sure we have enough antibiotics and prep her for surgery," he said. "Please, help me, Lord. This is my first patient and it is what I came here for," he prayed while leaning over the sink, scrubbing his hands.

It was a simple surgery and with a heavy dose of antibiotics, the little girl was up and around by the next morning. The grateful mother handed Thomas a bag of figs and an orange when he told her, the girl would be alright. He smiled. Things hadn't changed all that much from way back then. He still got paid in fruits and vegetables and would never get rich any time soon.

"You saved my little girl's life," she said in broken English. I am grateful. My husband refused to pay for it and was going to let her die, because she is only a girl," she said. "Thank you, Doctor, and may Allah reward you."

Thomas stood, stunned.

"That's right, her husband has the money to pay for this, but won't," Caleb whispered in Thomas' ear. "They probably already have several girls and no boy, so she is just another mouth to feed and therefore considered useless."

"You are kidding, right?" Thomas asked.

"No, I'm not. That is how things are done here among parts of the Muslim population; you better get used to it."

Thomas was too busy for the rest of the day to think about the situation. He fell into bed, dead tired from seeing so many sick and suffering people, that he was asleep by the time Melissa joined him.

Chapter 15

Thomas looked up from the microscope when a stranger walked into his office several weeks later. He was tall and thin, with the typical dark, close cropped beard of an Arab and wore a long, white tunic that reached down to his sandals.

Thomas sat up slowly.

"What can I do for you, Sir?"

"I am not here as a patient, but I need to talk to you in private, Dr. Peterson," the man said in broken English. "It is important."

"Who let you in here?" Thomas asked, cautiously. He had learned in the few weeks since the clinic opened to be careful about trusting the many different nationalities living in this part of the world.

"No one, Doctor. I slipped by the desk when the nurse looked away," he answered.

Now Thomas was alarmed.

"What do you want?"

"Please, I do not wish you any harm," the man said as he stepped closer. "I am a Christian Pastor and have come to ask you to speak to my congregation. I have a church on the outskirts of Tiberias, in a small village in the country. There are quite a few of us and we want to learn from the physician who walked with Yeshua."

"How did you hear about me?" Thomas asked, astonished.

"Your name is spoken with awe among those who believe, Sir, because you do not just say you are a follower of Yeshua, you act like Him by healing the poor. All of us, Palestinians, Arabs and Jews have heard of you, but are afraid to talk to you for fear of the religious authorities."

"But I have not spoken to anyone about my experience," Thomas said, "how could they have heard?"

The man smiled.

"A woman named Theresa goes around and tells people about how you spent three years in the ancient land of Israel in the company of Yeshua. She draws great crowds in the market place and in the streets of Tiberius with her tale. We all wonder why she has not been stopped. There are rumors that Yeshua Himself is protecting her."

"You still have not told me your name, Sir," Thomas said.

"I am Yusuf Ahmed. I am a Palestinian and the pastor of the church. We have to be very careful these days since to be a Christian is dangerous. Our church has been forced to meet in secret for fear of the extreme elements which have recently infiltrated our area. Will you come and talk to us?"

"If you are trying to scare me, it's working," Thomas said and smiled. "I have to speak with the person in charge of Shalom Outreach and see what he says before I can make a decision. I don't see why he would object, but it is better to make sure since I am the only doctor in the mission. This clinic is allowed to operate in this part of the country only if a doctor runs it. To put myself in a dangerous situation like this could be the end of our work if anything happens to me."

"I understand, Sir, but so much prayer has gone up before I came here, I am sure the Lord will make a way." Yusuf looked at Thomas with confidence and added, "You were sent here not just to heal the sick in body, but also the sick in spirit, do you not agree?"

"I do, Pastor and I will try very hard to come and speak to your people," Thomas said as he shook his hand. "It was good to meet with you. Please give the nurse a number where I can reach you and I will be in touch as soon as I know something."

There was much discussion with the team that evening around the dinner table.

"This can jeopardize our entire operation," Caleb finally said as he reached for the bread. "On the other hand, it is what we are here for."

"God has sent all of us to this place to be witnesses of His power," Theresa said with great emphasis. "He would not have sent you, Thomas, anointed and trained through a miraculous dream, if He did not want you to do more than just be a physician. I am convinced He has a special purpose for you and it isn't just being a surgeon."

"You have definitely spread the word about that, haven't you, Theresa," Thomas said with a slight frown, "and without my approval." Before she could answer, he turned to the others, "I want to make very sure all of you do not expect more from me than I can deliver. I know how to do surgery; I do not know how to preach or walk on water. Every single one of you is better qualified in spiritual matters than I am."

"That is where you are wrong," Theresa said and flipped a strand of her long, blond hair out of her face in an almost angry move of her hand. "You have been with Jesus, the rest of us have not." She looked at Thomas with a frown. "I wish you would stop telling us that you don't know anything spiritual, we know better and so should you."

"Are you saying I should be a preacher instead of a doctor?" Thomas tried not to get upset.

"Why can't you be both?" Meta said. "Jesus was."

Thomas looked at her, frustrated and angry.

"What are you saying?"

"I am telling you that the Lord did not just send you here to heal people with your talents as a surgeon. There are many who could do the same, unless you are trying to tell us you are the best He could find." She leaned forward, her eyes had a steely glint in them as she continued. "He sent you here to show His power and love for His people Israel; and there is no way you can tell me He is going to settle for your limited talents as a surgeon." She looked down at her plate, her petit body suddenly trembling with passion. "I am sorry, Thomas, I am tired of you telling us you don't know much. Trust me, we all understand that. As you saw with your own eyes, the Apostles didn't know much either and look what they accomplished. So stop whining and do what God sent you here to do – let Him use you the way He wants to and not the way you think He should. In other words, Jesus does not need your talents, all He is interested in that you obey Him when He opens the doors. If you go in your own power, we all agree, you would not be able to do much, but if you go and trust in Him, you will be exactly the same as the Apostles, weak vessels filled with the strength of the Lord."

The silence in the room was deafening. Thomas stared at his plate, his anger replaced by conviction. *Once again, his pride had gotten in the way and everybody knew it! What a jerk I am.* It was as if Yeshua stood and smiled at him with His knowing smile. *He knows. Oh God!*

"Well, that pretty well settles it whether you should go or not, doesn't it, Thomas?" Caleb finally said. "We all understand the danger that this will put this ministry in, but then, the Lord knows that, too. All of us will have to rely on His protection and strength, not just you, Thomas. We are behind you in this and together we will see what God will do in spite of the enemy all around us." He breathed a sigh of relief as he looked first at Thomas and then at the others. "Are we all in agreement on this?"

All eyes went to Thomas. He sat with his eyes glued to his plate, his face filled with apprehension and doubt. *I wish I hadn't come, Lord. I could be home in Philadelphia doing surgery and living a comfortable life and doing what I was trained to do. There is no way I can go out there and talk to people who expect me to be what I am not – a preacher. I really would like to go home if I cannot be a surgeon.* He looked up and tried to smile, but couldn't.

"You guys may have the faith and confidence in what I am supposed to do here, but I don't. I am a scientist, not a preacher, a surgeon, not a spiritual healer; and to go out there among people who are as alien to me as they can be, is ridiculous." He looked at Meta. "And no matter what you say, I am scared, confused and wish I could run away from all this." He put his head in his hands and sat in silence as the others looked at him with doubt and disappointment.

"Does that mean you are not going, Thomas?" Caleb finally asked.

"It does," he said without looking up. "I can't, because I can't be what I am not. Yeshua made a mistake when He picked me. He should have known better."

"Yahweh doesn't make mistakes, Tommy," a voice said from the doorway. "You are the one to go and you know it."

Thomas whirled around.

"Nana!"

"I can see I came just in the nick of time to set your head straight," she said with a broad smile before Thomas folded her into his arms.

"What are you doing here?" he asked when he let her go.

“I called Marcia Menendez in Chicago and asked her to take me to see my grandson preaching the Good News in the land of Israel. Don’t disappoint me or I will have something to say about it.” She looked at him with such love and affection, he couldn’t help but shrug his shoulders in a gesture of surrender.

“I have never been able to say no to you, Nana.” He turned to Marcia. “How did she ever talk you into this trip?”

“She didn’t have to ask me twice, especially since she paid for my ticket,” Marcia laughed. “As head of Shalom Outreach, it was time I pay a visit to our mission field anyway. I can’t wait to see the new clinic in action on Monday. I spoke with Eric and he and his team is coming here tomorrow. It looks like we will have a conference and I get to talk with everyone and see what God’s plans are.” She took a seat at the head of the table, while Melissa took Nana to her rooms to rest.

“I know you didn’t just come on the spur of the moment, Marcia,” Caleb said. “What is going on?”

“Things are not looking good and dark clouds are gathering on the world stage,” she said with a deep sigh. “The Middle East is a powder cag and it can explode at any moment. I have spoken with some folks in Washington and the situation looks grim. The new president may not be as good a friend to Israel as he said and has openly declared America will not help in case of an attack by Iran or the Islamic State. He even hinted that he will stop Israeli planes if they should decide to attack Iran before they can drop a bomb on Israel. From what I can see, Israel is alone and the only one who can help her is God.”

“Does that mean we will be asked to leave if it gets worse?” Caleb asked.

“Nothing has been said and I imagine we are ok for now. From what Senator Cranston told me the other day, we have never been this close to nuclear war since the Kennedy era,” she said. “We must be prepared to leave at any time.” She looked around the table with a smile and then fastened her eyes on Thomas. “It also means we don’t have long to spread the Gospel. Your purpose is clear, Thomas, you must go wherever God opens doors for you, no matter how dangerous it may seem. He will protect you and guide you, I have no doubt. Are you ready?” She leaned toward him with a look of expectation. “There is no time to lose.”

Chapter 16

Thomas woke up early. The sun was barely touching the horizon. It was Sunday and today was the day! Everything had been arranged for him to go to the small village almost ten miles outside of Tiberias, the name of which he had forgotten. He looked over at Melissa. She was still sleeping peacefully. He had not felt this scared since he took the final exam in medical school. He remembered, one day he was a student and the next day he was supposed to be a doctor. This was no different. Yesterday he was a surgeon and today a messenger sent by God to tell people whose language he did not understand and whose customs were even stranger, that Yeshua loved them.

I wish I loved them like you do, Lord. I fear them more than anything else and feel I have nothing in common with these people. Besides, Lord, I have no idea what to say that they have not already heard in their church. Please, if You do not give me the words when I get there, I will just stand there and freeze. My knowledge of the Bible is still not that great and neither am I. It would be different if I had as much faith as everyone here at Shalom Outreach, but You know I don't. Why did you pick me? All I ever wanted to be was a surgeon, Lord. You know I believe in You, but that is all I know right now. Everyone says it takes faith to serve You. Right now I don't have any. Please help me!

His stomach started to feel sick.

"I know you are scared, honey," Melissa said and reached for his hand. "Something wonderful is going to happen today, I can just feel it."

"Why can't I feel it?" he said with irritation in his voice. He felt the old anger rise in him toward Yeshua for leaving him clueless. "Why can't He ever talk to me in plain language I can understand instead of letting me grope in the dark? Doesn't He know I would do anything if I just knew what it is He wants me to do?"

"They call it faith, sweetheart," Melissa said with a chuckle.

He turned to her in anger.

"Wouldn't it be much easier if His will was made plain to me? I feel like I am in the middle of a storm, blind, helpless and at His mercy. What if nothing happens and I fail to convince them what I experienced was real? I am going to look like a fool. I swear to you, I will go back to Philadelphia and try to get my job back at Mercy hospital."

"Thomas, with all that has happened, how can you doubt He will be there with you?" Melissa asked in a gentle voice. She raised up on one elbow. "I tell you what, if you don't have the faith, I will have it for you. After all, we are in this together."

"You better, because I don't have anything but fear and doubt right now to the point I think I am going to be sick." He sat on the edge of the bed with his head in his hands, close to tears. " Please, Yeshua, help me, I can't do this without You."

An hour later, as he looked out of the car speeding down the highway, he wished he was in his carriage, Yeshua just around the bend, preaching to the multitudes on the hill. How good it would be to talk to Lucius or Helena. The fear got worse the closer they got to their destination. He was sure Yeshua had forgotten about him or was somehow busy up there in heaven.

"So this is where you were in your dream, Tommy," Nana asked. "I bet you remember the spots where Yeshua preached."

"I do, Nana, I just wish He would still be here and perform the miracles and feed the poor like He did then," Thomas said almost in a whisper.

"He is, Tommy," Nana said with total certainty. "He will do today what He did then and will show you His Glory."

He heard that same special tone in her voice she had when she told him to go and preach the Gospel on the day she accepted her Meshiah back in Philadelphia. "Put away your fear, Tommy, He is with you and so are we." She squeezed his hand.

The car stopped in front of a dilapidated, long, narrow, old building in the middle of nowhere. The front looked as if it was ready to collapse, being held up by a narrow door that squeaked as if in agony when Caleb opened it a few inches. They could not see any cars or sign that anyone was there.

"Are you sure this is it?" Thomas asked. "Maybe nobody showed up. Wouldn't that be nice," he added under his breath.

That's when the door was opened slowly from the inside and Pastor Ahmed waved them inside.

"Welcome everyone. Please, come on in, we are waiting for you." He pointed to a long, narrow room filled with hundreds of people crammed into rows of chairs, facing the front. "Dr. Peterson, if you and those with you will come up front, we have some seats for you."

The low hum of many voices had died down the moment they entered the room and every eye watched as Thomas and the team walked down the narrow walkway to the first row up front. After he introduced Melissa and the team, Thomas was asked to sit down in the first seat with a young man next to him which he hoped was the translator.

"I am Rashid Hafez and I will be translating what is being said," he said, his eyes sparkling with excitement. His English was amazingly good and in spite of his accent, Thomas had no trouble understanding him.

Pastor Ahmed stepped up to the microphone with a big smile.

"We are so blessed to have with us Dr. Thomas Peterson from America, the man who walked with Yeshua for three years. With him is his wife and grandmother, as well as the rest of the team from Shalom Outreach. Please welcome them." The crowd broke out in cheers and clapping and the Pastor had a hard time getting them to stop. "Much prayer has gone up for this event and I know many have come from many miles away to hear this brother tell us what happened that he should have been chosen to witness the ministry, death and resurrection of our Lord. Let's join in prayer, praise and worship now and after that I will ask Dr. Peterson to take over the meeting."

Thomas's heart was beating in his throat. This was it! He tried hard to remain calm, but noticed his hands were sweating and his mouth dry. He still had no idea what to say or how to say it, since every time he tried to make notes, his mind went blank.

Please, Lord, help me. I don't just want to talk, I want to share what You want me to share, but I don't know how to do it, because my mind is blank and nothing will come to me. It is as if I am unable to speak or think.

"Please, welcome our special guest and dear brother in the Lord, Dr. Thomas Peterson," he suddenly heard from far away. He walked up to the podium as if in a daze with Rashid following right behind him. At least he had gotten used to having a translator while working at the clinic during the last two months.

There was total silence as he looked out over the crowd. He could feel the atmosphere filled with an electrifying expectation he could not explain. As his eyes scanned across the crowd, to his horror he realized the first three rows to his right were occupied by people with obvious disabilities. He counted three crudely made wheelchairs, one stretcher and many with canes and walkers as well as children with deformities carried by their mothers. *Oh God!* This was more than his worst nightmare could have come up with. They had come to be healed, not by a scalpel, but by prayer! His first impulse was to run, but since that was not really an option, he turned to Pastor Ahmed, ready to tell him that they had the wrong idea about him. He was a surgeon, not a faith healer and this was all a sham. And then he heard his own voice.

"It was in this very land that Yeshua walked and sat on the hillside not too far from here, healing, preaching and caring for those who trusted in Him. It is here I heard Him tell that He would never leave us nor forsake us. On the banks of the Sea of Galilee He touched me, a hopeless sinner, disfigured by leprosy on the outside and sin on the inside, and made me whole. It was here I finally realized that on my own I can never be good, but with Him I can do all things." The words flowed as if someone else was speaking and Thomas continued.

"Before I tell you more, I want to share with you about a paraplegic, who was lowered through the tiles of the roof of a house in front of Yeshua. I knew there was nothing anyone could do, because he had a disease called MS and it was in the last stages. I stood close enough to see what happened. The Master looked at the man with a wonderful smile and forgave him his sins. When the authorities grumbled about that He dared to forgive Him, He simply told the man he was healed. I was one of those who watched him take up his bed and walk out." (taken from…

Thomas walked over to the wall where a stretcher stood with a young boy on it and said, "I have no idea what to say or pray other than what Yeshua did. I know without a doubt that I am not worthy or able to do anything for you, except ask the Lord to heal you in the Name of Yeshua." He put his hand on the boy and said in a gentle, barely audible voice, "Get up and walk, you are healed."

Nothing happened and the crowd watched in silence as Thomas slowly made his way back to the podium, ready to continue speaking. As he looked toward the young man, he suddenly saw the boy slowly raise up from the stretcher and carefully set both feet on the floor. His mother stood next to him, her face stunned as her son stood up on unsteady legs and then walked toward to where Thomas stood.

"He is healed!" the mother suddenly screamed. "My boy is healed! He has been paralyzed since birth and has never walked a day in his life. Look! He is walking!"

The people in the room jumped up, craning their neck and then shouting,

"He can walk, look, he can walk!"

The young man fell down in front of Thomas, crying uncontrollably as he grabbed his hands. "I can walk. Yeshua has healed me."

Thomas stood, totally stunned. He remembered the many scenes when the Lord touched all those who came to be made whole. He held onto the podium, his knuckles white. Yeshua had not forgotten him. He looked at Melissa, then at Nana and the team in the front row, their faces glowing with joy and amazement.

"Thank You, Master," he whispered over and over again, in total shock.

It was a long time until the crowd calmed down enough for him to take the microphone.

"What you have witnessed is the power of Yeshua in the same way I saw in my dream. He has not changed, but has sent me to do His work and share with you about His love and power to save, heal and bring many into His Kingdom before He returns. But not just me alone, He asks you as well to spread His Word of salvation to those who will listen."

He talked for another hour and shared more about what happened to him in his dream. At the end several people came forward to accept Yeshua and gave their lives over to Him. Thomas prayed for them as if he had done this all his life. Before he was finally ready to sit down, a middle-aged man stood in front of him with a confused look on his severe, hard face. Thomas looked at him with a friendly smile.

"What can I do for you, Sir?"

"I was sent here by the religious leaders to spy on Pastor Ahmed and on you. They are trying to close this church down and have authorized me to arrest the leaders of this congregation if I found any unusual religious fervor." He looked at Thomas with a mixture of anger and amazement as he continued, "I know the boy that got up off that bed. He belongs to the family of a distant cousin of mine. I can verify he has never walked before in his life. And yet, here he is." The man stared at Thomas. "I don't know what to think or what to do about this. There is no doubt in my mind that this is a miracle and yet how can that be? I believe in Allah and have spent most of my life punishing those who have offended him by refusing to worship him."

"Why don't you accept Yeshua and turn away from those who would persecute His followers," Thomas said with a warm smile.

"I will get killed if I do that, Dr. Peterson, you know that."

"Yes, I do know that, but I also know that if you do, you will gain much more than seventy virgins, but eternal life with the One you are persecuting. He loves you and is reaching out to you to be His instrument while there is still time before His return."

The man looked at Thomas with profound sadness in his eyes.

"I wish I had the courage to follow Him, but I have a wife and three children who would get killed together with me if I do as you say." He stood in front of Thomas, dejected and without hope. "I will not turn you in this time, just don't let me catch you again or many will die." He shrugged his shoulders in a helpless gesture. "I am sorry, there is nothing I can do," he said and abruptly turned toward the door in the back.

"What is your name, Sir?" Thomas called after him, but the man just waved one hand in a dismissive gesture and kept on walking.

Chapter 17

It was early in the morning several days later, Thomas stood at the edge of the Sea of Galilee. He looked for the simple, wooden fishing boats from the past, but spotted only a modern, sleek sailing vessel out in the middle of the lake. His eyes went north where Capernaum used to be and he remembered the many times Yeshua had walked along the lake, great crowds following Him, expecting a miracle. How he wished he hadn't wasted those many months, amassing riches, while allowing the true treasure of being with the Meshiah pass him by.

"Lord, I am still scared, a sinful man and not worthy to follow in Your footsteps. Yet that is what You want me to do. I will never understand Your reasoning or why You would have picked me for this job. There are so many others more qualified and knowledgeable of Your Word and altogether more spiritual than I am. I must be the most reluctant servant You have ever had." Thomas had spoken out loud as he walked along the shore. "I am neither a simple fisherman nor a learned scholar like Nicodemus, but a scientist, trained to believe what I can understand with my five senses. And yet here I am, sharing a dream and a vision of You walking along these shores two thousand years ago. Nothing about this sounds real or could have possibly happened scientifically, yet that is what You want me to share with others in this strange land." He stopped and dipped his hands into the water lapping against the sand. "I do remember that you sent me to tell Your people Israel, yet the boy You healed was a Palestinian. He is the enemy. Once again, You are not making any sense, but then You never have."

"Shalom, Sir." The voice came from close behind him.

"Shalom, to you," Thomas said as he turned around. "What a beautiful morning it is."

"Please forgive the intrusion, but I heard you talking and was intrigued by what you said." The stranger made no attempt to introduce himself. "It is certainly difficult to understand the mind of God, is it not? Scholars have tried for centuries, yet have not been able to."

"Are you such a scholar, Sir?" Thomas asked and suddenly realized he could understand everything the man said. "You speak fluent English, have you been to America?"

"I came to Israel many years ago from Russia and do not speak English."

"What language are you speaking then?" Thomas asked, puzzled.

"I speak Hebrew, of course and so do you." The man looked at Thomas with a frown on his face. "Why would you ask me if I spoke English?"

Thomas did not answer, but started walking without answering.

"My name is Thomas and I live in Tiberias," he finally said.

"I know who you are, everyone does. You are the man who healed the cripple and I want to know how you did that."

"I did not heal anybody, Sir. Please believe me, I am merely someone Yeshua used."

"I do not believe in this Christian Yeshua, I am a Jew. Not only that, I am a Rabbi."

"I can truly understand how you feel, Sir. I am a Jew like you, but unlike you, I was an atheist and did not believe in Yahweh or any religion until I met Yeshua.

"How could you have met Yeshua, He lived two thousand years ago and was a trouble maker of the worst kind." His tone was harsh. "He definitely was not the Meshiah we are waiting for like the Christians say." The man was trembling, his brown eyes filled with anger as he pulled on his curly, brown beard. He raised his short, stocky body up to his full height. "The God of Abraham, Isaac and Jacob curse you for turning to a false idol named Yeshua. You are not one of us, but a traitor to the faith." He was shouting now.

Thomas looked at him, astonished at his fervor.

"If you would allow me, Rabbi, I will show you in the Torah that Yeshua was indeed our Meshiah if you come with me to my house. I remember a man called Nicodemus, a member of the Sanhedrin in Jerusalem, who showed me the proof the day before they crucified the Son of God on a hill called Golgotha. Not only that, I was there when they put Him in the grave and saw Him after three days when He appeared to a group of us. According to

Nicodemus, this Yeshua is the only one who has fulfilled every single one of the prophesies dealing with the Meshiah in the writings of the prophets. He is alive today and wants me to tell His people how much He loves them before He returns." Thomas stopped and turned to the Rabbi, "The very fact that you can understand me and think I speak Hebrew when I hear you speak in English, means that Yeshua is reaching out to you in a special way, the way He did when I met Him in my dream."

"How dare you speak to me about the Torah and insinuating that I don't understand the prophesies. Your insane ramblings make absolutely no sense to me and I would strongly suggest you stop poisoning the crowds with your so-called message."

"Then how do you explain the healing?" Thomas asked in a gentle voice. "Do you really want to do the same thing the religious leaders did two thousand years ago when they killed the Meshiah in spite of the astounding miracles He did?"

"Lies, all lies," he yelled. "You are playing a sinister trick just like the man Yeshua did then and I will see to it that you will be stopped one way or the other, just like He was." He turned abruptly and walked back in the direction of Tiberias. "I will silence you, if that's the last thing I do," he yelled from a distance.

Thomas stared after him, astonished at what just happened. He looked across the Sea of Galilee. The sail boat was still gliding silently across the calm water. Except for the man, now quite some distance away, he was alone. A feeling of dread came over him as he realized the hatred and fear the Rabbi had shown towards him and knew it was not just real, but also dangerous. Maybe he should stick to surgery. And then he remembered understanding Hebrew and was understood by the Rabbi when he spoke English. That was no dream, that was reality and yet it was exactly the same as it had been back then. How could that be and how could he explain it to anyone? He decided not to tell the team, except Melissa and Nana. They would understand. He slowly turned and walked back to Tiberias.

"Are you sure it was Hebrew he spoke?" Melissa asked when he had finished telling her and Nana.

"Yes, sweetheart, I lived that way for three years, remember? Except then it was a dream, now it is for real and very frightening."

"Tommy, the Lord is trying to tell you He is with you. Do not fear, you have a job to do," Nana said as she took his hands in hers. "You are to continue to share and pray for people so Yeshua can heal them and help them to accept Him as their Meshiah. He will protect you until the work is finished."

"Then what happens, Nana?" He asked.

"I don't know, honey, that is in His hands."

"I want you to return to the US, Nana," Thomas said, looking at his grandmother with deep concern. "It is not safe here for you. The Muslim Brotherhood and IS are ready to kill Jews and Christians in this part of the world without hesitation. I don't know why, but I can suddenly sense danger all around us.

"Surely our government will protect us, should anything happen," she said with confidence.

"There is very little they can do, even if they want to. Besides, no matter how our new President tries, I am not so sure he can do much in the face of the religious hatred and turmoil in the Middle East. Our country isn't what it once was, and I doubt it will stand with Israel when the time comes."

"What makes you say that, Tommy? President Robert Amherst is a good man and has some wonderful ideas to get America back the way it used to be. He better be, I voted for him," she added. "He said he was a Christian when they asked him."

"Many people say they are Christians, Nana, that doesn't mean they are," Melissa said. "I heard the other day that more and more churches are empty and the young people don't go at all. People's values have changed and so has their faith. In these modern times they are looking for a god who promotes love in whatever form and faith in many different directions as long as it doesn't have anything to do with Christianity or Jesus.

"Before we left I heard about a new leader in the UN," Nana said. "He has been amazing in his ability to unite the faction of the world leaders, to the point, there is even talk that they want him to be Secretary General of the UN." She was suddenly thoughtful. "This is very strange, since he is Muslim and openly advocates hatred for Israel. His name is Mohamed Abdul Musharak and he is from Iran."

"This must have happened since we have come here," Thomas said. "What else do you know about him?" he asked.

"He is a very handsome, likable young man who speaks many languages fluently, including English, of course and advocates world peace," Nana continued. "I have listened to him and found him to be someone I could trust."

"Even if he hates Israel?" Melissa asked, astonished. "I am surprised at you, Nana.

"I never thought about that, since he promotes world peace and people getting along," Nana answered. "Everyone I talked to is taken with him; and with the way our politicians are these days, he is like a breath of fresh air. We need peace and with him being a Muslim, maybe he can stem the terrible tide of terrorism. He even hinted at a chance of a peace treaty between Israel and the Palestinians."

"Nana, according to the prophets there will never be peace until the end times, when the Antichrist rises up and leads the nations into a one world government," Melissa said. "This Mohamed Abdul Musharak sounds a little bit like him and we need to be careful not to be led astray by empty promises of peace. Remember, anyone who is against God's people cannot ever bring peace on earth."

Chapter 18

A month passed and life at the clinic was busy and rewarding for Thomas. Nana had gone back home. No one had asked him to speak since that time at the church and he was glad. He simply felt more secure in treating the sick than preaching the Gospel. Theresa continued to go into the streets of Tiberias to tell the people about Thomas and his dream. Yet somehow the response was not as great as in the beginning.

It was a busy Monday morning as usual with the waiting room packed to capacity. Thomas was finished with this third surgery and walked into his office to take a break, when a commotion coming from the waiting room stopped him.

"Thomas, we need you here," he heard Melissa shouting two doors down.

"What's going on?" he asked and was stopped by the shocking scene at the entrance of the clinic. Two EMT attendance brought in a stretcher with a man bleeding profusely, followed by four people covered in blood, holding each other up.

One of the attendance shouted something in Hebrew Thomas couldn't understand.

"Get me Mikail to translate," he shouted to no one in particular. "Melissa, get the OR ready. Take the man on the stretcher into room 1 and check the others if anyone else needs immediate attention."

"What happened?" Mikail asked.

"I have no idea. I need you to talk to the ambulance personnel, they are speaking Hebrew," Thomas shouted. It looks like a terrible accident."

A group of people suddenly came running through the front door of the clinic, shouting, screaming and pushing toward Thomas.

"There was a terror attack," Mikail shouted in Thomas' ear above the noise. "A bomb went off and killed dozens of people just down the street. Apparently we are the closes clinic to the scene."

"Tell the people to wait in the waiting room," Thomas said.

While he was speaking, one of the wounded collapsed on the floor surrounded by loud wailing and screaming. Thomas rushed over to the victim and saw that the man was bleeding profusely from a shoulder wound. Thomas could see that his arm was dangling in a bizarre angle and he was dying.

"Take him to room 2 and try to stop the bleeding, Melissa," Thomas yelled.

A woman suddenly stood in front of him, screaming at him in Hebrew.

"Mikail, what is she saying?" Thomas asked.

"She wants you to heal him like you healed the boy," Mikail said.

The other people in the group started to shout and cry out as well, pointing to their wounds. Thomas did not need anyone to translate what they were saying and looked at them and then shrugged his shoulders in a helpless gesture. And then, as if in slow motion, he reached out his hand and touched the man's arm.

"Yeshua, only You can heal this man. Just like before, I cannot help him, he has lost too much blood, but You can. I give him to You and ask that the bleeding stop right now, through the power of Your Name." He knelt down beside the man and held his arm and positioned it the way it should be, when suddenly, he felt the muscles move underneath the cloth. The man opened his eyes and smiled at Thomas.

"It doesn't hurt anymore." Thomas could understand him. "Look, I can move it."

Thomas was startled as he pulled the sleeve of his arm up past the elbow. After checking it carefully, he could not find anything wrong with it. He stared at it in wonder and then stood up with a big smile and reached out to a woman next to him with a large laceration on her scalp. It was bleeding profusely. He put his hand on the wound and prayed for it to stop. The rest of the wounded stood in silence as Thomas touched each one in turn and prayed for them. As he went from person to person, some sobbed, some stared and lifted their arms in praise. After he had touched each one, Thomas turned and walked into back to tend to the man on the stretcher. He was dead. He took a sheet and covered him gently with a sheet.

Stunned and overwhelmed by what had just happened, he sat down on the only chair in the room, his body shaking and put his head in his hands as tears began to stream down his face.

"Thank you, Lord, You are my God and my Meshiah."

After a while he heard shouting from the waiting room and went to check if anyone needed medical attention. The crowd rushed toward him when he entered and he had a hard time making himself heard.

"Please, calm down," he said as Mikail translated. "You have seen the power of Yeshua, the Son of God who wants me to tell you that He came to die on the cross for you and free you from your sins. He also sent me to let you know that He is your Meshiah, who wants you to know how much He loves you. He came for His people two thousand years ago, but they rejected Him. He has not given up on you, but wants you to accept Him as your Savior before He returns soon."

The people hung onto his every word, until a woman interrupted him.

"Why do you use a translator, we understand you just fine," she said in fluent American English."

Thomas knew immediately she spoke in Hebrew. He turned to Mikail. "What language does she speak?"

"I hear her speak Hebrew," Mikail said, astonished and confused.

"Stop translating and watch what happens," Thomas said and turned back toward the crowd.

"I want you to go next door to Shalom Outreach and ask for a women named Theresa. She will tell you more about your Meshiah and how you can accept Him into your life and be made whole, not just in body, but in spirit as well." Thomas smiled. "I still have work to do here at the clinic to treat the sick who have waited for a long time this morning." He turned to Mikail. "Why don't you show those who want to learn more the way to the Mission. Have Meta translate for Theresa while you come back to the lab."

The news reports confirmed later that there was a devastating attack by several suicide bombers in the busy streets of Tiberias. Over thirty-five people had been killed and many more wounded. The world mourned the dead, but never heard about those who were healed miraculously in a small clinic down the road. But the people of Tiberias heard and hundreds came daily to be touched by the American doctor who had walked with Yeshua. Most had to be turned away, because there simply was not enough time for the clinic to accommodate them all. Yet they came anyway, waiting patiently in the hot sun every day, just to get a glimpse of him. Many ended up in Shalom Outreach and were ministered to by Theresa and a team of local volunteers from Pastor Ahmed's church, who prayed for them and led a great number to the Lord.

After a few weeks, the clinic came to be known as the 'The Healing Place' among the locals. Thomas had started to pray with every patient before surgery, whether they were Jews, Muslims or any other religion and laid hands on those who wanted to accept Yeshua. He no longer wondered why God had chosen him, no longer complained that he was not qualified or spiritual enough, but accepted his purpose to reach the people of Israel and all others who came and tell them about Yeshua, their Meshiah.

At first the sick started to come from the surrounding areas as news of the clinic spread, and then from as far away as Jerusalem, Haifa and Tel Aviv. Many were healed and accepted Yeshua as their Meshiah, a never-ending stream of people in desperate need of being cured from their many incurable illnesses.

The miracle that went unnoticed by those who came was that Thomas understood and was understood by the people when he talked about Yeshua or prayed for them to be healed. Mikail had gotten used to stop translating when Thomas gave him a specific sign as he spoke. While he still heard Thomas speak only English, those he prayed for heard him in either Hebrew or Arabic. They both noticed that this did not work when Thomas treated his patients strictly as a physician and talked about medical matters.

For the longest time the rest of the team did not know, until he shared it with them over dinner one evening.

"Mikail and I are at a loss to explain it," he said. "I can understand this happening in a dream or a vision, but not in reality."

"There is actually a very good explanation for it," Theresa said as she reached for a bowl of delicious fruit salad, "and it is not the first time it has happened. Let me get my Bible and I will show you in the book of Acts the first time it occurred. As a matter of fact, let's finish eating and then we can go over it in our study later. I am a firm believer, if something happens that does not have a precedent or principle in the scripture, it is not from the Lord. It is the most important way to judge all things spiritual," she added. "And this definitely is the work of the Holy Spirit." She sounded excited.

After helping Petra to clear the table, they gathered in the living room and sat, each in their favorite spot.

"Why don't we open to the book of Acts, chapter 2, starting with verse 5. This is the place where the Holy Spirit has just come and filled the people in the Upper Room," she said. "It must have caused quite a noise since it says that people from all over came running to see what's going on. As Peter steps up and addresses the crowd, fourteen different languages were instantly translated as he speaks to them probably in Aramaic. The sad thing is, instead of knowing only God can do such a miracle, many dismiss it and contribute it to the Apostles being drunk." She smiled. "I have seen many drunks in my life, but none ever could do what Peter did, or even Thomas for that matter. And I am certain he doesn't drink," she added with smile. "The problem is, just like then, those who are threatened by the power of God will not stand idly by and let this happen, not then and not now."

She looked at Thomas with a strange look. "I have wondered for some time now why there is no resistance to our clinic or Shalom Outreach. The Lord has been gracious and has protected us so far, but I have heard rumblings in the streets when I go minister with my team. The Jews and the Arabs are beginning to realize something is going on they have no control over. All they know is, this place is drawing many people away from their faith. We must be prepared for the opposition to come, especially you, Thomas. I want to send an urgent letter to Chicago to have them get in touch with our supporters to pray for your protection and favor with the Lord for you and for all of us." She looked around the room. "Remember, we are not fighting people, but the enemy and he is not going to let this go on without causing trouble. He would want us to turn against the Jews and Muslims with hatred, but that is not what we are here for. No matter what happens, we are to love them and reach out to them with the love of Christ, no matter what they do to us." She sat back and let the words sink in for a moment and then went on. "What we are experiencing is almost the same as the apostles did. Allow me to read it to you."

"The apostles performed many miraculous signs and wonders among the people. (Acts 5:12) As a result, people brought the sick into the streets and laid them on beds and mats so that at least Peter's shadow might fall on some of them as he passed by. Crowds gathered also from the towns around Jerusalem, bringing their sick and those in torment by evil spirits, and all of them were healed." (Acts 5:15-16)

"Sound familiar?" she asked and looked around. "There is no doubt the same thing is happening here, so we should look to what is to come right after that in verses 17 through 21. "Then the high priest and all his associates, who were members of the party of the Sadducees, were filled with jealousy. They arrested the apostles and put them in the public jail. But during the night an angel of the Lord opened the doors of the jail and brought them out. "Go stand in the temple courts," he said, "and tell the people the full message of this new life."

"Are we ready for what is to come?" She looked at Thomas first and then the others with a tiny smile. "Are *you* ready to continue with our mission to heal the sick and spread the Gospel?"

Chapter 19

Thomas felt exhausted. It had been a grueling week of surgeries plus seeing countless patients from morning till night. He knew he needed a break. He suddenly felt a strong desire to see Capernaum, Nazareth and the spot where he knew his villa to be. There was something that drew him there. Intellectually he knew it never existed, but in his heart he longed to see the place where he met Helena and the others and just had to search for it – alone.

Without telling anyone on the team where he was going, he got in the car after breakfast and drove north toward Capernaum on Highway 90.

"I need to get away and will be back after lunch," was all he had said to Melissa as he kissed her on the cheek. "I love you."

His thoughts went to the time in the past as the car sped along the shores of the Sea of Galilee. The picture of Helena was still clear in his mind with her bright smile and winning, girlish ways. He loved her and missed her terribly. She would always be his little girl. He didn't dare think too much about Lydia, her stunning, simple beauty and slender, graceful figure. And then there was Octavia, the harsh woman with a soft heart underneath, in charge of the slaves. He cringed when he thought of Marcellus, the young boy who died because he refused to treat his wounds.

Thomas sighed deeply. It was all still so real as if it had happened yesterday. On a whim he turned off of the highway and followed the small road in the approximate direction he estimated the villa might have been. He tried to estimate the distance and slowed down when he thought he had come far enough and then stopped. He slowly pulled the car to the side of the road, looking across the rolling landscape, with a cluster of trees in the distance. The villa had been in the midst of one exactly like that. Of course it couldn't be the same, but it looked familiar nevertheless. He walked toward it and stopped, looking for any remnants that might still be there. But there was only the green meadow, interspersed with rocks as far as he could see. He sat down under one of the trees in the shade and leaned against the trunk with a deep sigh.

I have got to be crazy to come here. It has been two thousand years, even if this was the place, there would not be anything left to find, he thought and put his head down on his knees. Tears began to fill his eyes as he thought about all the people he loved and would never see again. *If they were never real, why do I miss them so much? The synagogue in Capernaum was real and yet I had never been there before. I knew the column where Yeshua stood and talked to me, that was real, why couldn't this be?* He sat and stared for a long time as if to make the villa appear, but it didn't. Except for the humming of insect, there was a wonderful stillness as he looked out over the green pasture.

"Yeshua, You could let me see them one more time," he whispered. "With all the miracles You have done, this would be such a small one and yet it would mean so much to me." He was so sure the house would appear before him, but of course it didn't and neither did Helena or the others. He felt foolish and started to get up, when he felt as if someone was making him sit back down. A great calm suddenly come over him. "*I am all you need, Thomas. My strength is sufficient and in My name you can do all things. Do not fear what is to come, for I will be with you till the end. I am the Alpha and the Omega, the Beginning and the End. Trust in Me and I will give you your heart's desire.*"

It was as if he was glued to the spot.

"Thank you, Yeshua. I am sorry I came here to find those who are not real and ignore You who was, is and always will be. You are sufficient and I thank You for all You have done so far. Please protect the team of Shalom Outreach and do not let the enemy hinder or destroy our ministry."

Thomas had a hard time getting up. His knees were weak and he stumbled against the tree trunk as if drunk. He took a deep breath and headed back to the car.

"You are just in time for lunch," Petra said as he walked into the mission. "We were wondering if you had gotten lost. The team is waiting for you in the dining area."

"You are just in time to hear the news," Caleb said and held up a letter. The expression on his face was grim. "This came in the mail today. "The city council of Tiberias has requested that we stop our operation immediately due to congestion in front of our building. They demand we move out within the next four weeks and find another place or they will to pull our permit to operate the clinic permanently."

"What are we going to do?" Meta asked. "They can't do that we haven't done anything wrong."

"They can and they will." Caleb sounded angry. "We are the foreigners here; they can throw us out of the country anytime they want without giving a reason."

"Can we ask Fouad Nabeth to help us?" Melissa asked. "He has some pull in Tiberias, especially with his father's name behind him."

"I don't think he can since his father would kill him and us if he knew his son was a Christian because of us," Thomas said.

"There has to be someone who was touched by this ministry who wants to repay us by helping with this situation," Theresa said. "There have been so many people who would be dead if it wasn't for Thomas, surely they will not allow this clinic to be closed," she added with some hope in her voice.

"I know someone who will help us." Mikail had been silent so far. "I have a lot of experience in dealing with people in the local government and can tell you they will never give an inch through reasoning."

"Who are you talking about?" Caleb asked.

"The Lord." Mikail grinned at the group. "You have forgotten He is the One who wants us here by talking to a Muslim in a vision. Do you honestly think He will leave us now at the first sign of trouble?"

"You are so right, Mikail," Theresa said, "we have forgotten that our God is bigger than the city of Tiberias."

They looked at each other with embarrassment.

"How easy it is to forget who is in charge," Thomas said and then told them what happened to him under the tree in the field. "He is with us and knew what was coming and yet He told me not to fear, His strength is sufficient. And so we will trust Him in this and rely on Him and not on any man. I would therefore suggest we do nothing until we hear from the city again. By then we will know what to do. In the meantime, we pray and go on with our work as before."

During the next week Theresa carefully spread the word without accusation or anger among the people in the streets of Tiberias that the city wants to close down the clinic. She told the team she had prayed and the Lord had instructed her to do it.

The work at the clinic went on as usual and the stream of those who asked for healing and prayer was undiminished. Just when everyone was sure the city council had forgotten about it, a car stopped in front of the clinic and a city worker posted a sign on the front door that the clinic would be closed by the end of the week. The man had to make his way back through the crowd waiting for the doors to open. A ripple of angry murmurs went through the line and then shouting as the news spread down the line. The poor man barely made it back into his truck and sped away.

By the time the team opened the door there was pandemonium outside with angry shouting and yelling and screaming. By noon the press was there in full force as people held up sick babies toward the cameras and screaming in anger and despair.

"Who is going to treat us now? We demand our clinic remain open. It is the only place that cares and Dr. Peterson is the only doctor who will treat us for free," they shouted. "He is the best thing that ever happened to us and the city has no right to close him down."

Caleb finally went outside to calm everyone down, not realizing the news cameras were there.

"Do you have a comment?" one of the reporters shouted.

"I am Caleb Weinstein, the Director of Shalom Outreach," he said with a nervous smile. "What can I do for you?"

"What can you tell us about the city closing down this clinic?" the reporter asked. "Do you think they have a right to do that?"

"They have the right to do anything they want and we will obey what they tell us to do," he said in a halting voice. "Although I am not aware of us having violated any laws or restrictions of any kind. All we want to do is give medical care to the poor in this area and I think we have been quite successful at that." He had gotten his bearing by now and smiled his charming, boyish smile. "It seems we have been more than successful at that according to the city."

"Are you going to fight this?" another reporter shouted from the back.

"No, we will not fight anyone, but obey whatever the authorities want us to do. For the rest we will trust God."

"Can we speak with the Doctor?" the first reporter asked. "Everybody has heard about his unusual methods of treating the sick."

"I am sorry, Dr. Peterson is here to treat the sick and wishes not to be involved with the legalities of this situation. He wants nothing more than to continue with his work should he be allowed to do so." Caleb stepped back inside the door and added with a friendly grin, "That is all I wish to say. Shalom, gentlemen."

It was the lead story on the evening news and caused a virtual fire storm of criticism and condemnation for the city council. They met in a hastily arranged emergency session the next day and unanimously rescinded the order to close down the clinic. A representative of the council appeared on TV the next day with an appropriate announcement. Thomas recognized a member of the council in the background. It was the Rabbi he had met on the beach.

A city truck came at noon to take down the notice. The driver left a letter explaining that an unfortunate misunderstanding had occurred and the city council hoped it had not caused too much of an inconvenience to the operation of the clinic and its valuable service to the poor.

Caleb waved the letter like a victory flag when he showed it to Thomas during surgery, holding the mask in one hand and the letter in the other.

"The Lord did it, Thomas. We can stay!" he shouted.

Thomas smiled underneath his mask.

"Like Mikail said, Yeshua is more powerful than any city government."

That evening Melissa snuggled up to Thomas as they sat in their tiny quarters, munching on a box of chocolate Nana had sent from the States.

"I am pregnant, sweetheart," she said with a smile, "and we are going to name her Helena."

Chapter 20

Life went back to normal after the furor with the city council died down. Only one thing had changed, everyone in Israel now knew about The Healing Place. Even the wealthy tried to get in, but were turned away.

"We are here for those who cannot afford to go to a regular doctor or clinic," the receptionist told them. "There is no exception. That is what the permit to operate was issued for and this is what we must do or be closed down," she informed them when they insisted to be seen.

Thomas and Melissa were ecstatic about her pregnancy. The team planned on an old-fashioned baby shower as soon as they heard the news.

"You will need a room for a nursery," Theresa said at their weekly planning session.

"And Thomas, you will need another RN when the time comes," Meta added, always the practical one.

"I will send word to Chicago and see if they can get someone for us," Caleb said. "I better do it right away, because it will take a while. Do you realize, you guys have been here for over a year. In a few weeks it will be 2018. I wonder what it will bring."

"I have a feeling it will be a year of turmoil all over the world," Thomas said. "And our little place will be no exception."

"What makes you say that?" Caleb asked.

"It's just the way the Lord talked to me under that tree. It gave me a feeling of impending trouble."

"You don't think the deal with the city council was it?"

"No, Caleb, that was just a mild beginning. We will face trials and persecution, maybe even worse than that in the days to come. These are only the beginnings of birth pains like the scripture says." He looked at Caleb with a strange, foreboding expression. "I have thought about this lately. "I spent three years in Israel and went through some horrendous times in my personal life as well as watching the Lord be put on trial and be crucified. Just like then, I became a doctor first, famous and sought after in this very area of the country, only to lose it all in a moments' notice. I am not saying I will become a leper, but something is going to happen to me to lose it all again and then be rescued by Yeshua. There is a growing feeling in my heart that this present reality will somehow mirror the old one in many important aspects. Except this time, I know the outcome. Whatever happens to me or to all of you, we will be with Him for eternity and that gives me peace."

There was a stunned silence around the table.

"Does that mean I will die in childbirth like Lydia did?" Melissa finally asked in a whisper.

"Of course not, honey." He took her hand. "The child Lydia carried was not mine and besides, the similarities will not be with everything, just the important overall things. This child will be a gift from the Lord to take away my longing for Helena. He told me in so many words under the tree when He said He will give me the desires of my heart." Thomas looked at Melissa with a loving smile. "We will have our own little Helena, you wait and see."

The following week Meta read in the society pages that Fouad Nabeth got married in one of the biggest social events in Tel Aviv.

"I hope those two are blessed by the Lord," she said. "I guess his father has not found out about him being a Christian."

"Let's hope he never does, it would be the end of him," Thomas said. "I have heard about the man since then and he is nobody to trifle with. There are persistent rumors he is connected with the Muslim Brotherhood or even the Islamic State," he added." And I somehow think Fouad knows it or he would not be so scared of his father."

"There have been several news reports that sleeper cells of IS are suspected in Israel, ready to strike at any moment," Caleb said, munching on a raw carrot. "Although with all the Israeli anti-terror measures, I cannot imagine how they could have gotten in."

"Look at our clinic, there are countless Arabs and Palestinians who live and work in Israel and then go home across the border in the evening," Mikail said. "I talk to them after I translate and have wondered about some of them. It would be easy to hide amongst the many honest ones who just want to work here and feed their families living in squalor across the border."

"There is a phone call for you, Dr. Peterson," Leona Caldwell said as she stuck her head in the door. "It sounds important."

"Ok, I'll take it, Leona." Thomas walked behind her to the office and picked up the phone. "Dr. Peterson here."

"Thomas, it is Fouad Nabeth. I can't talk long so I will get right to the point. I will be in Tiberias with my new wife and would like to meet with you and the team at Shalom Outreach. We would have to be extremely careful so no one sees us. Maybe in the evening hours would be best."

"Fouad, how good to hear from you. Congratulations on your wedding. Of course we would love to see you. Just say the word and we will have a special dinner prepared for you and your new bride." Thomas was excited. "We were just talking about you."

"Would next Saturday evening be ok with you then?"

"Absolutely, we are all looking forward to seeing you again."

Before Thomas could say more, the phone went dead.

Everyone was excited to meet Fouad's bride, but wondered what the visit was all about, since it was terribly dangerous for him and everybody at the Ministry to come here. Petra fixed her best meal of pot roast with potatoes, carrots and green beans and a Russian desert she would not say what it was.

"This rich, young man surely is used to much better food," she muttered, "but I bet every Ruble I have that this is the tastiest he has ever eaten."

The ladies helped clean the house and the men moved some furniture so they could all fit around the dining room table. It was a tight fit, but would have to do.

Fouad and his wife were right on time.

"Welcome Mr. and Mrs. Nabeth," he said with a big grin and hugged Fouad with a bear hug.

"This is my wife Nazra," Fouad said, pointing to a petit woman with large, beautiful brown eyes. Her thick, shiny, black hair was partially covered by a multi-colored scarf which matched her elegant summer dress, showing off a stunning figure.

"How nice to meet you, Nazra," Thomas said as he bowed to her. "Please come in and meet the others. We are all excited to see Fouad again and meet you."

The meal went well and Nazra proved to be a vivacious, personable young woman, who seemed to adore Fouad.

"I have heard so much about all of you," she said and smiled at everyone with an infectious smile. "It is good to be among fellow believers and to be able to talk about our Lord." She leaned against her husband and chuckled. "It was the greatest joy to find out after we were finally alone after the wedding that both of us are Christians. We are so blessed to have you as our friends since we cannot talk about this even in our own home except behind closed doors. We have to be so very careful with the servants. In time I want to get only believers to be part of our household, but that will take a while."

Fouad reached over and put a finger on her mouth in a loving gesture.

"You must try not to talk too much and let our friends tell us how things are going at Shalom Outreach, my love."

"Oh." She put her hand over her mouth and blushed deeply. "I do get carried away, don't I?"

"I don't think anyone here minds if you do, Nazra," Melissa said. "We are all delighted by your enthusiasm and beauty. Your husband is a very fortunate man to have such a lovely bride."

"I truly am," he answered. "Can you imagine how lonely she would have been all her life if I had not found Yeshua? How rare in this country to find such a perfect woman, especially since my father picked her for me." He chuckled. "If he knew, it would devastate him."

"Is there a special reason you came, Fouad?" Caleb finally asked. "I mean, we are glad to have you both here, but the danger to you and us is enormous."

"I do have a reason for coming," he answered. "Nazra and I want to go and live in America where we can be free to practice our faith and raise any children we might have to believe in the Lord Yeshua. We thought you could help us ask for asylum, because our lives would be lost if my family or hers find out." He took Nazra's hand. "There is no way we can keep our faith a secret in this country this close to our people." He looked at Caleb with hope in his eyes. "I have started to transfer my money to Switzerland and the Cayman Islands. We definitely would not become a burden to the US government, I assure you."

Caleb looked at Fouad for a moment and then answered, choosing his words carefully.

"I would love to help you, my friend and I will try as hard as I can, but I must tell you, with your father's dubious connections, you may not be allowed into the US. I know you don't believe there is anything to those rumors, but with terrorism rampant in Europe and in many other countries, America has tightened restrictions to the point that very few people from the Middle East are allowed in."

"But I have been there before, doesn't that count?" Fouad asked, disappointed.

"That was a few years ago, times are different now," Caleb said, trying to sound positive. "My uncle is a Senator. I will contact him and see if he can do something to help you, but it will take some time. Give me two weeks and I will know something," he added. "Just be very careful you two. We would not want anything to happen to you." He smiled reassuringly, yet the mood was subdued for the rest of the visit.

It was three weeks later. Thomas was on the shores of the lake early in the morning. It was his favorite spot, where he found peace and solace after a busy week at the clinic and alone with Yeshua. It was here he could walk where the Lord had walked, his faith renewed and feel fulfilled in the assurance of being in His perfect will. Since no one was out this early in the morning, he was free to pray out loud and raise his hands in thanksgiving for the daily miracles, signs and wonders at the clinic.

The picture of the little boy in braces yesterday came to his mind. He had stood helpless before the child when he realized there was nothing he could do since it was a severe birth defect of the spine. He knew the parents were Muslims, but when they asked him to pray, he told them about his dream and how he walked with the Son of God called Yeshua. When he came to the part of telling them that he himself had no power, but that they had to put their faith in the Meshiah, they bowed their heads and prayed with him. Together, they laid hands on the child and asked the Lord to heal him. The next day, the boy, walking without a brace and without pain for the first time in his life, came with his father, running up to Thomas, excited and smiling.

"Thank you, Dr. Peterson," the father said with Mikail translating. With the waiting room filled, he then shared with the people what happened with Thomas looking on, amazed and humbled as usual at the goodness and power of the Lord.

In the midst of his thoughts a voice suddenly said behind him,

"You will come with us, Dr. Peterson."

Thomas whirled around and faced two burley men of Arabic descent, dressed in black and one of them making sure he saw the gun under his loose shirt.

"What do you want with me?" Thomas asked, frightened. "I am an American citizen and you cannot make me come with you."

"We can and we will, Dr. Peterson. You are not in America, but a filthy infidel who has no rights in this country," the one with the gun said with a low growl. "Don't make us force you, it will be much easier if you come with us peacefully." He waved his hand in the direction of a dark limousine parked close by. "Let's go."

Thomas shrugged his shoulders in a helpless gesture and walked toward the car.

"Where are you taking me?" he finally asked.

"You will find out soon enough," the man said as he shoved Thomas in the backseat.

Chapter 21

Melissa woke up late since it was the weekend. She liked to sleep in whenever she could, unlike Thomas, who was an early riser.

She joined the team for breakfast. They were still talking about the wonderful miracle of the little boy, and when Theresa started the Bible reading, no one wondered about Thomas. It was not until an hour later, when he had not returned, Melissa started to wonder.

"Caleb, I hope he is alright, he never stays this late," she said when there was no sign of him by lunch. "Something is wrong, I am going to the shore and see if I can find him," she finally said, "anyone wants to come with me?"

"Of course, Melissa, Paul and I will go with you," Caleb said. "Let's check the clinic first, maybe he is in the lab doing some tests like he sometimes does," he added.

"That won't be necessary, I already checked there," Mikail said. "I am going with you."

By the time they got to where Thomas usually walked, there was no sign of him. A lot of tourist were walking along the shore and the restaurants were filled with the lunch crowd.

"Surely he would not have gone to lunch somewhere, would he?" Paul asked Melissa.

"No way," she answered. "He doesn't like crowds anymore since someone might recognize him and he hates that." She looked at the three, truly worried by now. "What are we going to do?"

"Why don't we call the hospital and see if he is there. Maybe he fell or got hurt somehow," Caleb said. He was dialing while he spoke, but found out, no one by that name had been admitted.

Melissa was near tears by now.

"Something terrible has happened to him, I just know it. Why did we wait this long to look for him?"

"Let's go home and see if we can call the police, maybe they have picked him up for some reason," Caleb said.

"He would have called from there," Paul said. "I am getting a bad feeling about this," he added as they got in the car.

By afternoon there was still no word from Thomas and Melissa was frantic.

"Should we contact the American Embassy?" she asked. "I am sure they would know what to do." She had been crying since they got back from the shore. Meta tried unsuccessfully to get her to rest for a while. "There is no way I can sleep right now. Besides, I don't want to be alone."

When Caleb contacted the Embassy, they told him a person would have to be missing for twenty-four hours before they could get involved and to call back in the morning.

There was a feeling of dread when they finally sat down and followed Theresa in prayer. There was nothing else to do.

"I wish I could say I am a mountain of faith right now," she started out, looking at everyone as they sat around the dining room table. "But that is what faith is, trusting God when our own strength means nothing and He is the only One who can help."

Thomas was astounded when the car drove into the drive way of Fouad's villa. The two men spoke Arabic and he had no idea what they were saying. His mind was racing. Why would their friend do this? Nothing made any sense.

"Get out of the car," one of the men said and shoved him toward the front doors. It opened as if someone had been waiting for them. He did not know the young man, but thought there was a family resemblance to Fouad. Maybe it was his brother.

Without a word, Thomas was waved in and followed the man to a spacious room with several chairs, couches and other fine furniture arranged tastefully. Everything reeked of money. He was shoved in front of an older man, sitting in a large leather chair, dressed in the long, flowing robes of an Arab. He had a severe face, covered by a grey, short beard. His dark eyes were overshadowed by heavy eyebrows and the smoke of an expensive cigar surrounded him.

He didn't speak for a long time as he studied Thomas standing before him.

"So you are the holy man who treats the poor of Tiberias?" he finally asked in English with a heavy accent. "Tell me, Dr. Peterson, do you know my son Fouad?"

"Yes, I do, Sir," Thomas answered. *Oh God!*

"How do you know him?"

"He sold us the building for Shalom Outreach." Thomas' mind raced, he had to be careful not give Fouad away. "It was a business deal, that's all. I do not travel in the circle of the rich, since I am only a doctor for the poor."

"Are you a Christian, Doctor?"

"Yes, I am part of Shalom Outreach and here on a medical visa. In order to open a clinic, the ministry has to have a physician to run it, Sir."

"Why would a rich American doctor come to this part of the world and treat the poor?" The man raised one eyebrow in disbelief. "Are you sure you are not here to poison the minds of the followers of Allah with your Christian beliefs?"

"We have no intention to poison anyone's mind, Sir and respect everyone's faith, including the followers of Allah."

"You are a liar, Doctor!" he suddenly shouted and stood up in front of Thomas. "You are a despicable infidel and have drawn many away from the true faith." His face had taken on a red, angry color as he shook his fist at Thomas. "Including that of my son, do you deny that?"

"I am not responsible for the belief of your son, Sir. He looks old enough to make up his own mind." Thomas tried desperately not to acknowledge that Fouad was a believer. "He sold us his building, that is all I know. What he believes or doesn't believe is none of my business, Mr. Nabeth."

"So you know who I am?" He sat back down. "Do you also know how much power and influence I have in this country?"

"I am sure you do, but what does that have to do with me?" Thomas was getting his bearing back. "I am an American citizen and there will be dire consequences if you do not let me go immediately. This is called kidnapping in my country."

The door opened at that moment and Fouad was led in by the men who had taken Thomas.

"Do you know this man, Fouad," his father asked him in a menacing, low tone.

"Yes, father, I do. He is the one I sold the building to. He paid a good price, too."

"Do you deny having any other dealings with him?"

"Father, I have always tried to obey you in every way all my life and have been a good son," Fouad said with respect. "Why are you treating me this way? I am a grown man and should be allowed to live my life the way I chose."

"Are you still a follower of the true faith?" his father suddenly shouted at him.

"I do follow the true faith, father and nothing can change my mind about that," Fouad said with conviction.

Suddenly Thomas realized he understood everything they said and knew the Lord was with him.

"How about your wife? There are rumors by the servants that she has left the faith."

"Nazra also follows the one God, father, no matter what the rumors say."

Yusuf Nabeth took a deep drag on his cigar.

"I had to come and find out for myself, son. You do understand that if I find out that you have become a Christian I will deal harshly with you according to the will of Allah." He walked over and kissed Fouad on both cheeks.

"Father, what have you done with Dr. Peterson? You have kidnapped him. Please, allow me to drive him back to the clinic," Fouad said.

"I guess that is alright then." Yusuf Nabeth turned to Thomas. "Dr. Peterson, please forgive the actions of an old man who acted in haste."

Thomas had no doubt that this man was neither old nor did he ever act in haste, but would do whatever it takes to get his way.

"I understand, Mr. Nabeth. It was nice to meet you, but it is time to return, my family must be terribly worried about me." He bowed low before the man and followed Fouad out the door.

"That was close," Fouad said when they were in the car. "I have no idea which of the servants told, but as you can see, we cannot stay here. Nazra and I may have to go to Europe, it is easier to get in there, as much as I would like to go to America."

"I understand. Your father is a force to be reckoned with. I agree, you should not wait any longer.

"Maybe Nazra and I can start planning for a vacation in London and simply stay there and ask for asylum. It will take us several weeks to sort out our life here and make a clean break without anyone finding out."

"Don't wait too long, my friend. It is too dangerous for you two to stay here any longer."

"I have a flat in London. We can stay there and live until our fate has been decided by the British government. Maybe we could still get to the US after a while from there." He looked at Thomas with sadness. "It is a pretty awful thing to have to flee from your own father." He sighed deeply. "I'm afraid London is the first place he will look after we are gone. His connections reach far and we probably still won't be safe even there, but it will buy us some time to figure out what to do and where to go."

Melissa threw herself in Thomas' arms when they walked in the door.

"I was sure I would never see you again," she sobbed. "Thank you, Lord for bringing you back."

Thomas shared what happened and the group was saddened to hear Fouad and Nazra had to leave Israel.

"Could your father get angry with Shalom Outreach after he finds out you are gone?" Caleb asked.

"He could, but I doubt it, Fouad said. "There is nothing to be gained by punishing you if I am out of his reach. He has no idea we are friends and it has to stay that way. I will probably not be able to get in touch with you for a long time, just to make sure."

"How will you and Nazra live?" Meta asked.

"Don't you worry about that I have funds in several different countries which allow me to live comfortably wherever we end up. That is one of the things I have to settle before we can go. It will take some fancy juggling to get it all done without my father getting wind of it," he said and got up. "I'm afraid I must go. I have gotten to love all of you and will miss you. I hope we will see each other again when the danger is over. Until then, may the Lord bless you and keep you safe. Nazra and I will keep you in our prayers." He hugged each member of the team and then left without looking back.

Chapter 22

Three weeks went by and they did not hear anything from Fouad. Thomas was sitting in the lab late one afternoon after the clinic had closed, his eyes glued to a microscope, when he suddenly heard Fouad's name mentioned on the radio. It was the only English speaking station he could find.

"Early this morning the decapitated bodies of the son of wealthy businessman Yusuf Abdul Nabeth, Fouad Nabeth and his wife Nazra, were found on the shore of the Sea of Galilee. According to police reports, it looks like the work of Palestinian terrorists. No suspects have been identified and Yusuf Nabeth has offered one hundred thousand dollars in reward for any information that leads to the apprehension of the killers of his son and daughter-in-law.

Thomas sat stunned, finding it hard to breathe. He knew this was not the work of terrorists, but an honor killing by his father. He must have found out Fouad and Nazra were Christians and getting ready to leave the country. *Oh God.*

A feeling of great loss came over him. He had become fond of Fouad and his lovely young wife. They had been so in love.

Would he be next? Would Yusuf Nabeth take his rage out against him or Shalom Outreach? His hands were shaking when he took out his cell phone and dialed Melissa.

"Honey, Fouad and Nazra have been murdered," he told her, but did not mentioned the gruesome details.

"Oh no, that is terrible. Do they know how it happened?

"I am certain it was ordered by his father. He must have found out about their plan to escape to London. I cannot even imagine how anyone can kill their own son because of religious differences," he said with deep sadness. "Such an unspeakable tragedy."

Melissa was crying.

"Are we going to be safe? What if his father found out we led him to the Lord, he will come after us," she said in a shaky voice.

"I doubt very seriously Fouad gave us away. He would never put our lives in danger willingly. He was a wonderful man and

Nazra could not have been more perfect for him," Thomas said. "Let me call Caleb and tell him. I am sure he will want to call Marsha Menendez in Chicago to inform her of what is going on. Not that I think that Yusuf Nabeth would dare to openly come against us, but the man is powerful and a fanatic, who will stop at nothing to get his way."

"Then you think we are in danger?" Melissa asked with alarm.

"No, honey, this is just a precaution, nothing more, don't you worry about it." He was sorry he had mentioned it to her. In her condition she did not need this kind of worry.

The team met in an emergency session that evening. Everyone was stunned and saddened by Fouad's and Nazra's death and there was an atmosphere of gloom in the room when Theresa walked in late.

She had brought her Bible and opened it before anyone could say anything.

"While we mourn the death of Fouad and Nazra, they did not just die a normal death," she said. "They died as martyrs to their faith in a way that is pointed out as special in the book of Revelation: "And I saw the souls of those who had been beheaded because of their testimony for Jesus and because of the Word of God. They came to life and reigned with Christ a thousand years. (Revelation 21:4)

She went on. "You might think that it is unusual for a father to kill his own son, but here too, the Lord tells us in Mark 13:1- 2 where Jesus describes the End of the Age, "Brother will betray brother to death, and a father his child."

"And in John 16:2 it says, "They will put you out of the synagogue, in fact, a time is coming when anyone who kills you will think he is offering a service to God."

"This is what happened to Fouad and Nazra. They may be dead to us, but they are very much alive and a part of those honored in heaven for their faith. That is why I would like for you to rejoice in spite of our loss. As Christians, we do not receive seventy virgins after we die, but a glorious eternity with the King of the universe and so rule and reign with Him in His Kingdom. Let me add, unlike Islam, there will be no continuation of subjugation of women in heaven, but everyone, women and men, will be counted as beloved children of the King." Theresa looked around the table and smiled. "This is not the time for mourning, but a celebration of life. The way things look, some of us may face the same fate. Are you ready to stand up for the Lord in these last days? He has shown us through many miracles, signs and wonders since we have opened this clinic, that He is with us and nothing that happens is by chance. We are here on His assignment and in His power. He sent Thomas to us in a miraculous way and has used him to spread the Gospel in a continued dramatic fashion. All this proves that we are a part of the end time harvest." She looked at everyone and then said, "You still have a chance to leave and go back to the States, but if you stay, you must be prepared to face what is to come."

After a long time, Thomas finally spoke up,

"The day Melissa and I drove out of our driveway in Philadelphia to come here, we both had the clear and unmistakable impression we would never see our county again. This is where we have been sent and this is where we will serve Yeshua until He calls us home, in whatever way He chooses to do that." He took Melissa's hand as he spoke and smiled at her. "I don't know that much about Revelation, but I guess I will get to live it in living color. We all are. And no matter how the enemy rages, Yeshua will win, that much I do know."

"Amen!" Theresa said and closed the Bible. "I want us to pray for Fouad's father that he may find the true God in the end. Although it is pretty hard for me right now to even try to love him, we all know that is what Jesus wants us to do."

A month later, a special delivery letter came from Switzerland addressed to Thomas. It was from a bank in Geneva.

"I can't imagine what this could be," he said to Melissa and sank into his chair. It had been a hard day as usual and he was tired and threw the envelope on the little table nearby. "I will open it later, I'm not up to legal or financial stuff."

"Do we have an account in this bank?" Melissa asked.

"No way, we would have to be a lot richer than we are, sweetheart," he chuckled.

"Here," she said and handed him the letter. "Open it, curiosity is killing me."

When he did, he stared at the document for a long time without a word.

"Well? What is it?" she asked.

"Fouad Nabeth has left me the sum of fifteen million dollars to be used for the clinic."

"You are kidding!"

"I am not. It states in here, he wrote a letter right after he got married, that if both he and his wife should not survive, he wants to make sure that the work of Shalom Outreach continues without ever having to worry about money. It is left to me in a trust fund from which I can use the interest to run the clinic with special exceptions to draw on the principle in emergencies. He also says he didn't leave it to the ministry, because his father could have it closed down and then contest the will. Since I am an American citizen, he can't touch me."

"Fouad managed to outmaneuver his father in the end, didn't he?" Melissa said. "I imagine that will not go over well with that evil man."

Thomas sat, deep in thought as he held the documents in his hand. Finally, he said,

"I think we should not tell the others about this. I will contact the bank in Geneva and have them send the monthly interest income anonymously to Shalom Outreach in Chicago with the stipulation that it will be exclusively used for this particular clinic. That way I am in control, rather than Chicago. It isn't that I don't trust them, but why tempt them with that much money. They might want to use it for some other good cause. The first thing I want to do is add on a small ICU ward to keep surgery patients for several days if necessary and then hire an additional doctor, several nurses and other necessary personnel we so desperately need.

"I am still concerned his father will find out and retaliate against you, Thomas," Melissa said. "We know he will stop at nothing, even kill his own son."

"Let's not worry about that, honey. The Lord has provided for us all that we need and I am quite sure He will not let one man hinder His work."

No one at the ministry in Tiberias or in Chicago had any idea where the sudden influx of funds came from, but the improvements they made possible turned the clinic into a small hospital. With the second doctor on staff, it gave Thomas more time to share his special message at meetings arranged by different churches in the area. He started to accept more speaking opportunities and began traveling across Galilee together with Melissa; although she was now in her seventh months and would soon have to slow down. They had found out it was indeed a girl she was carrying and Thomas already talked to his little Helena, whispering her name as he leaned over Melissa's belly every day. He couldn't wait to hold her in his arms.

It was on a visit to a Christian community they stopped at a restaurant along the highway. Melissa had a craving for fish and The Old Fisherman's Inn looked like the right place. It was quite crowded and they found one of the last tables in the very back of the restaurant, hidden away in a corner.

Half way through the meal, three men in black leather jackets walked in with large rifles in their hands. Without warning they pointed them at the people at the many tables, shouting Allah Akbar and started firing. Thomas instantly pulled Melissa under the table, put his body in front of hers and watched as dozens of screaming men and woman fell to the floor. Since they were out of the line of fire, he knew they were not in immediate danger, unless the gunmen came searching for them.

It was over in seconds and the gunmen ran out and drove off, laughing and waving their guns. Thomas moved so Melissa could get up and ran to where the many victims lay.

"I am a doctor," he shouted, "my medical bag is in the car. Melissa, go get it." He handed her the keys and started to triage the wounded. He found several dead and some wounded beyond hope. "Please, Yeshua, help me; I can't do this on my own," he prayed under his breath as he bent over a young woman holding her little girl in her arms. Blood was pouring from a head wound. Thomas saw that her child was dead.

In desperation he laid his hand on the girl's chest and asked the Lord to heal her. The woman looked at him with astonishment, but was too shocked to object. "I am Jewish," she whispered.

"That's alright, Yeshua loves you and your little girl just the same." He smiled at her as he laid his hands on her head and said so she could hear him. "Be healed in the Name of Yeshua."

Her wound stopped bleeding instantly and she leaned over her daughter and watched in amazement as the girl opened her eyes and said in Hebrew, “What happened, Mommy? I saw a beautiful angel who told me that Yeshua loves me. “Who is Yeshua?”

Thomas got up off his knees and ran to two bodies lying on the floor. It was an old woman who held her husband close to her body to keep him from moving. He had a gunshot wound in his abdomen and was moaning. Thomas knew if he didn’t get surgery within the next half hour, he would die.

“What is your husband’s name,” he asked the woman.

“His name is Philip,” she said. “Please help him, he is all I have.”

Thomas bent over the old man and placed his hand on his stomach and said,

“By Your Name Yeshua and through the power it holds over the enemy, I declare Philip healed.” The man’s eyes opened and he looked at his wife.

“I will be alright, my love, the pain is gone and I think I can get up.”

“How can this be, doctor, you did not do anything but pray,” she said, totally astounded. “I saw you, I was right here!” She began to cry as she helped her husband get up.

“Yeshua has healed him,” Thomas said and he knew he was speaking in Hebrew. “He is the great physician who has sent me to tell you that He loves you and that He is your Meshiah.”

“Where can I find this Yeshua, Sir?” she asked. “I want to know Him better.”

“Go to any Christian church and ask them to tell you about Him. I don’t have time right now, because there are others who need my help. “If you can’t find a church, come to Tiberias and go to Shalom Outreach, they will tell you everything you need to know.”

“Are you the American doctor who treats the poor and heals them? I have heard of you. My husband and I will find you, have no doubt.”

Thomas spent the next half hour treating the many wounded until the countless emergency vehicles arrived together with the press. Before he could stop her, the old woman and her husband rushed to the first reporter on the scene and told him the Doctor from Shalom Outreach had miraculously healed her husband. She was joined by the young woman who shared that he had brought her little girl back to life.

It was all 'downhill after that', as Thomas put it later, after the major TV stations descended on the site. Thomas was not allowed to leave since he was an eyewitness to the shooting.

When the authorities finally let him go, Thomas had missed the meeting at the church and they went back home instead. Several TV trucks followed their car to Shalom Outreach and soon the front of the clinic was filled with reporters waiting to get a glimpse of him.

The next day his picture was splashed across the front pages of every news outlet across the world, accompanied by headlines like AMERICAN DOCTOR HEALS VICTIMS OF SHOOTING and MIRACLE WORKER WALKS IN THE SHOES OF JESUS IN GALILEE, while another insisted PHILADELPHIA SURGEON CLAIMS TO BE JESUS.

The siege lasted for days and the clinic was forced to remain closed because of the crowds. He had countless phone calls from the States, but it was the one from his parents that upset him the most. His mother was hysterical in her ice cold way as only she knew how to be, while his father tried his best to get Thomas to return home.

Even Melissa's parents voiced their concern over the news reports and urged her to return home so her baby could be born in the US. They cited the violence as a reason, but she knew they were confused about Thomas turning from a surgeon to a faith healer.

It took a month for the furor to die down to the point, Thomas was able to return to the clinic without causing a near riot of people trying to be treated by him. He had been holed up in the Mission all this time, afraid to be seen in public, uncertain if he would ever be able to return to do surgery. With Shalom Outreach now a well-known Ministry the world over, offers of TV interviews, invitations by mega churches and even the Pope, as well as pleas for healing from the countless sick and dying continued to pour in daily. Thomas answered none of them and prayed for the day when he could go back to treating the poor and sharing his story. Through it all, he retained a clear understanding that his assignment, given to him by the Lord Himself, was not to reach out to the world, but to the people of Israel.

It was another month before he finally accepted a speaking engagement at one of the small churches in the country, about ten miles north of Tiberias. At first he was going to turn them down since Melissa's time of delivery was close, but she insisted that he go.

It was on a Saturday and the roads were not too crowded. Theresa told him it was to be a small gathering of Christians from the surrounding towns who met in a modest, little building in the middle of nowhere. The pastor was a good friend of hers and she had convinced Thomas it would be safe and out of the way, without large crowds or the press.

As usual, the area this close to Capernaum made Thomas think of Yeshua and how He would stand on a hill and teach the people. How he wished he could be there one more time, listening to the wonderful words of the Master and feel the peace each time He looked at him.

He almost missed the exit. He drove down a narrow road amidst fields of grain for about three miles, when he noticed columns of people walking on each side of the road. *Just like when they went to hear Yeshua,"* he thought.

As he turned around the bend, he slammed on the breaks. In front of him was a huge crowd, sitting on the grassy ground, facing a small podium with a microphone. It was incredible! It looked exactly the same as two thousand years ago, except this time it was not Yeshua teaching them, but him. *Oh God!*

He was ready to turn the car around and drive back the way he came, when a man in a flowing Arabic tunic opened the car door with a big smile.

"Welcome, Dr. Peterson. Thank you for coming, we have been waiting for you. I am Pastor Hassid. Come with me and I will introduce you to the many people who have come to hear your message.

"What happened to the small group you mentioned to Theresa, Pastor?" was all Thomas managed to ask before the excited man pulled him through the crowd toward the microphone.

"It sort of got away with us," he said with a disarming smile. "We have a translator for you. He is already up front. His name is Andrew and he is Jewish. He speaks good English."

Thomas nearly tripped over the rough surface of the grass and was glad they finally made it up front. The moment he stood next to Andrew, the crowd started shouting and clapping until Pastor Hassid finally managed to calm them down.

"I know you are excited, but if you don't be quiet, Dr. Peterson will not be able to talk," he said in Hebrew with Andrew translating. We all know who this man is and we also know he walked with Yeshua," he went on. "I am not going to take any more time away from what he has come here to share with us. We all expect great miracles and healings, because we have prayed in faith for this day." As he waved for Thomas to take the microphone, the crowd broke out in shouts again.

Thomas looked down from the podium and once again wished it was Yeshua preaching. *Please, Lord, I cannot do this, I am not You. Send your Holy Spirit and speak and act through me.*

"Before I start to tell you what I saw and heard in the three years I walked in this very place called Galilee, let me say with the Apostle Paul in 1 Corinthians 2:2-5, "For I resolve to know nothing while I was with you except Jesus Christ and him crucified. [3] I came to you in weakness with great fear and trembling. [4] My message and my preaching were not with wise and persuasive words, but with a demonstration of the Spirit's power, [5] so that your faith might not rest on human wisdom, but on God's power."

"I am her to tell you, if you want to see the power of God today, then you must look to Him and not to me. I cannot turn even one blade of grass green, not one." He smiled, "I can turn it brown, but not green, only He can," he said and pointed his finger upwards. "Do not do like the world does, who says I am a healer and miracle worker. I am not, but Yeshua is. The exciting thing is, He did it two thousand years ago and He still does it today. I am here to tell you, I was there in a dream when they nailed Him to the cross and laid Him in the tomb. But most importantly, I was there when He appeared to a group of us, risen from the dead and very much alive. He commissioned me to go to His people Israel to tell them He died for them first and then the world, yet they rejected

Him. In sending me now, He is giving you another chance before He returns. You are His people, for you He came then and now."

The crowd sat mesmerized as Thomas went on and shared his dream. When he was finished, hundreds came forward to accept Yeshua as their Meshiah. The sick came and as Thomas laid his hands on them, many were healed. The enthusiasm at the beginning of the meeting was replaced by a subdued reverence. The crowd watched in awe as some threw away their crutches, while others got up out of their wheelchairs, slowly at first, and then running and shouting toward Thomas. Once again, he did not need Andrew to translate, since he understood whatever language they spoke.

And so it came to be that Thomas, once an atheist surgeon from Philadelphia, preached to ever increasing crowds in the region of Galilee in Israel in much the same way Yeshua had done. The world had soon forgotten about Thomas, but the people of the Israel had not and came to hear him in ever increasing numbers, from as far away as Jerusalem, Haifa and Tel Aviv. Jews, Arabs and Palestinian turned to Yeshua in startling numbers, because the words of Thomas were accompanied by signs, wonders and miracles.

In the midst of it all, little Helena was born to the delight of her proud parents. The team spoiled and fussed over the baby as if she was their own since she made them feel like they were family. Even Karl, the giant of a man who talked to computers, turned to putty when he was allowed to hold her on rare occasions. Melissa was sure Helena would disappear in his huge hands, never to be seen again.

Yet in the midst of this seemingly peaceful time in their lives, dark, ominous clouds suddenly appeared on the horizon. On September 19, 2018 Iran announced it had a bomb!

Chapter 23

In the days after, Thomas could sense fear settling over the land like a thick, dark blanket. To his amazement, it caused the people to turn in even greater numbers to accept Yeshua as he continued to speak across the countryside of Galilee. Yet at the same time, the Jihadists grew bolder, since, with Iran's support, they suddenly had nothing to fear from the government of Israel. Terrorist attacks and bombings became an almost daily occurrence across the country and the Israeli government was overwhelmed by the sheer number of them, while at the same time preoccupied with preparations for the real possibility of nuclear war.

The Jewish religious authorities, in order to find a scapegoat for the chaos in the country, turned against the now quite large population of Christians and began a war of words, denouncing them as enemies of Israel and no better than the Jihadists. They were supported and even encouraged by the discrimination and even persecution of anything Christian across the world. It was estimated that Europe, after the influx of refugees several years ago, was now under Islamic control, psychologically and even to some extent politically speaking with Islam touted as the only peaceful religion. Listening to the eloquent words of the charismatic, young leader of the UN, Mohamed Abdul Musharak, the member nations of the UN were solidly on the side of Iran with the exception of Israel and the US. In the opinion of most people, it was time someone showed Israel they could not continue to mistreat their Palestinian neighbors by bombing them and get away with it.

In a speech to the nation, President Amherst, in a turn-around of his former stance, made it very clear that America would stand by Israel in case of a nuclear conflict and do all it can, to supply its closest ally in the Middle East with any help it needs. He promised to send warships to the Mediterranean Sea in a display of strength. However, the Iranian government, knowing full well, they were no more than powerless decoys, since they did not carry nuclear weapons of any kind in order not to inflame the situation.

Thomas looked out over the Sea of Galilee as he walked early one morning. He knew it was dangerous, but felt he needed this time alone with the Lord.

"I am trying to be without fear, Lord, but I am not doing a good job of it," he said out loud. "Things look bad and I know Shalom Outreach is in danger from every direction. If You don't protect us, it will not be here much longer. I am sure my work is not done yet, but I can't continue if we are shut down. It is a miracle that the authorities have not prevented me from preaching to the multitudes and I thank You for it. Allow me to go on and lead as many to You as time allows until You return. Have mercy on Your people Israel, Lord. The enemy is everywhere and there is no one to stand with her but You. Save Your chosen ones, Lord like You promise in Your Word. Protect those who You have already drawn to you. They are new in Your Kingdom, strengthen their faith and help them stand in Your Name in the terrible days ahead. Help me to be strong and not deny You like I did before, yet I know I will, unless You give me the courage. You did it for the Apostles back then, please do the same for me, even if, like them, I will lose my life. I will give it in exchange for Melissa and little Helena, if that is what it takes, just don't let anything happen to them."

Thomas was interrupted by a man coming toward him in the distance with determined strides. Something looked familiar about him. He strained to see who it was, when he realized it was the Rabbi from a year ago. The one who got so upset with him on the shore and the one he spotted in the background as a member of the city council, trying to shut down the clinic.

"Please help me say the right things to this angry man, Lord," he prayed as he stood and waited.

"You are still here, polluting my people with your heresy," the man shouted even before he reached Thomas. "This time I have the backing of the people, no matter what you do in your clinic, since you are no longer the doctor for the poor, but a heretic preacher."

"What is your name, Sir?" Thomas asked quietly.

"I am Yitzhak Sharim, a member of the religious council of the local synagogue. I have been sent to warn you to stop what you are doing or we will force you into silence by telling the people you are here to blaspheme our God and turn Israel away from Yahweh to worship this false Meshiah." He was trembling with rage. "Let me warn you, this time you will not stop me like you did before!"

"Rabbi, you may be able to stop me, but just like two thousand years ago, the message of Yeshua cannot be stopped by human hands, no matter how hard you try. If it is not me, then it will be someone else, for your Meshiah is mightier than you and will not stop sending His messengers, until His purpose has been fulfilled, drawing to Him every one of those He has chosen." Thomas looked at the Rabbi with compassion as he continued," He came for you as well, Yitzhak and for all those who decide to acknowledge Him as their Meshiah. Search your Torah and read the words the prophets foretold about Him, Yeshua has fulfilled every single one of them." Thomas reached into his pants pocket and took out a card. "Here, I have printed on here where you can find what has been prophesied about Him, read it for yourself," he said and handed it to the Rabbi. Before the astonished man could answer, Thomas turned around and walked away.

As soon as he entered his home, Melissa handed him the phone.

"Your Mom is on the phone. She is very upset."

"Hello, Mom, how are you?"

"Thomas, I am totally beside myself and insist that you return home. With the situation the way it is, there could be a nuclear war any day and all of you would be killed. Please, Thomas, I can't stand this anymore. Please, come home." She was sobbing uncontrollably and then his father came on.

"This has gone on long enough, Thomas. We have been abandoned by you, rejected, humiliated and frightened by your behavior over the last two years. We have a granddaughter we have never seen and probably never will. Enough is enough! I can no longer handle your mother's outbursts of anger and fear for your lives. We are getting too old for this." His father was trying hard not to shout.

"Dad, I love both of you and understand how hard this must be to hear all the bad news about what is going on here. We are fine, nothing has happened to us and the Lord will protect us, whatever happens," he said with as much love as he could. "Please understand, I have a purpose to fulfill for our people and I am not going to run out on it just because it looks a little dangerous here right now. You have raised me better than that." He suddenly heard his father crying and it broke his heart. "I am sorry, Dad," he said, close to tears. "I am so very sorry. I love you and Mom." He looked at Melissa with a helpless shrug. When his father stopped crying, he said in a gentle tone, "Dad, go see Nana and let her explain to you about Yeshua. If you want to help me, let her tell you how to accept Him into your heart. You don't have to make a decision, just listen to her without interrupting and without preconceived atheistic ideas. He is our Meshiah, of that I have no doubt."

There was silence until his father hung up the phone without a word. Thomas sat down and cried.

"I risk my life for strangers every day to bring them to Yeshua, but I can't convince my own parents that He is the One. I preach to thousands that without Him there is no salvation and yet I see my mother and father going to hell, because they won't believe in Him." Melissa stood beside him and wrapped her arms around his shoulders.

"It's not too late, Thomas, there is still time. Give Nana a chance to talk to them and most of all, give Yeshua a chance to draw them. He can do what you can't."

"Maybe I should fly home and talk to them myself?"

"You do what the Lord tells you to do, but be prepared that they may not let you back into the country," she said.

"You are right, I hadn't considered that," he answered and then told her what happened at the shore.

'This is a powerful man among the religious community," Melissa said, worry showing in her voice. "He can certainly do what he threatens to do and close down the clinic, can't he? And there is nothing we can do about it."

"Maybe the purpose of the clinic has been fulfilled and what is left is for us to concentrate on sharing the Gospel," Thomas said.

"I had never thought of that possibility," Melissa said.

"We have the money to operate without Shalom Outreach if they close it down and turn it into a strictly Evangelistic Mission if the worst should happen."

"Would the rest of the team stay with us I wonder?" Melissa asked.

"I imagine some of them would, while others would transfer to Jerusalem, Tel Aviv or Haifa. Since we own the building here, the authorities cannot force us to leave unless they get the government in Tel Aviv to expel us from the country. I doubt they would do that, since the US is the only friend they have left, no matter how weak American support might be at the moment."

Two days later, in the middle of the morning, the clinic was bombed. A man, his face covered by a black mask, threw a small, homemade explosive into the waiting room filled with mostly women and children. While no one was killed, there were several wounded children, who were treated by the medical team. The damage to the clinic was minimal and the incident was dismissed as the work of a Palestinian youth. Until one of the nurses found a note underneath one of the chairs, hidden way against the wall several days later. LEAVE ISRAEL OR DIE. Thomas suspected the Rabbi, but of course could not prove it and the team decided to ignore the whole thing. With such minimal damage and no one seriously hurt, they knew nothing would be done about it anyway. But it left everyone on edge.

"We have joined the rest of the Israelis, living in constant fear of being killed by her many enemies inside and outside the country," Meta said over lunch several days later. "It has become a way of life for many years now, but has gotten much worse lately. It never ceases to amaze me how the world can hate such a tiny country for no other reason than they don't want it to exist."

"It is only about as big as New Jersey," Thomas said, "with a fraction of the number of people of the nations who want it gone. According to Iran's leaders, their entire reason for building the bomb is to wipe Israel off the face of the earth."

"If the United States or any other country was hit by only a fraction of missiles Israel has been hit with over the years, there would have been retaliation on a massive scale long ago and the world would be appalled," Caleb said. "Instead, Israel is blamed for defending its borders and accused of atrocities against those who attack it constantly by shooting back."

"If you have ever doubted that this is a spiritual battle rather than an earthly one, this is the proof, Theresa said. "This is where the Meshiah comes from and by coming has changed the fundamentals of life, our laws and morals not just in the Western world, but everywhere else. Christianity is still the only religion which advocates love for your enemies in its purest form. And still, it is now being persecuted worldwide for no other than religious reasons and because it will not conform to the sinful ways of the world. What we thought of as unacceptable behavior only a short few years ago, is now accepted as normal. For example, homosexuality, abortion, living together without marriage and many others. To think of these things as sin makes people uncomfortable, so they call those of us who believe they are, old fashioned, narrow minded and bigoted. The way our world is these days, makes Sodom and Gomorra look like a convent." Theresa was visibly upset and had stopped eating. "I believe it is time the Meshiah comes back, there is no way the world is able to continue on this immoral, unspiritual and violent course."

"I am ready to go any time the Lord wants to come," Leona said with deep conviction. "I wish He would hurry up. What a joy it will be to reign with Him instead of watching everything we know and love be trampled by a world gone upside down."

They finished their lunch in silence, each in their own thoughts, when Thomas' cell phone rang.

"Hello."

"Thomas, this is Bob Durham."

"Bob, how wonderful to hear from you. It has been two years. I hope nothing is wrong?" Thomas shouted with excitement.

"Nothing is wrong, my friend. But I do want to tell you that my wife died in a car crash a year ago and I have been at a loss to know what to do with my life since then."

"I am so sorry, Bob."

"So am I, Thomas. She was the love of my life, but that is not why I am calling. I want to come and be a part of your ministry. I know it is sudden, but not for me. I have been praying about this for some time. What do you think?" Bob sounded excited.

"You do know how dangerous it is here right now?" Thomas asked, incredulous. "This is not the time to be in Israel as a tourist or wanting to spend a few weeks on a mission trip."

“That is not what I want. This would be for the duration of whatever comes. I want to be a part of the end time harvest and what better place than being in the eye of the storm.”

“That is definitely what it would be, my friend. Of course we could use you, but are you sure you realize the danger? What about your kids, what would they say?” Thomas asked, thinking about his parents.

“My kids are busy with their lives and not really interested in the things of the Lord. Besides, Marsha has all my paperwork together and Eric has agreed to accept me, so there is nothing to stand in the way. Actually, I will arrive in Haifa in two weeks.”

“We are getting a new doctor,” Thomas said to the group after he hung up. “His name is Robert Durham and he is an Orthopedic surgeon from my old hospital in Philadelphia. He is also on the board of Shalom Outreach in Chicago.”

“That man has a lot of chutzpah,” Meta said with admiration in her voice. “We could use another doctor, especially since Dr. Rashad quit. I never quite trusted him to be a Christian.”

“I think he was, but you are right, I was never that certain myself,” Caleb said.

“With Bob Durham there is no question,” Thomas said. “He is a wonderful, kind and committed man who is sold out to the cause. He is the one who brought me to Shalom Outreach when I was rejected at Mercy. It will be an honor to serve with him.”

Chapter 24

Bob Durham arrived on a Saturday afternoon. Caleb and Thomas picked him up at the airport. He looked all the same, a man in his sixties, of medium height and a little more round in the middle than Thomas remembered. His close cropped, red beard and hair to match stood out like a shining light. His ruddy complexion rounded out the perfect picture of what everyone would think an Irishman should look like.

"Thomas, old boy, you lost some inches where I gained them. It is so good to see you. And you, Caleb, I remember meeting you in Chicago once some years ago. Still running the show, hey?"

"I am, Dr. Durham," Caleb said with his brightest grin. "It is good to have you join us, isn't it Thomas?"

"You will call me Bob like all my friends, young man. At my age you can call me anything you want and I will listen," he said laughing. Looking around in the airport, he said in awe, "So this is Israel, the land I always wanted to visit. This is what I call God's country, literally."

"It is that," Thomas said. "Wait till you see Galilee. It looks very much like the way I saw it, except for the cities."

They arrived at Shalom Outreach in time for dinner and Bob Durham met the entire team. Little Helena was fascinated with his red beard and pulled on it as hard as she could every time he held her.

"She is a wonderful child," he told Melissa and Thomas. "What a blessing," he added with some sadness in his voice. "My grandsons are nearly grown and quite disinterested in this old man. You, my little angel, will just have to make up for it."

"The way she is handed around in this house, she is not shy at all as you can see," Melissa said, "but thinks everyone here is part of her family. And they are," she added and looked around with a smile.

"And we are so glad to add you to it," Thomas said.

Bob Durham proved to be a tremendous asset to Thomas, not just in the clinic, but also praying for people at the meetings. They were fascinated with his red hair and beard, and especially the children surrounded him wherever he went. With his jovial demeanor he brought many to the Lord as he shared about the Yeshua in a unique way, geared particularly to them. Not long after he got there, he started a bible school for young people in the waiting room of the clinic on Sunday afternoon. In no time, they had to turn children away until he added another on Saturday morning. Mikail volunteered to help with translating, since most of them were Jewish from the poor section of Tiberias. Before long, the old familiar song rang throughout the clinic on weekends, 'Jesus loves the little children', translated into Hebrew by Mikail.

It was on a Thursday afternoon several weeks later, two policemen walked into the clinic and asked for the Director. Thomas had just finished his second surgery when the receptionist called him up front.

"I am Dr. Peterson, what can I do for you?" he asked with Mikail translating.

"Do you have someone working here by the name of Theresa Ryan?" one of them asked.

"Yes, we do? Is anything wrong?"

"Could we talk to you in your office, Doctor?"

"Of course, follow me." Thomas was getting nervous. This did not sound good. He knew Theresa and two local volunteers had gone to their weekly street mission in downtown Tiberias.

"We are sorry to inform you that Theresa Ryan was killed in a brutal attack an hour ago by unknown assailants as she and two others with her were gunned down in a barrage of machine gun fire. We are truly sorry for your loss and will try to do anything we can to find out who did this."

Thomas stared at the two men, trying to comprehend what he had just heard.

"Are you sure she is dead?" he finally managed to asked.

"Yes, Sir, there is no question about that."

"You need to tell her husband, he works here as well," Thomas said and picked up the phone on his desk. "Paul, please come to my office right away. It is urgent."

Paul Ryan was a quiet man and stared at Thomas without words and collapsed in the chair after he heard the news.

"We need someone to identify the body at the city morgue, Doctor," the policeman finally said, clearly uncomfortable.

"I will see to it, officer if you will give us some time to deal with this," Thomas said and pointed to Paul. "Does it have to be her husband?"

"No, anyone from the organization will do."

"Thank you, officer, I will handle it," Thomas said and closed the door behind them after they left.

"Paul, I am so very sorry. Theresa was the most important part of this ministry, because she held us together spiritually with her strong faith and trust in Yeshua. Please accept my condolences. I will have someone stay with you in your quarters." He turned to Mikail. "Could you get Bob in here? Would that be alright with you, Paul?"

Shalom Outreach closed the doors the next day as everyone gathered in the Mission in shock and filled with fear. They had found another note under the same chair as before. THIS IS THE FIRST, THERE WILL BE MORE. LEAVE ISRAEL NOW.

"This is when we need Theresa, to help us cope and trust the Lord," Caleb finally said into the silence. "I don't have the words to deal with this," he went on as tears filled his eyes. "She was the glue that held us together and the lifeline to Yeshua. What are we going to do now?"

No one said anything until Bob Durham spoke up.

"I didn't know her as well as you did, but what short time I worked here, there was no doubt she was a godly woman who was ready at a moment's notice to give her life for the Lord. Like us, she knew the risks and without fear, she went among the people of Israel to share the Good News. We grieve with you Paul, because there are no words to help right now that will make you or us miss her any less, but we are here for you as fellow workers in the harvest of the Kingdom of God. Theresa has finished the task the Lord gave her to do and I know beyond a doubt He welcomed her into His presence as his beloved daughter and a martyr for His cause. There is no greater reward, no greater honor than that. She gave her life for the people of Israel that they might join their Meshiah in eternity." He looked at everyone with an expression of sorrow and hope. "We are all here, because we are part of the same harvest, the same danger and the same hope. Like the Apostles gave their lives in the service of Yeshua, so might we be asked to do the same and take comfort in the words of Paul, "to live is Christ and to die is gain." (Philippians 1:21) "All we can do is what Yeshua did when they nailed Him to the cross, forgive those who did this terrible thing. Some of you may not be ready for it, but un-forgiveness is poison in the life of any believer."

Paul sat in stony silence when Bob finished. Leona and Meta cried, while Melissa held Helena close to her as if to protect her. The men in the group stared in silence, trying not to show any emotions. Finally, Thomas spoke up,

"Thank you, Bob. I remember clearly when I stood in front of the cross as Yeshua spoke those famous words of forgiveness over those who were killing Him. I couldn't imagine then how He could do that, until now, as He is asking us to do the same. We are all in a special place, a special time and asked to do special things. And just like He, we may be asked to give our lives as Theresa did. Knowing her the way I did, she did not mind at all to die for her faith, because to her it was a badge of honor to be counted worthy." He turned to Paul. "She loved you very much, Paul, but she loved Yeshua more by going out into the streets among those who would want to take her life. You will see her again in eternity among the honored martyrs, reigning with Christ the way He promised. Let hope sustain you, Paul, not grief. Allow faith to help you carry on and the love of Yeshua strengthen your resolve to continue the work here. I know that is what she would have wanted for you."

A week later a letter came from the city council of Tiberias. After expressing their condolences, Shalom Outreach was told that from now on, any activity promoting religious beliefs or open gatherings within the city limits, must be approved first by obtaining a license. Failure to do so could jeopardize the permit of Shalom Outreach to operate the clinic. It was signed by the Rabbi from the shore of the Sea of Galilee, Yitzhak Sharim.

When Caleb went to city hall to obtain a permit, it was denied on grounds it was too dangerous in view of recent events. Apparently the Rabbi Sharim had done his homework this time and closed every door for any more ministry within the city of Tiberias, other than the clinic.

The entire team went to the funeral of the two volunteers who were killed with Theresa. It was a quiet affair and just one of many in recent months with terrorists carrying out their gruesome acts almost at will, with the police nearly helpless because of the sheer number of them.

Theresa's body was shipped to the US and she was buried in her small home town of Lynville, Pennsylvania by her parents and siblings. Caleb and Thomas sent a letter of condolences together with words of praise for the wonderful work she had done.

It was not surprising that nothing came of the investigation of who killed her and her two volunteers. Bob took over her job of counseling and Bible teaching at Shalom Outreach and after a while, life seemed to go on as it had before. Paul was even more quiet than before and had finally turned to Bob to talk about his grief after he returned from the funeral in the US. It was as if the Lord had sent him just in time to replace Theresa.

Before any more restrictions could be put on open meetings in the countryside of Galilee, Thomas obtained a permit from Haifa, covering the entire region. Since then he spent less time at the clinic and more on the road, drawing huge crowds wherever he spoke, with miracles, signs and wonders occurring daily. With the nuclear threat from Iran looming over the county like a cloud of fear, thousands came to hear the message of hope, deliverance and healing by the Meshiah Yeshua. Since Iran breathed threats to destroy Israel on a daily basis, the people came from Jerusalem and the rest of the country and accepted Christ in such astounding numbers that even the government in Tel Aviv became aware of it. They sent an envoy to Tiberias and were welcome by the Rabbi Yitzhak Sharim, who was only too happy to inform them of Shalom Outreach as a hotbed of agitators and heretics, who poisoned the people against the Jewish faith. Since Israel had always been tolerant of other religions, no measures were taken against the ministry – for now.

Chapter 25

The shrill sound of the special emergency alert signal from the radio made Thomas stop in the middle of surgery. Without having to call him, Mikail came rushing in to translate for him, a mask over his face.

"We interrupt our broadcast to bring you this special news bulletin from Washington. The President of the United States has been shot an hour ago on his way to a veteran's memorial service in Arlington National Cemetery. He was flown to Bethesda Hospital, but no details whether he survived the attack or who is responsible are available. The US military has been put on highest alert worldwide and all military installations are closed to civilians for an indeterminate time. Vice President Roland Kendrick is standing by at the White House in case he is needed to take over. According to informed sources, he and the President disagree sharply on whether to stand by Israel in case of an attack by Iran. The Vice President is known to be a great supporter of the UN General Secretary Musharak. Informed sources out of Tel Aviv state, that if President Amherst does not survive this attack, Israel will have lost its only ally in the West and will face the threat of Iran alone. Stay tuned for more information as soon as we have it.

No one said a word as Thomas continued with his surgery. Fear gripped his heart to the point he had trouble concentrating. *Israel stands alone against the world bent on destroying it and we are right in the middle of it!*

That evening over dinner, the team sat in stunned silence as they got the news that President Amherst had died on the way to the hospital. Roland Arthur Kendrick was now the new Commander in Chief of the most powerful nation in the world and a friend of the enemy of Israel.

"There is no hope for Israel," Caleb said. "If God doesn't intervene, His people are doomed."

"We know better than that," Bob said. "For thousands of years the Lord has taken care of his chosen people, He is not going to stop now. He will not forsake us any more than a father can forsake his children. No matter how bad it looks, the enemy will not win this one, trust me. It is up to us to spread the hope and assurance that the God of Abraham, Isaak and Jacob will come to our rescue and defeat the nations who would dare stand against His chosen people. And all of us here will be witnesses. Instead of fear, we need to stand in faith and spread the Good News of Meshiah Yeshua until He returns or calls us home, whatever comes first.

The crowds at Thomas' meetings grew even larger as hopelessness and fear spread across the land. There was a marked increase in depression and suicides among the population as it became clear, President Kendrick stood with Mohamed Musharak when he announced in his acceptance speech, America would not risk getting involved in helping Israel should Iran decide to attack.

Anti-Semitism rose dramatically worldwide with bombings of synagogues and Jewish cemeteries. In Turkey a Jewish school, filled with hundreds of children was blown up and over fifty of them died with many more wounded. In France, immigrant gangs stormed a synagogue during services and raped dozens of women and killed over twenty-five men. In Germany, flags with the swastika emblem printed on them, were draped over several synagogues by a right wing group of demonstrators.

But it didn't stop there, many Christian churches and synagogues across Europe and even some in the United States, were burned or desecrated by right wing fanatics, blaming Christians and Jews for the turmoil in the world. Soon after President Kendrick took office, all mention of God or Jesus was banned from official documents in the US, schools and other government facilities. One of his first official act as President was the elimination of prayer in the Senate.

Large companies soon followed suit, adhering to strict regulations of political correctness. Even some of the major denominations fell in line with them and preached adherence to a more tolerant society.

Jews and Christians were discriminated against in subtle ways and the name of Jesus became the preferred cussword across the land. Christmas was changed to Winter Festival and Easter was renamed Spring Holiday. No religious decorations were tolerated outdoors, even in private yards, for fear of offending someone. No calendars with religious holidays mentioned could be found; and it seemed, without much fanfare or opposition, God was eradicated from the official economy and moral thinking of the Western world.

To the surprise of the team at Shalom Outreach, the clinic was left untouched by the general turmoil and many came to seek much more than physical healing. Bob had changed a back portion of the clinic into a counseling center, where different members of the team prayed for those who wanted to know more about Yeshua. Over a short time, hundreds came to the Lord under the guise of seeking medical help. As word spread, the back room became known as the 'SRS', short for Soul Refuge Sanctuary. Anyone who wanted prayer or counseling was instructed to ask to speak with 'Theresa'. This password was established by the team in honor of Theresa Ryan and was given only to those who wanted to become a Christian, sent by neighbors, family and friends who knew about it from their own encounter.

In the last two years, because of the preaching of Thomas, churches had sprung up everywhere. Some underground, some in homes and others in inconspicuous buildings in the cities, while still others simply met in a field on the edge of many towns across Israel. Thomas and Bob and other mature believers visited them as often as they could, instructing and helping those who became their leaders. Once a week, these in turn came to the SRS to get instructions on the Christian faith and how to study the scriptures and teach their congregation. By now, a large net of these groups had been established and grew in spite of the opposition of the religious authorities. So far, they could do little to stop them, since the policy of religious freedom was still in effect in Israel. Yet Thomas knew the Rabbi was working tirelessly on changing that.

And that change came one day in the person of the new Prime Minister of Israel named Ibrahim Berger. Just as the American President had done, he pushed a new law through the Knesset which outlawed all public religious gatherings, except the ones held in the synagogues. Almost instantly, riots and demonstrations broke out among the Muslim community and spread across the country with terrible violence and terror attacks, especially in the cities.

The Christian churches quietly went underground, but like throughout history, the moment they did, the number of believers grew in spite of it. Thomas was no longer able to hold his meetings in the country, but was forced to speak to smaller groups in smaller places. He stopped doing surgery altogether and devoted all his time to spread the Gospel with Melissa and Mikail at his side. The authorities didn't notice, since the number of patients in the clinic had outwardly increased under the cover of SRS, the clandestine Soul Refuge Sanctuary. And since the clinic still served the poor for free, due to the money Fouad had left to Thomas, the city of Tiberias was only too happy to allow them to continue to operate in spite of constant pressure from the Rabbi Sharim. He had been elevated to a high leadership position in the local synagogue and wielded enormous power in the religious community, not just in Tiberias, but in Haifa as well. Even the government in Tel Aviv had started to consult him on religious matters, but especially on how to deal with 'foreign' religions. In spite of his new responsibilities, Thomas knew he kept a close eye on Shalom Outreach with a hatred that was hard to explain. Knowing this, the team prayed for him daily for the Lord to touch his heart somehow. However, only Bob had the faith to believe the Rabbi would ever change.

It was on a hot summer day and Thomas, Melissa and Mikail were driving home from a meeting in Haifa. The golden grain waved gently in the wind on both sides of the highway and reminded him of the past. How many times the Lord had walked here with His disciples, picking the pods of grain along the edge of the fields at lunch time. A vineyard in the distance basked in the sun and a small herd of sheep grazed peacefully next to it.

"This looks just like it did then," he said. "I don't know why, but my carriage with the two sleek horses somehow fit better into this tranquil landscape. We think our technology is everything, but having experienced both ways, there is something to be said, traveling across this beautiful scenery at a leisurely pace." He sighed deeply. "There are many times I still get homesick for it and wish I could love this land today the way I loved it then. It is still hard for me to imagine it was only a dream." He reached over and turned the radio on. "Let's have some mus…" the piercing sound of the emergency alarm system filled the car.

"This is an alert from the Ministry of Defense in Tel Aviv. It has just been confirmed that an Israeli plane has shot down a suspicious Iranian aircraft over the waters off the coast of Israel heading toward our country. It exploded in a huge fire ball far enough off the coast to pose no danger to the population. While not confirmed yet, it is suspected to have carried what is commonly called a 'Dirty Bomb". We are urging people to leave the beach immediately to avoid radioactive contamination. It is important to understand that this is not a nuclear weapon by any means, but made from regular bomb making material like dynamite mixed with a low dose of nuclear particles. It affects a very small area and the only damage is within the immediate blast area. Since it was destroyed over the water, there is absolutely no danger to our country or the people. The evacuation of the beach area is simply a precautionary measure. The government is asking people to stay calm and wait for more instruction by staying tuned to your radio or TV."

Thomas turned the radio off with an angry twist.

"This is terrible," Melissa said, her voice filled with horror. "Are you sure this is not a nuclear attack and they are trying to hide it from us?"

"Sweetheart, if it was a nuclear bomb, we would all be dead by now," Thomas said and put his hand on her arm. "A dirty bomb is more designed to cause panic than damage. It will not harm us, sweetheart."

"Thomas, do you think it is time we go back to the States, we have Helena's future to think about. I am scared for her and for all of us. We can leave before it gets any more dangerous." She was crying hysterically. "The next thing will be the real thing I just know it. We will all die a terrible death. How could we stay here, you should have listened to your parents and gone home. I want to go back to the US, please Thomas, take us back." She sat up straight in the seat. "I can't breathe, please help me, I can't breathe."

Thomas stopped the car on the side of the road.

"Melissa, listen to me, take a deep breath. That's good, now another. There you go, you'll be alright, you are having a panic attack." He reached over and took her in his arms. "There, that's better. Everything will be alright. Listen, if you want to leave with Helena, that is fine. I understand and will do everything I can to get the two of you out of Israel, tomorrow if you want. For now, relax and lean back and look at the beautiful scenery outside. The Lord will take care of us, I am sure of it. The minute we get home I will call the airlines."

"Will you come, too?" she asked in a whisper.

He answered in a calm, gentle tone,

"Please, understand one thing, I have a purpose to fulfill and will stay here until the Lord tells me to leave. And so far, He has not done that. I cannot expect you or any of the team to feel the same and will ask them when we get back, if any or all want to go with you." He looked at her with a reassuring smile. "I will trust Yeshua to keep me safe until it is time to go home, whether that is to the US or heaven, it doesn't matter."

Melissa did not say a word and neither did Mikail.

Lord, I trust You and will not desert You like I did before. My place is where You say it is, no matter what comes. You have chosen me for this work and I will be faithful to the end. Please be with Melissa and tell her what to do, whether to stay here or go; and Holy Spirit, show each member to the team as well. And Lord, don't forget to defend Your chosen people Israel now that the whole world stands against them.

They drove on in silence for a long time and Thomas thought Melissa was asleep until she suddenly spoke in a clear voice,

"My place is with you, Thomas. I remember some time ago I told you I would have faith for us both when you didn't have any, now I am asking *you* to have enough for both of us. If you want me to stay, Helena and I will stay and all of us will face together what must come to pass as foretold in the scriptures long ago."

"I cannot make that decision for you, sweetheart," he answered with a sad little smile. "You ask the Lord and then do whatever He tells you to do." Thomas turned around and said to Mikail, "The same goes for you and the team. Neither the Lord or I will hold it against you if you go back."

"I have nowhere else to be. Most of my life has been in preparation for this assignment and I will not abandon it now,"

Mikail said with deep conviction. "Whatever comes, I am ready to serve Him and if need be, die for Him."

"I don't think I could ever take Helena away from you, Thomas," Melissa said. "I know I am terribly scared, but as long as I am with you, I can make it. Like Mikail says, I also have nowhere else to be since this is where the Lord has put us, no matter what comes." She looked at Thomas and then at Mikail. "We are a team in the Kingdom of God and the enemy is not going to scare us away, is he?" She reached for the radio knob and turned it. "Let's find that music now.

"The death toll is in the hundreds," the announcer was saying. "The city of Berlin is in chaos with thousands clogging the highways to get away. I repeat, terrorists have detonated a dirty bomb in the financial district of Berlin an hour ago and several bank buildings have been damaged. It is not yet clear if there is any radioactive fallout, but people are not taking a chance and are fleeing the city in the thousands. The chancellor of Germany is expected to give an update in a moment. Stay tuned for more information."

The announcer stopped and then said, "I have just been handed a note saying that another bomb exploded in London a moment ago. It is too soon to tell what is going on. This seems to be an all-out attack on Europe by Iran or IS, although so far, no group has taken responsibility for it. It is entirely possible, more cities are going to be hit and fear is gripping the nations. All air traffic has been halted and all EU borders are closed as of now. Apparently there is now chaos in every major city with people not knowing where to go or what to do. This is a catastrophe of major proportions and our government has advised to suspend all travel within Israel for the moment until the possibility of more bombs here has passed."

Thomas reached over and turned the radio off.

"Let's hurry and get home," he said quietly.

Chapter 26

Fear gripped the world as three more dirty bombs were found in the cities of Brussels, Paris and Madrid. While the damage in each was minimal, the psychological impact rose to such proportions, it drove many to violence and hatred as people fled the cities, not knowing where to go or what to do. The economic fallout of plunging stock markets caused billions of loss worldwide for nearly every stockholder on a scale never seen. To the detached observer, it seemed incredible that a few rather harmless bombs could have brought the world to the edge of the abyss.

The team was sitting around the dinner table in the evening, discussing the events.

"Do you realize how the Lord has protected Israel in all this?" Bob asked. "In stealing a plane from Iran and trying to use it to bomb this country from the air, He made sure it was the only bomb that detonated harmlessly over the ocean.

What IS thought was an especially effective way to hit Israel, turned out to be the perfect method to keep it unharmed. This is the first miracle of how God is coming to the rescue of His people, you wait and see." He looked around the table at everybody with a triumphant smile, "He is going to render Israel's enemies powerless and I can't wait to see how He is going to do it."

"It is a shame America has abandoned its friend and ally at a time of desperate need," Thomas said with sadness. It will pay a terrible price for its unfaithfulness. God has not changed His mind about His people. From the beginning He told Abraham in Genesis 12:3 "I will bless those who bless you, and whoever curses you I will curse; and all the peoples on earth will be blessed through you."

"God has kept His word. Through Yeshua He blessed the whole earth. And since He is a God who does what He says He will do, look at Germany. When that nation killed six million Jews, it lost six million of its people as Germany was totally destroyed. The only reason it recovered in such a miraculous way after the war was the fact, that for decades the German government gave millions of dollars every year to Israel in restitution for what Hitler had done." Thomas looked at the team with a solemn expression. "Why do you think America rose to such heights in such a short time? From the beginning, every President we have ever had, supported the Jews, except two. And look what is happening as a result, its world power is gone and it is crumbling from within. God's promise of blessing those who bless Israel and cursing them who abandon it in its greatest need, is still very much alive. He is a God of justice and mercy. I pray that He will be merciful to America in the days to come in spite of our sins against Israel."

"The way I see it, it is actually safer here in Israel right now than elsewhere in the world, since the Lord is watching over her," Caleb said. "This is totally amazing. And that brings me to a point I wanted to discuss. With everything that is going on, if any of you want to return to the States, as soon as air traffic returns to normal, I will understand if you do. I know you all have families who are worried sick about you and want you home. Just let me know and Shalom Outreach will pay for your flight home." He looked around. "Is anyone ready to head home?"

No one made a move.

"I don't have a family to go back to," Meta finally said. Remember, mine has disowned me because I became a Christian. This is home for me now."

"My memories with Theresa are here in this house," Paul says. "She would not like it if I left when everything is the way it is."

"My computers would give up the ghost without me," Karl said. "I am learning Hebrew so I can talk to a girl I am interested in." He smiled a sheepish little smile. "I haven't told you before, but I think we are getting serious."

"That's wonderful," Melissa said. "Will it be a Jewish wedding?"

"No, her whole family is Christian. They came to the Lord in one of Thomas' meetings. Her little brother was healed of some disease, I forgot what it was. That's how they heard about Yeshua."

"What's her name?" Thomas asked.

"Rachel Gottlieb. She is a tiny little thing and I am totally crazy about her," he said with an embarrassed little laugh.

"It looks like I have to stay for the wedding, doesn't it?" Leona said. I love weddings. Like the rest, where else would I go? This is my home and you are my family."

At that moment, Petra entered the room, wiping her wet hands on the apron.

"We are asking everybody if they want to go back to the States, Petra, but then you are an Israeli citizen, aren't you?" Caleb asked. "That means you're stuck with us."

"Who would cook for you and keep the place clean if it wasn't for me? I might as well stay here as long as you want me," she said and looked around the table.

"We would definitely starve to death without your good cooking, Petra," Mikail said before anyone else could answer. "I vote we keep her if she continues to fix some of that good Russian food."

"That leaves me, Bob said, "and everyone here knows I'm not leaving until they carry me out in a pine box." He laughed. "Then again, I'll just wait till the Lord comes back, then I won't need it."

"How about you, Thomas and Melissa?" Caleb asked.

"We are here until the Lord calls us home, one way or the other," Melissa said before Thomas could answer.

"Well, it looks like no one is going anywhere," Caleb said with a happy grin. "I will inform Chicago, they will be elated, because I don't think they could find anyone right now to come here, given the situation."

It was three days later, in the late afternoon, when the Rabbi Yitzhak Shamir, together with two other men wearing the yarmulke or Jewish head cap, entered the clinic and asked to speak to Thomas.

"I will get him for you," the receptionist said as she picked up the phone. "Please have a seat, gentlemen."

As soon as Thomas heard who wanted to speak with him, he called Caleb. He was nervous, this did not bode well.

"We are here on behalf of Tel Aviv and demand to see the back of the clinic," Rabbi Shamir said without introducing the men. "We have it on good authority that you are in violation of your permit by running a church in those rooms. This is a medical facility as you might recall," he added with venom in his voice.

"Please, come with me, gentlemen, I will show you the area you are talking about," Caleb said. "These are counseling rooms for those who have psychological problems. Dr. Robert Durham is in charge of it. I can assure you that we are not holding church services here," he added as he showed them the rooms. "As you can see, this doesn't look like a church sanctuary, does it? I don't know who told you such a thing, but there is no truth to it."

"Our informant also said that there are a lot of healings and fake miracles going on here, Dr. Peterson. You can't tell me that you are not involved in that?" His voice was starting to rise in anger.

"You are right; people are being healed through our medical services," Thomas said in a calm voice. "That is what this clinic is here for, isn't it? I don't know anything about fake healings, Rabbi. Whoever gave you that information is mistaken."

"I promised you I will close you down and I will not rest until I have accomplished it, Dr. Peterson. This may not be the day, but it will come, trust me."

"There is nothing I can do to stop you, Rabbi, but just like in the days of Yeshua, His message will continue to go out. Not because of me or this clinic, but because He is the Son of God who wants to reach His people Israel with His love." Thomas' voice was filled with kindness. "Did you read the scriptures from the prophets I gave you? If you had, you would understand that He has to be the Meshiah, who is still reaching out even today and save, heal and deliver His people in these perilous times."

"How dare you preach to me, Doctor!" the Rabbi screamed at Thomas. "I will destroy you if that is the last thing I do and cleanse my country of the greatest heretic next to this cursed Yeshua. And look what happened to Him, be careful that you do not meet the same fate." He was shaking, is face red with anger. Before he could continue, one of the men with him took his arm and pulled him toward the door.

"We will see ourselves out, Doctor. Thank you for talking to us," he said and led Rabbi Shamir out the front door.

"That went well," Caleb grinned. "You have a way with words, Thomas."

Thomas sat in a chair and took a deep breath.

"Did you notice we did not lie? The way he asked the questions gave us a chance to tell the truth and yet not be discovered. Thank You, Lord."

"I wonder who tried to give us away," Caleb said.

"There is no telling. With so many people coming through here, there is bound to be one who tells someone and they in turn tell someone else; you see what I mean," Thomas said. "I am surprised this hasn't happened before and it will happen again. I am not going to worry about it, the Holy Spirit will give us the words, just like He promised in the scripture, as long as He wants this clinic and SRS to stay open."

The next day they tightened the precautions for the back room ministry by asking that those who told a person about it, had to come and vouch for them. In spite of it, the stream of people asking to know more about Meshiah never let up.

It was the same in many other places, not just in Israel, but also in the Middle East and the rest of the world. Millions gave their lives to Yeshua and while some of the established churches lost many of their members, the ones who were alive with the Spirit, grew at an astounding rate.

The fear which had gripped the population, divided the rest of the people into two camps. Some looked for religion, others for pleasure. Many strange cults sprang up with some of their leaders claiming to be the Messiah, leading countless people astray while taking their money at the same time. Others plunged into immorality and perversion as had never been seen before. The latest craze in entertainment was called pleasure palaces and could soon be found in many big cities. The tragedy of the sex trade took on horrendous proportion as it became almost normal for young boys or girls to disappear, never to be seen again. Marriage became a rare occasion among the younger set and homosexuality the preferred choice of true love. Pornography was now a dominant force and infiltrated TV, the internet and the movie industry to a degree never before seen.

Largely unaware of what was going on in the world, the team stayed busy as time went on. It was as if God had put them, the clinic and the ministry in a cocoon until their assignment to reach His people was fulfilled. Thomas was on the road almost every day to various places, not just in Galilee, but even as far as Jerusalem,

Tel Aviv and other larger cities. Some of the churches in these places organized large meetings for him to share his message. In spite of the restrictions placed on Christians not to assemble other than in the synagogues, the authorities for some reason did not interfere.

It was in one such meeting, held in a large auditorium in Jerusalem, Thomas had an uneasy feeling of being watched. He couldn't explain it and didn't say anything to anyone except Melissa. They were in a small room down the hall from the auditorium. They had made it a habit to spend some time in prayer together, just the two of them, because he could be more honest about his doubts, fears and feelings of inadequacies than if other people were present.

"When are you going to learn to trust the Lord to be there when you need Him?" she asked on this day. "He has never not shown up, Thomas, why would today be different?"

"I don't know, something is going to happen and I feel terribly nervous. It has been a long time since I want to tell the Lord that I am a surgeon and not a preacher," he sighed. "He doesn't listen anyway when I start on that argument, so I might as well forget it and go out there."

"You have ten minutes, honey. We have prayed and put all this in His hands, there is nothing else you can do but trust Him."

"That's easy for you to say, you are not the one standing in front of all those people, not knowing what you are going to say until you say it." He looked at her, his eyes filled with doubt, fear and anxiety. "I have no idea why I feel like this today."

"It is time, Dr. Peterson," a voice said from behind the door. "We are ready to start."

"If the Lord doesn't step in today, I am not going to make it," he mumbled to himself as he opened the door and walked down the hall to the stage door.

A crowd of several thousand people greeted him, cheering, clapping and shouting the moment he walked up to the microphone.

If they knew how I really felt, they wouldn't do this, he thought and waved, smiling. *I feel like such a hypocrite. Please, Yeshua, help me!*

"I don't have anything to tell you today other than I would much rather be in surgery," he said in a halting voice. "I don't have anything to give you other than myself and that is not good enough, and neither do I have any power to heal, convict or change your heart unless Yeshua sends His Spirit. So if you came to see me, please get up from your seat and go home. If you only came to see miracles, please don't stay, because I can't perform any." He looked over the crowd with a look of helplessness as he went on. "Like I said, the only thing I know how to do well is surgery and since you are here, it looks like you don't need any this evening."

The crowd laughed, thinking he was trying to be funny.

"Maybe you don't understand," he went on. "I am not trying to be humble or make a joke, what I am saying is how I truly feel tonight." He stood and looked at the crowd in silence for what seemed like a long time. Not a sound could be heard in the huge hall, because the people finally realized he was serious.

Suddenly, a man in the back stood up and slowly walked up to the front. No one stopped him or asked who he was or what he was doing. As he came closer, Thomas could see tears streaming down his face and he held his hand out to him and the man joined him at the microphone. He was dressed in brown dress pants with a matching shirt and tie. Thomas knew he was Jewish by the yarmulke on his head. His face was clean shaven except for a mustache and he definitely looked like an educated man. As if guided by an unknown force, Thomas held out the microphone to him without a word.

"My name is Samuel Rosen. I was sent here by the authorities to check out this meeting. I am Jewish, but I don't really believe in anything and am part of a select group of people in the government that wishes to do away with religion in Israel, since it makes it impossible for our nation to ever be accepted by the rest of the world. My assignment this evening was to prove you a fraud, Dr. Peterson and declare Yeshua a myth."

Thomas looked at the man with confusion and wondered why he was holding a pair of thick glasses in his hand.

"Let me explain what happened," Samuel Rosen went on as he held the glasses up to Thomas. "I have an eye disease which will render me blind within the next six months. They have already performed five surgeries and want to do one more. If that doesn't work, I will never see again." He turned from Thomas toward the audience as he continued. "I was sitting in my seat tonight as Dr. Peterson was telling us that he couldn't do anything unless Yeshua does it. I was sure his words were part of a gimmick, because he is a fraud and can't do anything and so is Yeshua, when suddenly, my vision became blurry. I took my glasses off, thinking they had become foggy somehow and cleaned them. When I put them back on, my vision was even worse and I took them off again. That's when I realized I could see everything around me clearly, even you, Dr. Peterson, way up on this stage." He was crying so hard by now, he had to stop talking. When he finally composed himself, he looked at Thomas, "You were right, you cannot heal anybody, but Yeshua can and He did. I believe I have 20/20 vision."

Thomas, awed and overcome with wonder as always when he saw a miracle, realized that tonight he hadn't even said anything about his dream or his faith. Yeshua had proved to him that He didn't need his words, just his obedience to be willing to go and share His message.

"There is nothing I can say or do that will top what has just happened. For those of you who have come to meet Yeshua personally, please come forward and our counselors will pray with you. For those who have come for healing, don't hesitate to make your way up here, this is a special time to see what the Lord can and will do if you trust Him instead of me. I have no idea how long this will take, but if there is no time left for me to speak, that is perfectly fine, I think Yeshua is saying and doing all that is necessary."

Thomas never got a chance to speak and yet hundreds came to the Lord and countless were healed. And Samuel Rosen was one of them.

Chapter 27

It was a week later. The headlights of the car behind Thomas were blinding him to the point, he nearly went off the road. He was returning from a meeting in Haifa. Melissa had to stay home since Helena had a cold. He did not remain long after the meeting and left Bob in charge, while he headed back alone, since he had a difficult surgery planned in the morning. It was one only he had the expertise to do.

Totally blinded, he suddenly felt his car being pushed and the jolt snapped his head back against the headrest first and then forward against the steering wheel. He immediately stepped on the gas, but was unable to shake the car closely behind him. He panicked and had no idea what to do as he was pushed onto the side of the road. Another car sped in front of his and blocked him in.

"Get out," a man said in a gruff voice as he knocked on the window with his gun. "Get out or I will help you in ways you won't like."

Thomas slowly opened his car door and stepped out without a word. He knew it wouldn't do any good to ask what they wanted, they would either kill him right away or take him somewhere, who knows where.

He was shoved into the car in front of his and landed face down on the seat. Before he could sit up, they sped off into the dark. *Oh God!* There was no need to blindfold him, because it was pitch dark outside.

They drove for quite some time, until they reached an estate with an iron gate. It opened silently as they approached and shortly, the car drove up to a large three-story house with an impressive, ornate front entrance. A man in some sort of uniform opened the backdoor as soon as the car came to a stop and waved for him to get out. Thomas was escorted to a small door a few feet left of the front by two others. No one spoke a word as they shoved him inside. He had a hard time seeing in the dim light of the hallway and couldn't make out any details. Finally, at the end of the hall, he was pushed into a small room with a simple bed with a metal frame and a thin mattress. The first thing he noticed was a bath connected with the sparse surroundings. That was something to be grateful for at least.

When he was alone, he checked out his surroundings in the dim light coming from the bathroom. He could not find a light switch or a lamp of any kind in the bedroom. The only place to sit was the bed since it was all there was in the way of furniture. The walls looked a dirty gray in the low light and there was no window in the room. It definitely had the feel and look of a jail cell.

He laid down with a sigh. There was no telling where he was or who abducted him and he knew he would have to wait till morning to find out. He stared at the ceiling with a feeling of resignation and then worried about Melissa and the team. They would be frantic, with no idea where to look for him. As he prayed for them, he felt a calm come over him.

"Yeshua, please give them peace and give me strength for what is to come in the morning." With that he fell asleep.

His watch showed it was shortly after six when the door opened and an old woman showed up with a tray of food. Without a word she put it on the bed and left. He was surprised to find a boiled egg, a slice of bread and a thick piece of what looked like cheddar cheese. The steaming cup of strong coffee tasted good and together with the rest of the breakfast, made him feel better. He had time to wash his face in the small sink. Unfortunately, they had not left a toothbrush or a towel.

The dark was getting on his nerves and he couldn't wait to get out of his confinement. But it was not until three hours later until a young man came and motioned for him to follow him along many hallways and doors and finally crossed a courtyard and then entered a large room with ornate, expensive furnishings. The rich tapestry on the walls and colorful tile on the floor reminded Thomas of the villas in his dream. With a motion the man ordered him to stand against the back of the wall and wait.

After ten minutes a door on the far end of the room opened and Mohamed Yusuf Nabeth, Fouad's father walked in. He seemed taller than Thomas remembered him. His face looked gaunt and angry as he sat down with a heavy sigh and waved for Thomas to step closer.

"You do have a way with invitations, Mr. Nabeth," Thomas said. "I guess kidnapping is your favorite one. All you had to do was ask and I would have come to see you."

The old man looked at Thomas with an expression of utter hatred and said in fluent English,

"Because of you I lost my son and I will never forgive you for tearing him away from the true faith."

"He is the one who came to me, Sir," Thomas said. "And he is the one who chose to accept Yeshua as his God."

"Be silent, infidel swine. Have you not done enough by killing his soul, now you have taken his inheritance as well. He was screaming.

"What are you talking about, Sir?" Thomas tried to remain calm.

"You took fifteen million dollars from him and I want it back. It does not belong to you, but to me, his father," he said, a little calmer.

"I thought you are a wealthy man and I was not aware that you are in need of it, Sir," Thomas answered. "Fouad left it to me in his will and I knew nothing about it before then. If you had not had him killed, it would still be his and not mine."

He watched as the man's face slowly turn red from the neck up before he exploded,

"You wretched son a dog, how dare you accuse me of killing my son. I will have you flogged and shot for saying such a thing," he shouted as he waved his walking cane at Thomas. "I swear I will kill you and feed your miserable body to the vultures if you don't take it back."

"I will not, Mr. Nabeth. I believe you call it an honor killing. Where is your honor now that your son is dead, together with your beautiful daughter-in-law and your unborn grandchild?" Thomas continued before the old man could answer. "While your god demands the life of your children when they chose another faith, my God tells me to reach out in love and pray for them until they come back to Him. Yeshua tells us to love our enemies while Allah tells you to kill yours. Which god do you think is the better one of the two? Turn to Yeshua and He will forgive you for what you have done."

There was silence. Mohamed Nabeth stared at Thomas, his body shaking with rage. Finally, he waved to the young man waiting by the door and growled menacingly,

"Take this miserable infidel and beat him until he is dead."

Thomas followed the man to another part of the house until they came to a courtyard. He pointed for him to sit on a stone bench and then disappeared down a hallway.

A well-dressed man in western clothes came out of another door.

"I am sorry for this, Dr. Peterson. My father is given to terrible outbursts since my brother and his wife died." He stretched out his hand toward Thomas, "I am Yusuf Nabeth, Fouad's brother. You would do well to forget what you have heard and seen here. I will have someone drive you home."

"Your father has dementia, doesn't he?" Thomas asked gently. "I can clearly see the signs. "I could order some medication for him to stop the progression if you come to the clinic. They have made great strides in that field."

"That is very kind, Sir, but my father suffers more from grief and guilt than a physical ailment. And for that there is no cure," he added with sadness.

"That is where you are wrong, Mr. Nabeth. "Yeshua will forgive him if he turns his life over to Him."

"That is not our way, Doctor. He thinks he has done it for Allah and even if he wanted to, there is no way he could change."

"How about you, Sir?"

"I don't believe in any of this nonsense, because religion has always been the engine that drives this sort of madness, no matter which one it is."

"That is how I used to believe, until I met Yeshua. He is different because He asks us to love our enemies instead of killing them."

"That may be true of Him, but it certainly has not been true of His followers throughout the centuries, has it?" Yusuf said with a slight smile. It made his face suddenly less severe. He reminded him of Fouad.

"I really got close your brother, Yusuf. He was a kind and gentle man who loved his wife Nazra and always tried to obey his father in all things.

"I know, that is why it was such a stunning surprise when he decided to become a Christian. He must have really believed this Yeshua was God or he would never have gone against Father," Yusuf said, stroking his dark, short-cropped beard thoughtfully. "He was happy with Nazra and this Yeshua, I do know that."

"I was an atheist and felt like you do about religion," Thomas said, careful not to push the subject.

"What happened to change your mind?" Yusuf asked.

"It's quite a story, are you sure you want to hear it?"

"Yes, I feel I owe it to my brother's memory to understand what he died for."

And so they sat on a bench in the courtyard of the Nabeth villa in Haifa, while Thomas shared about his dream with another son of Mohamed Yusuf Nabeth, one of the richest man in the country and a devout Muslim and hater of all that is Christian.

When he was done, Yusuf sat, stunned.

"You are telling me that an angel appeared to my brother and told him to get in touch with you?"

"Yes, that is how I met him. He came to Shalom Outreach, because he was instructed to talk to me. I have the rest of our team as witnesses. Trust me, we were petrified when he showed up, because the Director of our mission knew who your father was and what he would do to us if he found out about our financial dealings with Fouad," Thomas said. "In the end your brother and Nazra were a few days away from fleeing to England and live there to get away from his wrath. Unfortunately, one of their servants gave them away and we are pretty certain your father killed them."

"So am I," Yusuf agreed. "That is why he is literally losing his mind, knowing he killed his son and his family. He found out through the autopsy that Nazra was pregnant and that is what drove him over the edge." He looked at Thomas. "You were kind in calling his state dementia. It is much more than that. There is no forgiveness with Allah, because he commands us to do the very thing my father did, therefore, he cannot ask for it and has to live with his regret and guilt for the rest of his life. The worst thing is, it is this regret that puts him against Allah's will. That's why I want nothing to do with religion. I am part of the new generation and lived in the West too long to follow such barbaric practices." He sat for a moment before he went on, "I am however, intrigued by your story. You are a doctor, an intelligent man, a scientist and not given to wild imaginations. I have heard about Yeshua all my life, but was taught He was only a prophet. Maybe a good one, but lower than Mohamed." He shifted uneasily in his seat. "What if you are right and this prophet is the true Meshiah?" He smiled at Thomas. "Mind you, I am no friend of the Jews, and to believe that a Jewish prophet could turn out to be God's Son, is a stretch for me."

"I understand, Yusuf. You know where you can find me if you ever want to know more or are ready to accept Him. I will always be there for you."

Thomas got up and they shook hands since the driver had come in to take him back to Tiberias.

"May Yeshua show you like He did your brother, Yusuf and may He bless you and touch you with His love in the days to come. I am certain our meeting today was not by chance, but the will of God." With that Thomas left. He was amazed at the way the Lord had made a way to reach this man, who otherwise would have never had a chance to hear the truth.

Chapter 28

When Thomas returned, the clinic was in turmoil. While he was gone, a bomb had been thrown into the waiting room yesterday morning. With seven people dead and twenty-four wounded, Shalom Outreach was once again in the limelight. By the time he got there, everyone had been checked for injuries and the city morgue had picked up the dead. He was grateful to the Lord that none of the team members had gotten hurt.

Since these attacks were common now, the police did not have the time or the resources to investigate more than was absolutely necessary, especially since it happened at a Christian medical facility. Anti-Christian attitudes among the city government was high, especially since, once again, Thomas and his ministry was the focal point of the headlines.

Because of the crowds of reporters and many curiosity seekers clogging the front of the clinic, they had to close the doors to all patients. Besides, it would take several days to repair the extensive damage to the waiting room area. This gave the team some time to evaluate what happened and come up with more effective security measures to avoid a repeat of this kind of tragedy.

"There is no doubt, we are all in danger," Thomas explained to the team when they gathered in the board room. "There is also no doubt that it will get worse. While there is no information yet on who did this, with the many enemies we have, it is certain that it could happen again."

"As head of Shalom Outreach, I must urge you to put your affairs in order." Caleb's voice had an urgency to it. "We are a prime target not just for the terrorists, but also the Jews because of our belief. The only assurance Shalom Outreach can give any of you is, you will die a martyr if you are killed, because there is no real protection other than God's grace and mercy to allow us to operate here until His purpose is fulfilled." He shifted uncomfortably in his seat. "Once again, I must ask you to think about returning to the States if you think you cannot take the risk of losing your life. Please, be assured, there is no shame if you decide to leave, God will understand and so will we." He looked around the table with his usual smile. "We will even give you a farewell party."

Thomas and Melissa looked at each other with a look of reassurance and then he said,

"Melissa and I will stay and serve the Lord right here, no matter what happens."

No one else spoke up, but each looked down at their hands. Thomas could sense fear in their hearts.

"I am reminded of the many Christians who died in the arena, facing lions and other wild beasts centuries ago. All we can ask of the Lord is to give us that kind of faith should we ever need it," he said as he looked at everyone with a grave expression. "We have nothing else with which to defend ourselves from what may not be wild beasts, but people, every bit as ferocious in their tactics to kill us as the lions were in those days." He leaned forward across the table as he continued. "Remember, the Lord did not save them from death, but allowed them to become martyrs and join Him as His precious children in His Kingdom. What I want to make very clear, just because we are working for His cause and purpose, does not guarantee that we will not lose our lives in the days to come."

"All we can do is be ready to face Him at a moments' notice," Bob spoke into the silence. "Our hope is not to be rescued from getting killed by the Lord, but to join Him in heaven if we should meet that fate. That is why His message is called the Good News and that is also why the Apostle Paul states that "For to me to live is Christ and to die is gain." (Philippians 1:21) "It was easy to read when we were sitting in church at home, safe and so sure we would never have to face persecution. It is not nearly as easy to live it in living color like we are asked to do right now," he went on. "Theresa has run the good race; no one knows whether we will be asked to do the same. The question for us is not if we could get killed or not, the question is, do we have the faith to believe in the hope Christ promised us. Let's face it, we all have to die someday; are we willing to stand ready now to do it for the Lord or wait until old age or sickness take us eventually?"

Bob looked at the group with a radiant smile. "I know where I am going when I die and so should you. As Christians, this assurance and knowledge is what sets us apart from the world. They cannot take our spirit, just our body and that would wear out anyway." He pointed at himself with a grin. "Look at mine, it is showing wear and tear now. I don't mind at all if the Lord sees fit to take me home before it really goes downhill."

Before he could go on, Petra came into the room. She was out of breath.

"Turn on the radio. There is terrible news out of South Korea," she shouted. "North Korea threw the bomb!" She was shaking with fear and started to cry. "They finally did it; they threw an atomic bomb and probably killed millions of people!"

"Oh my God, help us," Meta cried. "This is the end of life as we know it." She started to sob uncontrollably as she laid her face down on the table.

Thomas looked at Melissa and took her hand in his.

"We are not done with our assignment here," he whispered, "it is not time yet."

"How much worse can it get?" she whispered back and squeezed his hand tightly. "I am scared."

The group looked at Thomas.

"What is going to happen to the people in that country?" Caleb asked. "What are the symptoms of radiation poisoning?"

"No one can say for sure, because it depends on how strong the bomb is, whether people are indoors or out, the proximity to the explosion and the direction the wind is carrying the fallout. Death is highly likely and radiation poisoning is almost certain if one is caught in the open with no mountains or building within a radius of 0-2 miles from a 1 megaton airburst. There is a 50% chance of death from a blast which extends 0-5 miles away. Since we do not know where the bomb was detonated, whether in the country or a city, it is hard to say how many people died. Without knowing all those details, it is very hard even for the scientists to give us a clear picture of the damage. One thing we know for certain, this is a catastrophe of unimaginable proportions."

"This pretty well makes it certain that we are entering the end times, doesn't it?" Meta asked. She had stopped crying. "I will not give in to fear, because I will trust the Lord," she said with determination. "All this means, the Lord is coming back soon and we will be with Him forever."

"We will be alright, you will see," Bob said. "Our job is not done until the Lord returns. Until then, we do what we have done until now, heal the sick and minister to those who want to know Jesus. That is what we have been commissioned to do until we are called home, one way or the other."

"It will take about a week to fix the clinic," Caleb said, always the practical one. "I will contact a company whose owner is a Christian. He will give us a good price."

"In the meantime I will keep up my schedule with the meetings," Thomas said.

"The rest of us will prepare the clinic to be re-opened. There are a lot of catching up we can do with paperwork and re-stocking our supplies," Melissa added. "I have neglected doing those necessary things and now is as good a time as any to do it."

Two days went by. It was eight o'clock at night when there was a knock on the front door. Everybody was sitting in the common room watching a football game on the English-speaking channel. Petra had made popcorn and several pitchers of iced-tea.

"Who could that be?" Caleb said and got up to answer it.

A man in a dark suit stood outside.

"I am with the Tel Aviv government, may I come in?" he said in a hushed tone.

"What is it you want, Sir?" Caleb said with apprehension in his voice.

"Please, Sir, it is urgent that I speak to you." The man looked around nervously. "I mean you no harm, just let me talk to you for a minute."

"Ok, come on in." Caleb opened the door reluctantly. "What can I do for you, I am the director of Shalom Outreach."

"I know who you are, Mr. Weinstein. I am here to speak with Dr. Peterson."

"I am Dr. Peterson, what can I do for you?" Thomas answered.

"I must ask you to come to Tel Aviv with me, Doctor, it is urgent. I must also ask you and your team not to tell anyone where you are going."

"I am an American citizen, Sir. Unless you have official papers from your government, I will not go with you, because I have no idea what this is all about or who you are." Thomas sounded firm.

"I will explain everything to you on the way," the man said.

"You will explain it to me now, Sir."

The man hesitated and then stepped toward Thomas.

"Ok, I will tell you, but you must understand that this is a top secret matter. Several lives depend on it and that includes mine."

"Come in and sit down with the rest of us in the living room and tell us what is going on," Caleb said and pointed to the rest of the team.

"My name is Stephen Raffael. I work in the office of Prime Minister Ibrahim Berger. The Prime Minister has sent me to take you to his private residence, where he wishes to speak with you. It is about a matter that must be discussed in secret. I am the only person who knows what it is about, but I have been instructed not to reveal it. All I can tell you, it is urgent and cannot wait." The man wiped the beads of sweat from his forehead as he said, "Please, Dr. Peterson, you must come with me now, before it is too late."

"I cannot imagine what the Prime Minister of Israel wants to talk to me about, but I have a feeling I will find out," Thomas said. "I will come with you if you permit me to bring Dr. Durham with me."

"I am sure that is fine, Doctor," Stephen Raffael said with great relief. "But we must leave now. My car is waiting a little way down the street."

No one spoke much on the way to Tel Aviv as the black limousine sped through the night. Thomas could not imagine what this was all about, but could not say anything to Bob with Stephen in the car. When they arrived at a black, iron gate on the outskirts of Tel Aviv an hour later, it opened silently. A guard waved the car in without delay. When they stopped at the front door of the large villa, a uniformed guard opened the car doors. Stephen motioned to follow him inside.

Once inside, they entered a large, beautifully furnished foyer, which reminded Thomas of his own house back in Philadelphia. Before he had time to look around, a door opened and a short, distinguished looking man with gray hair and an expensive gray suit came out to greet them.

"Dr. Peterson, I am delighted you could come on such short notice. I am Ibrahim Berger, welcome to my home." He turned to Bob. "I see you brought someone with you."

"This is Dr. Durham, Prime Minister," Stephen said, "Dr. Peterson insisted he come with us."

"That is fine, Stephen, you may leave us now. There is no need to put you in danger any longer. Thank you for a job well done."

"You really are the Prime Minister," Thomas said with a smile. "I wasn't sure whether to believe Stephan."

"I am, Dr. Peterson. I am sure you are curious why I have asked you to come."

"To say the least, Sir. What business could a country doctor like me have with the head of the government of Israel?"

"Please follow me, gentleman, I will show you." He waved for Thomas and Bob to follow him and stopped in front of a door at the end of the hall. When they entered, a woman sat in a chair, holding a book in her hand. She looked up when the Prime Minister kissed her on the cheek. She was in her late fifties with dark hair surrounding a face filled with deep lines and eyes marked by pain. A loose, colorful gown hid her full figure. It was her smile that gave her full, round face a warm glow which came from deep inside.

"This is my wife Miriam and she is waiting for you to pray for her, Dr. Peterson."

"You are kidding!" It slipped out before Thomas could stop himself.

"I know what you're thinking, Doctor, my husband has banned all religions except Judaism and here he is asking you to pray for me to Yeshua." She turned to the Prime Minister with a loving smile and went on, "He may not believe in the Meshiah, but I do." She looked at Thomas. "You see, Doctor, I have a brain tumor that will kill me in a few weeks and there is nothing anyone can do about it, except Yeshua." She looked at Thomas with a warm smile. "Ibrahim loves me enough to smuggle you in here so you can lay hands on me and pray that the Lord might heal me if it is His will. I am ready to die, but Ibrahim does not want to face this terrible world without me by his side. I told him about you and how you have healed hundreds of people all over Israel, why not me?" She looked at Thomas with an expression of hope in her brown eyes. "You see, Dr. Peterson, I went to one of your meetings several months ago and saw many people get healed. Someone on your team prayed with me to accept Yeshua as my Meshiah. Although I have had to hide my new faith because of my position as Ibrahim's wife, I have prayed to Him every day. He is the One who impressed me to have you come and pray for me."

"The reason for the secrecy about this is hopefully obvious to you, Dr. Peterson," her husband said. "If it was known that my wife is a Christian and that I allowed you to pray for her, I would have to resign and possibly face charges of treason."

"How do you feel about Yeshua, Prime Minister?" Bob asked. "Do you believe He is the Meshiah?"

"I do not, Dr. Durham. I leave religion up to my wife, maybe she can have faith for both of us."

"It doesn't work that way, Sir," Bob said with a smile. "Each of us has to accept Him as our Savior to gain eternal life."

"I did not ask you here, gentlemen to preach to me, but to indulge a dying woman's wish. Since I am going to be gone for a few days, tonight was the only time I could spare to do this." He sounded slightly irritated.

"I am sorry, Sir, please forgive my zeal, but I have seen too many astounding miracles to let any chance go by to share what I know to be the truth." Bob did not sound sorry at all as he looked at the Prime Minister with boldness.

"Do you need anything for your ceremony, Dr. Peterson?" Ibrahim Berger asked, trying to hide his impatience and doubt as best he could.

"I have everything I need, Sir, which is the faith to do what I saw Yeshua do when I walked with Him two thousand years ago." Thomas turned first to Miriam and then to Ibrahim as he went on, "You see, Yeshua never did anything that looked or sounded like a ceremony when He healed the multitudes. All He did was, He spoke a word of healing or even just looked at somebody and they were healed. And then one day He told His followers, "...whoever believes in me will do the works I have been doing, and they will do even greater things than these, because I go to the Father." John 14:12

"And that is why I go around and tell my story and then simply do what Yeshua did. It is not in my own strength or power I do them, but in His Name." Thomas turned to Miriam and laid his hand on her head and spoke one simple sentence, "Miriam, in the Name of Yeshua, be healed."

"That's it?" Ibrahim Berger said in astonishment. "That's all you are going to do?"

"There is nothing more to do, Sir," Thomas said and smiled at Miriam. "You are healed, go with your husband on that trip he is taking tomorrow. All will be well." He turned to the Prime Minister. "Take her with you and see the Glory of God. Do not give me any credit, because I did not do this, but Yeshua did. Turn to Him and allow Him to change you in ways that will change the destiny of Israel. Yeshua told me to go to His people before He returns and gather them into His Kingdom. Will you help Him do that, Ibrahim?"

Miriam stood up and put both hands on her head.

"I will go with you tomorrow, Ibrahim, my head has stopped hurting for the first time in two years. The Lord will allow me to be by your side when the enemies of Israel will surround us and God will come to our rescue. What a privilege it is to be a part of it all." She hooked her arm into her husband's and added, "Let's show our visitors out so they can get back to Tiberias, it is late." Then she turned to Thomas and Bob and said, "May the Lord bless you and keep you, and may His face shine upon you in the days to come."

Chapter 29

The next day Thomas saw the Prime Minister and Miriam on TV. She looked radiant and full of energy as she reached out to the crowds. *Thank You Yeshua, you have given me favor with the Prime Minister of Israel, just like You did with Pontius Pilate by healing someone in his family.* An uneasy feeling came over him. *It didn't help to change anything then, Lord, will it be different this time?*

"The Lord is good, wouldn't you say, Thomas?" Bob asked as he joined Thomas in front of the TV.

"He is and I thank Him for it," Thomas said in a thoughtful tone. Nothing may come of this, on the other hand, this did not happen by chance. I have a feeling God is going to use Ibrahim Berger in more ways than just helping us."

"It doesn't hurt to heal the wife of a Prime Minister," Bob continued. "Surely, the Lord has every intention to touch Ibrahim Berger and then get him to take away the restrictions on religious freedom he instituted not too long ago."

"I have learned one thing, Bob, God does not do things the way we think He will or follow our logic. Let's face it, His ways are not our ways; but whatever His plans are, He will bring them to pass without our help, you can count on that."

And so, in spite of what had happened, nothing changed and Thomas did not hear from Ibrahim Berger or Miriam in the days that followed. The world had become a place filled with fear and turmoil after the bomb fell in South Korea. Several million had perished in the aftermath and many more started to show severe signs of radiation poisoning. The country became virtually isolated from the world, since all traffic was permanently suspended because of the radiation contamination.

Europe was still in turmoil, with people expecting the same thing to happen there as Iran became bolder each day by flaunting its nuclear power at every turn. America was helpless to do anything, as it refused outright to be drawn into a confrontation with its leaders. Fear and hatred took over reason and tolerance, as countless survival groups sprang up across the country, advocating resistance to the government by promoting anarchy. They found fertile ground in all States, but especially in the South. Liberal groups everywhere, but mainly in the North, blamed religion and especially Christians and Jews for what was happening. With the President's backing, they influenced the government to shut down churches and synagogues across the land. And since several liberal supreme court justices had been added to the highest court of the land, they instituted new laws, curtailing religious freedom in the United States in ways no one ever thought possible.

How strange, if Thomas and the team had lived in the US, they would not have been allowed to operate their clinic, since all medical facilities could now only be run by the government. This included all privately owned religious hospitals and clinics.

Thomas had a feeling of foreboding as he drove toward Capernaum. He had insisted to go by himself in spite of everyone's objections. There was an overwhelming desire in his heart to talk to the Lord at the column of the temple ruin, where he met Yeshua two thousand years ago. The world was crumbling and yet his ministry was doing well and the clinic was filled with patients and those who wanted to meet Yeshua. In spite of the threats last time, the Rabbi Shamir had not bothered them in any way, which was strange. He heard rumors that an unknown authority from the government in Tel Aviv had put a stop to any kind of interference by the city of Tiberias against Thomas or the clinic. Maybe the Prime Minister was responsible for that, but no one knew for certain.

The sun stood high in the sky and the heat was oppressive when he entered the ruins of Capernaum. No one was there as he walked slowly toward the temple. Instantly, a strange sense of calm came over him when he reached the place where his carriage had stood. In his minds' eye he saw Esther get off the carriage with his help, bent over and in terrible pain. He even remembered the face of the Pharisee who objected to her wanting to be healed on the Shabbat. That's when Thomas realized, today was Shabbat.

I have come to talk to You, Lord. My heart is heavy and I don't know why. Something is going to happen and I will need Your strength when it does, of that I am certain. Thank You for

Your favor and power that You have poured out on the ministry and me. Thank You for the love that I feel when I go and share the Gospel. I remember, I didn't like it here when I first arrived, but You have filled my heart with love for Your people and even their enemies. Thank You for the rich harvest of souls we have gathered in Your Name. They stand ready for Your coming in the clouds to take them home with You. So, why is my heart so heavy?

He stood motionless, waiting for an answer, when, suddenly, a tall man, dressed in white appeared seemingly out of nowhere.

"Why are you troubled, Thomas? The Lord is with you and what is going to happen is ordained by Him. Do not be afraid of what must come, but take heart, because it is part of His design. For a while, it will look like the enemy will win, but never fear, God is with you and nothing can stop the purpose He has for you and His people Israel. "In this world you will have tribulation, but be of good cheer, I have overcome the world. (John 6:33) Remember these words well, Thomas, for they are given to you so that you may not forget when the enemy comes in like a flood."

Thomas stared at the angel, unable to speak and fell on his knees, his head touching the ground in the spot where Yeshua had stood.

"Please, help me, Lord," he whispered. "I am not strong enough on my own for what is to come." He finally got up and a wave of fear flooded over him that he felt like he was drowning. "Lord, I can't do this, please do not let it happen. I am not strong enough and my faith is weak," he spoke into the silence and remembered Yeshua in the Garden, begging the Father to take the cup from Him. "Not my will be done, Yeshua, but Yours," he heard himself say with trembling and felt so weak, he had to sit down at the base of the column. With his head in his hands, he sobbed, *I don't even know what is coming, but I am already so afraid, I want to die right here and now, Lord. As always, I think You should have chosen someone else for this job, I am just not good or strong enough.*

"Are you alright, Sir?" a voice asked. "Maybe you are overheated and need some water?"

Thomas looked up and saw a woman standing before him, handing him a bottle of water.

"Thank you, I am fine," he said and got up, hoping she did not notice he had been crying.

"You are American?" she asked, "so are we." She pointed to a group of people behind her. "We are from Atlanta and have come on a trip to the Holy Land with our Pastor." She wiped her forehead, "No one told us it would be this hot."

Thomas loved her beautiful southern accent and smiled.

"I am Dr. Peterson. I live in Tiberias with my wife and daughter."

"Oh my goodness gracious, you are the American Doctor who heals people. I have heard about you. How exciting to meet you!" She stretched out her hand. "I am Katy Pepper. Would you mind if I introduced you to my group? They would be tickled pink to meet you." Without waiting for an answer, she called out to the group behind her, "Come on over you all, we have a celebrity here."

Thomas cringed and realized his time alone with the Lord had come to an end.

In the following days, Thomas started the outdoor meetings again, hoping that the Prime Minister's order would protect him from the city authorities. No one bothered them for a while, until one Sunday morning, a group of official looking cars drove up. Many hundreds of people sat on a grassy hill on the outskirts of Tiberias, listening in rapt attention to Thomas. It was the Rabbi Shamir and his fellow religious leaders. Without hesitation, he walked up to the microphone and took it out of Thomas' hand with an angry gesture.

"People of Israel, why do you listen to this Gentile's heresies? Are you not the children of the God of Abraham, Isaak and Jacob? Why do you offend our God by turning to other gods in these troubled times? This Yeshua, this foreigner calls the Meshiah, is a fraud and will lead you to everlasting shame and destruction. Listen to the voice of the one and only God, instead of this lost son of Israel, who preaches heresy and abomination in the sight of Yahweh. Our God is the One who brought our forefathers out of Egypt into this land and warned us not to worship other gods unless we draw His anger. Yet you have turned to this Yeshua, who came to deceive and lead our people astray. Everything he says is a lie, designed to destroy your soul in the sight of the one and true God of Israel. I am telling you, everything this foreigner says is also a lie. Listen to your religious leaders, who have studied the Torah and have come to save you from this man and his false god." He pointed his finger at Thomas in anger.

"How about the miracles he performs, how do you explain them?" someone in the crowd shouted.

"Deception and lies," the Rabbi shouted back. "He is a doctor and knows how to make it look like a miracle when it is nothing but a drug-induced, momentary improvement. He is a charlatan and liar, who is after your money."

"He has never asked for money," the same voice answered, "and he treats the poor for free."

"Lies, all lies. I am on the city council I know what's going on." The Rabbi was shouting now. "Is it not enough that America is abandoning Israel against Iran, must we also abandon our faith to this foreigner? We stand alone against the world; and those who used to be our friends are now side with our enemies. The God of Abraham, Isaac and Jacob will not forsake us when the time comes, but will destroy the nations who dare stand against the people of Yahweh. He is the One who will rise up and save us in due time and not this imposter Yeshua. If you agree with me, stand up right now and walk away from here and so save your soul from the wrath of the living God."

Thomas watched in amazement as about five hundred people stood up and left to stand on the sidelines. His heart was heavy as he realized they would be lost when the Lord came for His own after being so close just moments before. He knew it was time do take the microphone away from the Rabbi and reached out to take it from him. Before he had a chance, the people who stood on the side, rushed up to the small podium, shouting, yelling and waiving their fists.

"Get out of Israel, you heretic. Leave our city and go home Yankee!"

Thomas looked at the team and nodded for everyone to leave before things got out of hand. The crowd cheered, clapped and shouted obscenities after them until they escaped into their van. The last thing their heard, was the Rabbi reciting the *Shema, "Hear oh Israel, the Lord is One."*

No one said anything on the way home, until Caleb asked,

"Nothing like this has ever happened before. What are we going to do now, Thomas?"

"From what the angel told me at the temple in Capernaum, it is going to get a lot worse. He warned us so we can prepare our hearts and minds for what is to come. One of the ways to do that is to make sure, our hearts are clean and we are right with God and man, so that the enemy does not have a foothold when we ask the Lord to help us." Thomas turned around from the front seat, facing the others. "The first thing we must do is forgive the Rabbi Shamir. I know that is what Yeshua would do. The second thing is to contact our people at home and tell them we love them. I have a feeling our time of peace and freedom is coming to an end. Just make sure, you don't tell your families, just remind them to pray for the ministry. Lastly, go before the Lord and ask Him to show you where you need to clean up your act and then ask Him to help you do it." Thomas' face suddenly lit up with a bright smile as he said, "Remember, we know how the book ends. We also know it is no walk in the park what happened before it's all over. Our God reigns! He knows exactly what is going on and there is nothing the enemy can do unless God allows it. For this He sent us over here and for this we will stand in faith until the Lord returns. Think of it, what an honor to be counted worthy to save His people before He comes."

Chapter 30

The next day the city health inspector arrived at the clinic for a surprise inspection of the medical facility. As Thomas feared, he found multiple major violations of various health codes and without much fanfare closed the clinic down. There was no doubt in anyone's mind, Rabbi Shamir was behind it.

Five days later, each of the members of the team, including Thomas, got a notice from Tel Aviv, ordering them to leave the country.

"I have to get in touch with Stephen Raffael, the man who came to get us to pray for Miriam," Thomas said. "I am not sure what his role was in all this, but he does have the confidence of the Prime Minister." He turned to Caleb. "You and I are driving to Tel Aviv to the private residence of Ibrahim Berger. If he is not there, I am sure Miriam, his wife, will see us."

An hour later, they were on the way.

"Do you know how to get there?" Thomas asked Caleb.

"I googled it and have it in my GPS," he answered with a grin. "Our real problem will be to gain entrance. With the way things are, I am sure the residence is protected like a fortress," he added. "But then nothing is impossible with our God, is it?"

When they arrived at their destination, the tall, iron gate looked impregnatable. As soon as they stopped the car, an armed guard approached them and ordered them to roll down the window.

"We would like to see the Prime Minister or his wife, please," Caleb said in Hebrew.

"I'm sure you would," he answered in English. "May I ask what your business is with him, Sir?"

"We are friends of his and want to ask him for help with something," Thomas said.

"Could I see some identification?" the man asked.

They gave him their passport and waited as he checked them out.

"I am sorry, but the Prime Minister is at the office at this time of day. Why don't you go there and try to see if he will see you?"

"Could you call inside and ask Miriam if she will speak with us?" Thomas asked. "I am certain she will see us."

"Sir, it is not my job to call the residence about visitors. There are extensive security measures to be completed before you could ever gain entrance," the guard said. "Like I said before, please try at the ministry in the city, maybe you will have a better chance."

At that moment, a black limousine drove up to the gate.

"You will have to move your car, Sir, I have to open the gate," he said with urgency.

"That looks like Miriam in the car," Thomas said and held his hand out and waved.

"Thomas, is that you?" It was Miriam. "Please allow these men inside, sergeant," she said to the guard. "They are good friends."

"They are not on the list of visitors, Madam," the sergeant said. "I am not allowed to let them pass."

"I insist that you do, even if you have to call my husband's office. Just ask Mr. Raffael, his personal secretary, he knows these gentlemen."

After about ten minutes, he waved them on through the gate and before long, Thomas and Caleb were sitting in a spacious living room, drinking coffee with the wife of the Prime Minister of Israel.

"I was supposed to be gone to a meeting today, but it was cancelled," Miriam said. "God always know what He is doing, doesn't he?"

"I can see you are feeling well," Thomas said as he took a cookie off of a silver tray.

"The tests showed no sign of the cancer," she said with a radiant smile. "The Lord healed me, Dr. Peterson."

"What does your husband think about it?" Thomas asked.

"He has been watching me closely, not sure if it will come back. Every morning he asks me if I have a headache and every morning I tell him I am fine. I never say anything about the Lord, but I can see, Ibrahim is beginning to be curious about Yeshua and his power to heal people. That's why he rescinded his order and allows religious freedom again in Israel against the advice of his cabinet. There are rumors that he has become a Christian, but they are not true. I would know. He is intrigued, but that is all. And I don't dare pressure him about it. My healing speaks louder than any words I can use." She looked at Thomas with a questioning look. "Why have you come to visit me, is there a problem?"

"As a matter of fact, there is, Madam," Thomas said and told her of the closing of the clinic and the meetings being disrupted by the Rabbi Shamir.

"That sounds just like the man," she said, "I am familiar with him, he hates anything Christian and has great influence with many members of the Knesset."

"Can you speak with your husband and see if he can have the clinic re-opened and the Rabbi stopped from coming to our meetings?" Thomas asked.

"This is not as easy as it sounds, Dr. Peterson. Rabbi Shamir is a force to be reckoned with, not just in religious circles, but also in political ones. If he knew my husband would take the side of a Christian ministry, the consequences could be disastrous for Ibrahim." She smiled at Thomas. "But I will talk to him and see what can be done. I can't promise anything, but he or I will let you know through Mr. Raffael." She got up and Thomas and Caleb knew the meeting was over. "Thank you so much for your obedience in coming to pray for me. May the Lord bless you both in the difficult days ahead." She handed Thomas a business card just before they walked out the front door. "Here, Dr. Peterson, take my private number and use it only in the direst emergency. And make very sure you do not give it to anyone, no matter how tempting the situation might be. Do not even tell anyone you have it."

Two weeks later, the city informed Shalom Outreach that the clinic could re-open if all the violations would be corrected to the satisfaction of the city health inspector. During that time, the team had meticulously fixed, repaired and improved everything that had been cited. By the time the inspection was over, all was found in order and the clinic opened its doors the following day. No one ever found out if Ibrahim Berger had a hand in changing hearts at city hall, neither were they ever contacted by Stephen Raffael.

The atmosphere at the meetings had changed, however. The crowds were decidedly smaller, with hecklers interrupting continuously. Thomas knew they were sent by the religious leaders in Tiberias, with Rabbi Shamir as their leader. He imagined the man was furious when the clinic re-opened and the meetings were held just outside of the city limits. Rumors were, he had been reprimanded for his efforts against Shalom Outreach by Tel Aviv, but that could not be confirmed.

Thomas was having breakfast with Bob one morning. The clinic was running smooth and the number of those who came in secret to the back room to know more about Yeshua had increased dramatically.

"Nothing has changed much in two thousand years," he said between bites. "The religious leaders are still raging against Yeshua and His followers, trying to discredit them as heretics."

"The real sad thing is, they, just like then, are still waiting for their Meshiah and ignoring His miracles now in the same way they did then," Bob answered. "Will they also persecute us and the believers in Israel in like manner?" he asked, looking at Thomas thoughtfully.

"So far, the Lord has protected us, but I keep remembering what the angel said to me not too long ago and it leaves me uneasy," Thomas said. "Something is going to happen, and it isn't going to be good. All we can do, is continue with what we are doing until He tells us otherwise," he added. "To change the subject," he said as he took a sip of coffee, "Melissa is taking the baby to a meeting for new mothers in one of the churches in Haifa. Some lady is teaching on how to discipline and deal with our children growing up in this anti-Christian environment of today. Meta is going with her."

"Are you sure they will be safe?"

"There are two ways to live with the danger we live in," Thomas said. "Melissa and I discussed it last night when she told me she wanted to go. One is, you can stay home and become a prisoner or decide to live with it and go about your normal business. I am not saying to ignore all precautions, but trusting the Lord to protect you when you are out in the world is a part of our faith, is it not? Besides, who would want to hurt a woman with a baby?" he added.

"Let's hope you are right, Thomas," Bob said and got up from the table. "It is time for us to go to work.

It was not until that evening, after the clinic closed, Thomas and the others realized, Melissa, Helena and Meta had not returned from Haifa.

"Has anyone heard from them?" Caleb asked, looking at Thomas.

"I have been too busy all day to answer my phone," he said as he searched for his cell phone in his pocket. "No, there is no call or text." An ominous feeling of dread spread over him. *No, Lord, not this. Not Melissa and the baby. Please!* He was screaming on the inside, but no words came out as he stood, looking with dread at the team as he dialed Melissa's cell. It went straight to voice mail.

"Let's not assume the worst," Caleb said. "We need to call the church they went to. After that the police and the hospitals to see whether they had an accident." He turned to Leona. "You get right on that, please. Have Paul and Karl help you. Bob, you try the number Miriam gave you for an emergency and talk to her. Thomas, try to raise her or Meta on their cell again."

"No need, Leona said, "I have already done that several times, it is going straight to voice mail on both."

In spite of all their efforts, there was no trace of them and the mood at Shalom Outreach turned from worry to panic.

Chapter 31

Meta was enveloped in total darkness. The moon was hidden behind a thick cloud cover as she ran through the open field away from the city of Haifa. She had no idea in which direction she was fleeing, all she knew, she had to get far away from the nightmare of the last few hours.

"Please, God, help me," she said between sobs. "I can't run anymore." That is when her foot hit one of the many rocks strewn across the field and with a piercing cry she fell to the ground, holding her right ankle. She knew it was broken by the nasty cracking sound she heard as she hit the ground. Whimpering in pain, she laid down on the grass, resigned to her fate. They would probably catch her and take her back to that horrible place. For the rest of the night she cowered low to the ground, kept awake by the excruciating pain until, finally, just before dawn, she fell asleep.

She woke up with a start when she felt something touch her shoulder.

"Are you hurt?"

She looked up into the face of an old man with an even older looking pipe in his toothless mouth.

"I think I broke my ankle; can you get help?" she asked in Hebrew.

"It will take a while, Miss. I am a simple shepherd without a car. I would have to walk to Haifa to send someone."

"No, don't do that!" she cried out in panic. "Is there another way to get me to a doctor to set my foot?"

"I am too old to carry you, although you are a little bit of a thing, aren't you?" he said with a friendly grin.

"Do you have a cell phone, Sir?" Meta asked.

"I do, but I don't know how to work it. My son gave it to me, but I really have no need for it," he said as he searched his pants pocket. "Here it is, he even charged it for me last night."

Meta took the phone and dialed the number of Shalom Outreach.

"Leona, it's Meta. Please, I need help. I am in a field near Haifa with a broken ankle, can you come and get me?" She turned to the old man, "Does this place have a name?"

"It's called the Shepherd's valley and is about three miles south of Haifa," he said. "The road is right over there," he went on and pointed toward the highway in the distance.

"Leona, I will wait for you by the highway, three miles outside of Haifa. Hurry, I don't want to be seen, so you have to look for me on the left side of the road." She hung up before Leona could ask any questions and then, leaning heavily on the old man's arm, started the long hobble toward the road. It took quite some time until they reached it and she sank down on the grass, exhausted.

"I will keep a look-out for your friend's van," he said.

"It will be a while, my friends are coming from Tiberias," Meta said, trying not to cry out because of the pain.

"That is indeed far away and we will have to wait a long time," he said. "I will have to go back and tend to my sheep, but I will keep an eye out for you as I bring them closer to this place." With that he slowly walked back to his little flock in the distance.

It was two hours later, when she spotted the van. With supreme effort she raised herself up on one elbow and waved with the other hand until it slowed down. She began to cry when she saw Thomas, Caleb and Mikail jump out and run over to her.

"Meta, are you alright?" Thomas shouted as he bent over her. Where are Melissa and Helena?" He looked around in panic when he didn't see them.

Meta looked at him, unable to say the words.

"Where are they?" He shouted. "Tell me, are they alright?"

Meta's eyes filled with tears.

"No, Thomas, they are not."

"What are you saying, Meta?" Caleb asked with dread in his voice.

"They are dead." Her voice was without emotion. "They will never be alright again."

"No God, no!" Thomas made a guttural sound like a wounded animal. "No, please God no! It is my fault, I let them go when I knew it was dangerous." He crumpled to the ground, sobbing and shaking, covering his face with both hands.

No one spoke for a long time until Mikail finally said,

"Thomas, we have to get Meta to a doctor, her foot is broken."

"I don't care, I just want to die," he said in a monotone voice. "I lost my little Helena all over again. Please, God, let me die." He started shaking and sobbing again.

"Meta, let's get you in the van," Caleb said. "Can you hold out until we get to the clinic or do we need to find an ER in Haifa?" He asked.

"Not Haifa, please don't take me to Haifa, I want to go home!" She was shouting and then added in a whisper, "Please, take me home, I just want to go home."

It took a while to lift her into the van and get her foot situated in a way it was supported sufficiently. When Thomas refused to get up, Caleb and Mikail lifted him by the shoulders and forced him to sit up.

"Thomas, we cannot stay here without attracting unwanted attention," Caleb said. "Please, get up and go sit in the backseat of the van with Meta. She needs medical attention."

"I don't care," he moaned.

"You will care enough to stand up and get in the car," Mikail suddenly shouted. "Right now!"

Amazingly, it worked. Thomas raised himself up with an extreme effort and slowly climbed into the car without a word. He did not ask what happened, nor did Meta volunteer any information during the long, silent trip home. When they got closer to Tiberias, Caleb called Leona at the office. When she put Bob on the phone, he asked him to be prepared to fix Meta's foot as soon as they got to the clinic.

"Is everybody alright?" Bob asked.

"No, they are not," was all he answered and hung up.

Thomas went straight to his room and locked the door behind him. Bob fixed Meta's foot and put a cast on it. She had not said a word before the procedure, even when he asked her what happened. All everyone knew so far was, Melissa and Helena were dead. Each member of the team tried to make it through the day without breaking down and crying in front of the patients. When they finally closed the doors after the last person left, they gathered around the dining room table. Petra had fixed spaghetti, everybody's favorite. Only Karl managed to take a plate full, while the others just picked at the food.

"Did someone tell Thomas to come for supper?" Caleb asked.

"I did," Petra said, "he said he wasn't hungry."

"We have to talk to Meta and find out what happened," Bob said. "The authorities have to be informed that something terrible took place in Haifa. I have tried to speak to her about it, but she won't talk. I am pretty sure she is in shock and we will have to wait till morning. I have given her a sedative to help her sleep."

"What do you think happened?" Paul asked.

"There is no telling, all we know is it was traumatic, given the emotional shape she is in," Bob answered. "She may not be able to share tomorrow either, we will have to wait and see."

The next day was Shabbat and the clinic was closed. One by one the team quietly sat down at the table early in the morning and waited in silence to see if Meta was able to share. No sound had come from Thomas' room and no one dared to ask him to come down for breakfast.

And hour had gone by when Meta came out, walking on crutches.

"Have a seat," Leona said, "I will get your coffee."

"Thanks." She sat down with a heavy sigh, holding on to the cup with a tight grip. Her face was a stony mask and her eyes looked empty. With her disheveled, curly hair and loose-fitting gown, she looked like she had just gotten out of bed without bothering to brush her teeth or wash up.

"Can you tell us what happened, sweetheart?" Bob asked in a gentle tone. "We need to know so we can inform the authorities."

Meta looked at him with a strange look and said in a monotone voice,

"I don't know if I can ever talk about it, it was too horrible."

"You can try, Meta, dear, it is important," Bob went on gently. "We will wait until you have finished your coffee and maybe have some toast and jelly, like you usually have in the morning."

"I wish that is all it would take to make me feel better." Meta began to cry. "I will never feel better, not ever."

"Yes, you will. With the Lord's help you will," Bob said as he took her hand. "We are here for you as well," he added and put his arm around her shoulder. "Tell us from the beginning what happened yesterday since you left here with Melissa and little Helena."

Meta reached for a napkin and blew her nose before she started in a halting voice.

"We arrived in Haifa at the church and went to the meeting. There were a lot of women there and it was very informative. We went to lunch in the city at a nice little restaurant on a side street from the church. When we walked back to the car, a van drove up alongside of us and two men jumped out and forced us into the back before we could scream for help. The people on the street probably thought they were there to take us home and didn't make any attempt to stop the men.

Once inside, the car sped away fast and we had no idea where they were taking us since they were talking in Arabic. It was not long, when we stopped and were told to get out of the car. Helena was crying and one of the men yelled at Melissa to make her stop. She tried by holding her close and talking softly to her, but she was hungry and wouldn't stop. That is when he hit Melissa with his gun and she fell to the ground. I saw a big bruise on her face when she got up and pleaded with him not to hurt her baby. He laughed and pushed her toward a door on the side of a building. I have no idea where we were, because all I saw was a tall wall on all sides.

I was pushed by the other man and ordered to follow Melissa. We were put into a small, dark room with no windows and dirty, bare walls. There was one narrow bed in the room, nothing else. A metal bucket in the corner served as a toilet. Helena was screaming by now, but since we weren't given food of any kind, there was nothing Melissa could do to make her stop.

We were in this room for two days. No one brought us food or water. On the second day, Helena finally stopped crying and just whimpered in a most pitiful way that broke our hearts. Melissa was beside herself with concern for the baby, but there was nothing she could do but let her suck on her little finger. On the morning of the third day, a man came in and motioned for us to follow him. We were weak with hunger and thirst and had trouble walking. He led us into a courtyard, where we saw a bucket of water standing in the corner. We ran toward it and drank until we were full. Melissa managed to get some into the baby's mouth before the man pulled her away. The water tasted foul, but it didn't matter.

He pushed us to the other side of the yard through a door. We found ourselves in a large room with a group of young men sitting at a table, drinking and laughing. They paid no attention to us at first, until one of them walked over to Melissa and made her follow him to the where the others were. They said something to her in Arabic. The only word I could understand was American or a word sounding similar to that. I also heard the name Peterson. From that I surmised they knew she was Thomas' wife.

I could see Melissa tremble as she stood, holding on to Helena, who was asleep from hunger. One of the hoodlums walked over to her and said in English,

"You are the American infidel whore who is married to Dr. Peterson?" he asked her.

"Yes," Melissa said. "What do you want with me?"

"That is not for me to say, I just translate," he answered.

"Who are these men?" Melissa asked.

"We are the new generation in the service of Allah and not connected with any group. We support ourselves by doing jobs no one else wants to do, like this one with the Rabbi Shamir. He wants to get rid of your husband, because he is a Christian swine and infidel, who leads the people into heresy."

"Why would you care; you are Muslim?" Melissa said with astonishment.

"We care, because he is paying us handsomely."

"What are you going to do?" Now she sounded scared.

"I don't know; I am only the translator."

"But you are not translating," she said. "Maybe you can tell your friends I won't tell the authorities they have kidnapped American citizen and let us go."

"I can't do that. The Rabbi has paid us already and we have to do what he wants."

"What is that?" Melissa didn't sound so scared anymore.

"Kill you."

Meta moved uneasy in her seat and then began to cry.

"I can't go on; it is too terrible what they did then. She began to tremble and it made her spill her coffee. Bob gently took the cup out of her hand.

"Meta, it is alright; if you want to stop for a while, we can just sit here and let you gather your thoughts. Would that be alright?"

"Yes, I guess so." She calmed down a little and even took a piece of bacon. "I have not eaten in three days, I think."

"Oh my goodness, dear, you must eat before you go on," Bob said and put some eggs and three strips of bacon on a plate and handed it to her. "Here, this will make you feel better."

She ate until there was nothing left on her plate and then reached for more. The team sat very still during all this, not wanting to interrupt Bob's expert handling of getting Meta to talk. After a half hour had passed, Meta was finally done eating. She leaned back and wiped her mouth.

"I guess I was really hungry."

"Can you tell us the rest of the story, Meta?" Bob asked, careful not to push her back into silence.

Meta looked at him with such sadness, it broke his heart and then continued in a detached, monotone voice,

"They took Melissa and little Helena outside to the courtyard. All the men followed. After a while I heard triumphant shouting and yelling and then they came back in and started drinking again. No one paid any attention to me and I crept out of the room to the courtyard to find Melissa." Meta started to sob uncontrollably and threw herself on Bob. He held her tight and stroked her hair gently.

"It's alright, baby, it's alright, you are safe." When she calmed down, she went on, still trembling,

"I found them both laying on the ground, beheaded."

"Oh my God," Bob blurted out in shock. "Oh my dear God."

It was at that moment he saw Thomas standing in the doorway, motionless. Everyone stared at him, frozen in horror.

"God had nothing to do with this," Thomas said in a strangely calm voice. "Any God, who would allow something like this to happen to my wife and child after I have served Him faithfully, is not my God any longer. I hate You, Yeshua, for you have betrayed me and my family and I will never serve You again." His face was void of emotion as he turned and walked out.

Chapter 32

The authorities came. Since Meta was unable to tell them anything about the men or where the house was, nothing was done. No one believed her when she told them Rabbi Shamir had ordered the killings. After all, he was a respected religious leader, incapable of committing such a crime. The bodies of Melissa and Helena were never found.

Weeks went by and Thomas staid in his room. He refused to speak to anyone, do surgery or honor his commitment for his many scheduled meetings. He had not shaved since that day, nor dressed in anything but his old jeans and a ragged t-shirt, while lying on his bed, staring at the ceiling in total silence. Petra put his meals in front of his door, but many times he never touched them.

It was a month later, when he suddenly appeared at lunch. The team was shocked to see he had lost at least twenty pounds, his gaunt face was covered by a thick, unkempt beard and his hair had not been combed or washed for a long time.

"Thomas, it is good to see you," Caleb said. No one else spoke.

"I am going home."

"You do realize Shalom Outreach, the clinic and this ministry will be closed down if you do?" Caleb answered.

"I don't care."

"Do you want to talk about this?" Bob joined in.

"No."

There was silence, no one else dared to say anything. Finally, Caleb spoke again,

"We need you, Thomas."

"I don't care, let Bob take over."

"We already tried, the authorities did not accept his application and insist, it is you or nobody. This is their best chance to get rid of this ministry without violating the religious freedom clause. That is why Rabbi Shamir did what he did, he knew you would not stay and so get rid of you without any suspicion falling on him."

"It doesn't matter, let him win; I have already lost everything I care about." Thomas had not looked up from his plate during the entire conversation.

"How dare you wallow in your self-pity!" It was Meta. "Do you really think you are the only one who is hurt? I was there and I will never be the same, but I know I still have a job to do here. We all do. Yeshua did not bring us this far so you can throw it all away, because you hurt." She was angry. "We are all hurt. So stop your whining and continue to do what God has brought you here to do. This is not all about you, Dr. Peterson and neither are you going to find any more peace or happiness by running back home. People there will point their finger at you and smirk, because they will be sure you were wrong to follow Yeshua. Is that what you want?"

"How dare you!" he shouted. "How dare you think you hurt as much as I do. They were my life, there is nothing else for me." He was shaking with anger.

"Oh really? You have the market on pain now, do you?" She raised her small frame up and suddenly seemed tall. "Let me tell you about pain. The whole world is falling apart, millions have died and chaos reigns everywhere. The anti-Christ is getting ready to take over and unless we continue to spread the Gospel in our little corner, people will go to hell. Don't you see, we are the only ones who have the answer and crawling into a hole of self-pity is not going to help anyone. We are not fighting the pitiful Rabbi Shamir, but Satan himself, trying to destroy God's last call to His people. And whether you like it or not, bigshot, unfortunately you are the one He still wants to use. For the life of me, I don't know why, but then He has always used the losers to do something great."

Thomas looked at her. For the first time since that day, his face showed some life. Although he didn't say anything, everyone knew, he was waking up from his nightmare. They watched his eyes fill with tears as if in slow motion, when, suddenly, he put his face in both hands and sobbed pitifully.

"I have railed against You, Yeshua," he finally managed to say. "I have hated You and cursed You. Please forgive me, I am sorry. I am not worthy to do this, I never have been and still wish You would choose someone else. But if You don't, I will stay and finish my purpose." He raised his head after a long while and then looked at Meta and said, "There is a mountain of faith and determination in that tiny body of yours."

"Welcome back," Bob said, relief showing in his voice. "We have all come through a terrible ordeal, but as always, the Lord has been there throughout. It is time we give Him thanks and ask for directions of where to go from here." He looked around the table. "The first thing we need to get out of the way is to forgive Rabbi Shamir." A groan went through the group, but before anyone could say anything, he continued. "Remember when the Lord hung on the cross, dying? If He had not forgiven those who killed Him, His purpose could not have been accomplished, because the Father counts un-forgiveness as sin. And since Yeshua was incapable of sin, He had no choice but to do what He did. That is why He expects us to do the same if we are to accomplish His purpose for us." Bob looked at the team and went on, "It is not just for our spiritual well-being we do this, but more so that the purpose of God might be fulfilled through us."

Thomas looked around the table. It was as if he had woken up from a nightmare. The last four weeks were a hazy, unreal memory. The thought of Melissa and Helena still caused pain as if a knife went through him. He knew it would be a long time until he got over it, if ever. He reached over to Meta and took her hand.

"Thank you for waking me up and for being there with them when it happened."

"Thomas, they are both with Yeshua and are waiting until you can join them. Just hold on to that thought and you will be able to go on," she answered as she squeezed his hand. "Both Melissa and Helena loved you more than anything."

Thomas was never the same. While he returned to the Lord and prayed to forgive Rabbi Shamir, his heart remained broken. No one ever saw him smile or laugh again. And while he took up surgery, he did not accept any speaking engagements anywhere. As time went by, the number of people coming to the clinic to search for Yeshua became less each day, until finally, they stopped altogether. It was as if the light had gone out of Shalom Outreach ministry, just as the Rabbi had hoped it would.

Chapter 33

The next Saturday Eric Foster, the head of Shalom Outreach for Israel came for an unexpected visit. The team was expected to attend a meeting late in the afternoon to discuss the status of the ministry.

Thomas decided he would not attend and was annoyed when Eric insisted he come and join them.

"From what I have heard and seen here, this ministry is in trouble. Other than the medical facility, there is no spiritual outreach whatsoever. Why is that?" he asked when everyone was seated.

No one answered.

"Thomas? Can you guess what is going on?"

"I am doing what I was sent here to do, heal the sick and work as the doctor for the poor," he said, "and that is all I'm responsible for."

"What about your meetings?"

"I don't do those anymore."

"I know; can you tell us why not?" Eric asked.

"I no longer feel anointed; what else can I tell you?" He sounded almost petulant. "Why are you singling me out, Eric? There are others here you could ask the same question."

"They did not walk with Yeshua for three years and were told by the Lord to share the Gospel with His people before He returns."

"Then He should not have allowed my family to be killed."

A stunned silence hung over the room.

"I thought you asked Him to forgive you for your anger. Did you mean it?" Eric held his breath.

"I thought I did, but apparently, this is the best I can do. He should have never picked me, I just don't have what it takes," Thomas said with defiance. "I just don't care anymore, I guess."

"What would it take for you to start caring again, Doctor?" Eric asked, frustrated.

"I honestly don't know."

"I have orders from Chicago to give the ministry two more months and then, if nothing changes, it will be closed down. We can use every one of you in other places to spread the Gospel and pray for people to accept Christ." He turned to Thomas, "Except you, Dr. Peterson, you can go back to the US if you want."

"That sounds fine with me." He got up. "I will be in my room." With that he left.

A month went by and nothing changed. The team was starting to prepare to leave by not re-ordering supplies. A gloom hung over the clinic as everyone did their assigned duties, no more. They stayed in their rooms in the evenings, unlike before, when they sat together and played games or watched the only English speaking channel there was. Thomas did not associate with anyone and preferred to be alone. He had notified his parents that he was coming home.

It was one of those evenings as he lay on his bed, lonely, angry and sad, when, suddenly, the words of the angel came into his mind with crystal clarity.

"Why are you troubled, Thomas? The Lord is with you and what is going to happen is ordained by Him. Do not be afraid of what must come, but take heart, because it is part of His design. For a while, it will look like the enemy will win, but never fear, God is with you and nothing can stop the purpose He has for you and His people Israel. "In this world you will have tribulation, but be of good cheer, I have overcome the world. (John 6:33) Remember these words well, Thomas, for they are given to you so that you may not forget when the enemy comes in like a flood."

Thomas sat up with a jolt. He had forgotten! His mind was suddenly filled with anger on the one hand and guilt on the other as he saw the face of Yeshua before him, the way He used to look when he had done something wrong. *Oh God!*

"How can I serve You, Lord when I feel so dead inside? How can I please You when I am angry with You for taking my family from me? If You don't raise me up, I have no choice but to leave and fail You and miss the purpose for which You brought me here." He was praying out loud and realized, it was the first time he was talking to the Lord in many months.

A peace came over him, gently, without warning. He knew Yeshua had heard him.

"Please, help me," he whispered, "I don't know what to do. I need Your love, Your power and Your Holy Spirit. I am willing to go out into all the world and be You voice again, but I can't make it happen on my own." He was crying, but this time they were tears of relief instead of sadness and hopelessness. "I want to come home, Lord, to the place in the middle of Your perfect will. Forgive me for trying to handle things on my own, for my anger against You and for how terrible I have treated everyone around me here at the ministry. Once again, You have shown me that I cannot be righteous without You. How many times do I have to go through this lesson until I get it?"

Thomas laid back on the bed, exhausted, but filled with joy for the first time since that day and went to sleep, smiling.

He got up the next morning, feeling alive. When he arrived at the breakfast table, shaved, nicely dressed and with a smile, everyone stared at him in disbelief.

"What happened to you?" Meta asked.

He walked over to the coffee pot and poured himself a cup and put it on his place. After filling his plate with a stack of pancakes and pouring a generous helping of syrup over it, he sat down and ate without saying a word.

The last one to arrive was Paul Ryan. After he sat down with his food, Thomas looked up from his plate and said casually,

"Leona, how long would it take to get me back on the speaking circuit?"

"What?"

"Do you still have churches who want me to speak?"

"I have a whole list of them, all you have to do is say the word." She sounded totally surprised. "You are serious?"

"Yes, I am." He looked at Caleb. "I had an encounter with the Lord last night and He healed my heart and freed me from the prison of darkness. I will stay and serve Him and be His voice like before and take His Good News to His people Israel, just like He told me to do from the very beginning." He smiled at everyone as he went on, "The Lord reminded me of the words the angel spoke to me the last time I went to Capernaum.

"Why are you troubled, Thomas? The Lord is with you and what is going to happen is ordained by Him. Do not be afraid of what must come, but take heart, because it is part of His design. For a while, it will look like the enemy will win, but never fear, God is with you and nothing can stop the purpose He has for you and His people Israel.

"In this world you will have tribulation, but be of good cheer, I have overcome the world.'" (John 6:33)

Remember these words well, Thomas, for they are given to you so that you may not forget when the enemy comes in like a flood."

"The problem was, I forgot about those words and let the enemy overwhelm me for these many months. But his game is over and the Lord woke me up this morning with a renewed sense of hope, power and purpose." He looked directly at Caleb as he went on, "I will not be going home, but going out into all the world and preach the Gospel again. And then he looked at everyone and said, "I want to ask your forgiveness for my awful behavior over these past few months. I wish I was a better person and Christian, but like Meta so eloquently put it the other day, the Lord uses the losers to do great things."

Meta blushed while everybody laughed.

"I didn't mean it, Thomas."

"If you didn't, you should have. I was a pitiful, selfish jerk."

"But we all love you anyway," she said, "don't ask me why."

Within a week the invitations came pouring in and so did the crowds. Soon the back room of the clinic was once again filled with people seeking to know about Yeshua. If it hadn't been for Melissa and little Helena missing, life at Shalom Outreach had returned to normal.

But normal could not possibly describe the state of the rest of the world. Because of the constant nuclear threat in North Korea, Iran, between Pakistan and India and even some of the Middle Eastern countries, earth was a powder cag waiting to go off at any minute. This instability, together with people filled with fear and anxiety in the face of economic collapse worldwide, cried out for someone to bring law and order to the nations. And that someone was none other than the new leader of the UN, Mohamed Abdul

Musharak. In his latest speech to the World Council of Churches, he hinted at the new idea that a one world government was the only way to bring peace to a world at the brink of emotional, economic and political collapse. His speech brought positive reactions from many nations around the world, clamoring to be included in his plans. Even many mainline denominational churches supported his ideas and scorned and ridiculed those who tried to warn people that this was the anti-Christ.

The team listened to the latest news on TV and an uneasiness filled the room as they listened to Musharak tout his new ideas of world peace and brotherhood among all religions. They cringed as he mentioned that the only people who didn't agree were the Evangelical Christians and suggested strong measures to deal with them by demanding their pastors submit every sermon to a panel of city leaders before they are allowed to preach it.

The next news segment was a terrible shock.

"This is just in from Tel Aviv. In a surprise move, the Prime Minister of Israel, Ibrahim Berger has been ousted from office by a unanimous vote of the Knesset this afternoon for subverting Jewish traditions and values by having converted to Christianity. It is estimated that in recent years, Christianity in Israel has increased at an alarming rate, largely due to the American Doctor Thomas Peterson and his outdoor meetings. In spite of recent efforts to stop his proselytizing, it is reported that his meetings go on unhindered due to the protection of the late Prime Minister Berger. A prominent religious authority named Rabbi Yitzhak Shamir is looking into the matter and will no doubt advise the new head of government on the situation.

"That does not sound good," Thomas said in a light hearted tone. "They have no idea who they are messing with. Yeshua's plan is not going to be pushed aside by the Rabbi, no matter how hard he tries. I can't wait to see what is finally going to bring the man down to the point he has to acknowledge that Yeshua is the Meshiah."

"I am upset about the Prime Minister," Bob said. "On the other hand, isn't it wonderful he has found Jesus? I wonder if the Lord used Miriam or someone else."

"I am afraid there will be tougher times ahead with a new Prime Minister," Caleb said. "The Knesset is going to make sure he is not favorable toward Christians, which could mean we will get closed down. It would be a shame, now that we just got going again."

"The way the Lord told me, we will not be stopped until our work here is done, no matter how the heathens rage against us," Thomas said with conviction. "I don't think we should worry about it until it happens and then He decides whether stay open or get closed down. Either way, there is nothing we can do about any of it, but do our jobs until we are called home," he said and pointed his finger upwards.

Chapter 34

"Son, you have to come home, your mother is gravely ill." Thomas took a deep breath before he answered. "Dad, I will come as soon as I can. What is wrong with Mom?"

"She has stage 4 colon cancer. As you know, there is nothing that can be done." His father sounded heartbroken and close to tears. "She refused to go to the doctor and have it checked out, no matter what I said. You know how she is and now it's too late. All she talks about is, she wants to see you one more time."

"I will be there, Dad, I promise."

Thomas was on the plane the next day.

Lord, I know she doesn't know You, please allow me to show her how much You love her by sending Your Holy Spirit to ready her heart by the time I get there. I could not bear the thought of her dying without You, it would be worse than losing Melissa and Helena. He sat in the narrow seat by the window and stared into the brilliant blue sky over the Atlantic Ocean.

"I have been meaning to ask you, Sir, you look like that famous Dr. Peterson, the one who heals people," the woman next to him asked.

"I am, but I can't heal anyone, Ma'am, only He can," Thomas answered and pointed his finger upwards.

"I don't believe in all that faith healing stuff, but even your critics say, you have done some pretty spectacular things. Are they right?"

"They are, but again, I can't turn one blade of grass green, only God can, there is a big difference."

"I wish I could believe like you do. You see, my son?" she pointed to a young man next to her, "he wanted to see Israel before he dies. We are Jewish and it has been his dream to walk in the land of his ancestors. I am a widow with limited income, but I scraped together enough to fulfill his wish."

"What is wrong with him?" Thomas asked.

"He has lung cancer. The doctors have tried everything, chemo, radiation and every other remedy they can think of, but it hasn't done any good. Jeffrey, that's his name, now has trouble breathing and is on oxygen all the time."

Thomas hadn't noticed the small, portable tank before. The young man had his earphones on and had not heard what his mother was sharing. He was in his early twenties, gaunt and pale and his labored breathing was quite evident. It was emphysema in the last stages.

Thomas suddenly remembered the man at the Pharisee's house as he knelt before Yeshua and begged for his life. He never forgot the relief and joy as he took his first normal breath.

"Jeffrey, do you mind if I ask you a question?" he said as he leaned over passed his mother.

Jeffrey took his earphones out with a frown on his face. Thomas could tell, he did not want to be disturbed.

"What is it you want to ask me, Sir?" he asked, trying to be polite. "As you can see, I can't talk much."

"I know; I am a Doctor."

"He is that famous faith healer, Jeff, the one we've been hearing about, remember?" his mother said.

"Oh, are you going to do one of your magic tricks and heal me?" the young man said with a cynical smile.

"As a matter of fact, I want to pray for you, but it isn't magic I offer, but Yeshua and His power."

"We are Jews and don't believe in Him," the woman said before Jeffrey could answer.

"Do you want to believe in Him, Jeffrey?" Thomas asked gently. "He wants to heal you if you accept Him as your Meshiah."

Jeffrey looked at Thomas for a long time and finally said,

"I don't have anything else going for me, do I? Why not try Jesus."

"How dare you, Dr. Peterson, you are leading my son away from our faith with your heresy." She sounded frantic as she turned toward her son.

"Don't listen to him, you are a Jew and we don't believe in this Jesus. Do not disgrace our faith and me by falling for his talk." She had raised her voice enough, people in the next row turned to see what was going on.

"Mom, stop! You are not the one dying, I am. We have tried everything; this is all I have left. Please, for once, let me make a decision without you interfering." He leaned over passed his mother and said, "I give my life over to this Jesus. You say He is the Messiah. If He is, then I believe in Him. My life is at an end and I have nothing to lose."

Thomas took the young man's hand and said in a low voice,

"Yeshua, I ask you to accept Jeffrey into your Kingdom. He is giving You his life, take it and restore his body to health like You did before so many years ago. Thank you, Lord."

He let go of Jeffrey's hand and leaned back in his seat and went to sleep for two or three hours, until breakfast was served. When he looked over to where Jeffrey had sat, the seat was empty with only the oxygen tank on it.

"He took it off an hour ago," his mother said, angry. "Look what you've done. This is dangerous, but as a doctor you already know that."

At that moment Thomas saw the young man coming down the aisle. He smiled at Thomas, his face no longer pale, but a healthy pink. "For the first time in months I can breathe normal," he said as he sat down in his seat. Jesus has healed me, mother."

"That is ridiculous, put your oxygen back on, you will not make it without it," she said with panic in her voice.

"Look at me, mother, do I look sick to you? I am fine, don't you understand, Jesus healed me, because I can breathe normal and my strength is back." He took her hand and held it. "How come you are not happy for me, Mom?"

She looked at him, confused and scared. "I don't understand; how can this be?" she said, looking at Thomas.

"I don't know how, all I know is that Yeshua lives and touches people even today. He wants to touch you, too, Ma'am if you do what your son did and turn your life over to Him."

"I don't know, I'm going to have to think about this some more, but thank you." She turned away from Thomas with an expression that left no doubt, she was done talking about it.

It took many more hours with the lay-over in Boston, before he finally made it to Philadelphia, where his father picked him up at the airport. He hadn't realized how much he had missed him till he hugged him.

"It is good to see you, Dad. How is Mom?"

"You have lost a lot of weight, Thomas," Abraham answered. "Mom is frail and in pain. She is not good, son, I am glad you came."

"What's the prognosis, as if I didn't already know."

"Pete Vasser, her oncologist, gives her only a few days."

"Are you kidding?" Thomas said, shocked. "you didn't tell me it was that bad."

"I didn't want to worry you; you have had enough death to deal with lately."

"It was terrible, but I am fine now, Dad. God saw me through it and He will see us through this as well."

"I wish I had your faith, son."

"You can have it, all you have to do is ask," Thomas said, carefully not to overdo.

Thomas felt nostalgic as they drove up to his parents' house. He had grown up here and some of the large trees in the yard had been little when he was little.

"Make sure you don't show your shock when you see your mother," Abraham said with sadness in his voice as they walked into the house. "She looks pretty bad.

It was worse than he thought. Sylvia, a petit woman to begin with, had shrunk down to a skeleton as she lay in the hospital bed, set up in the family room.

"Tommy, my wonderful boy, you came," she cried out in a weak voice when he entered. "You have no idea what it means to see you one more time before I die." She held out her arms to him and he knelt by the bed and laid his head on her chest.

"Mom, I'm here. I love you and missed you," he cried. "I won't leave you again, I promise."

"Sweetheart, I don't have but a few days, so I believe you." She smiled a knowing smile as she held him and stroked his hair. "My goodness, you have a lot of gray these days. It looks very distinguished I must say, but then you were always a handsome boy right from the start."

"Mom, I missed you. Leave it to you to tell me I'm getting old." He smiled at her, his voice filled with love. "I love you."

"I love you, too. I wish I could have been a better mother, but I did the best I could." Her breathing was labored as she went on.

"The reason I wanted to see you once more is, that I want to tell you how much joy you have been in my life and to ask your forgiveness for not telling you more often how much I love you. What a blessing you have been for your father and me. I know we have not always agreed about things, but that is all in the past. I want to die in peace, knowing, you know that I could not have asked for a better son."

Thomas was crying as she spoke and took her hand in his.

"Mom, I know you realize you are dying. I have come to tell you about Yeshua and how much He wants you to accept Him so you can be with Him for all eternity. Will you do that?"

"Thomas, you are asking me to do something I don't believe in or know how to do, since I don't even believe there is a God. I am content to go into the ground into nothingness, what difference does it make what I say or do right now? All I ask, that you stay right here with me and then let me go in peace when my time comes."

"Yes, Mom, I will," he said, tears streaming down his face. *Yeshua, don' t let her die without You, I beg You. Do it for me, if not for her. You have used me to bring thousands to You, would it be so much to ask to do it for one more? She is my mother, please don't let her be lost forever, I couldn't bear it.*

The nurse touched his shoulder.

"Dr. Peterson, your mother needs her medication."

Sylvia Peterson slipped into a coma the next day and died peacefully two days later with her husband Abraham, her mother-in-law Nana and her son Thomas by her side.

Once again, Thomas could not understand why Yeshua had allowed it to happen and let his mother die without saving her. The loss was deeper than when Melissa and Helena died; at least he would see them again. Strangely, though, his grief did not turn to hatred or anger, just profound, abject sorrow at the thought he would never see his mother again.

Only his Nana understood the depth of his feelings and the two of them held on to each other for comfort during the funeral. Thomas looked at his father. Abraham looked broken with grief to have lost his soul mate of so many years. Thomas realized he was alone now, with his only son far across the ocean in Israel. In spite of the many people attending the funeral, he was certain his father felt isolated and wanted to join Sylvia.

Thomas saw many of his former collogues. Most of them kept their distance or shook his hand briefly and walked on. He heard some whispering and felt their curious stares as they thought him to be the strange, famous faith healer from Israel.

"Healed anyone lately?" Mark Kosack said in a loud voice. "You are quite the guy, aren't you?"

"Hello, Mark, I see you haven't changed much, still the diplomat, hey?" Thomas grinned as he shook his hand. "God bless you."

There was an embarrassing silence among the people who heard Mark Kosack.

"Thomas, our condolences for your loss." It was Berry Vance, another surgeon. "Kathy and I are also sorry about the death of your wife and child. How are you holding up?"

"I am going to be alright, Berry. Thanks for caring. It has been a difficult year for me, that's for sure."

"Are you going back to Israel to your work?" his wife asked. "We keep up with you through the news."

"I am leaving in a few days." Thomas said, surprised at their kindness. He had not known them well.

Many came and were glad to see him, but many stopped by out of curiosity to meet the "Philadelphia surgeon who thought he was Jesus".

Early the next morning after the funeral, Thomas sat in the lanai, looking out over the lush, green garden his mother had cultivated over the years. He held a cup of coffee in his hand when his father walked in, joined by Nana.

"You are up early, Tommy," Nana said. "It seems the time change is still messing you up."

"I don't think that is what it is, Nana, I am used to getting up early with the clinic opening at eight."

"Tell us about your clinic, son," Abraham said. "I would like to come see it."

"There is no reason why either one of you or both cannot come with me when I fly back in two days," he said. "I would love to have you."

"It takes a little more planning than that, I'm sure," Abraham said, "but that is not such a bad idea. With Sylvia gone, this house is going to cave in on me."

"Why can't you move in with Dad, Nana? That way neither of you would be lonely."

Nana looked at Abraham.

"You know, that is not such a bad idea. I will need someone to take care of me as time goes on and you need someone to keep the house, what do you think, Abe?" She sounded excited.

"There, that's settled. Now if you do as well with arranging for a flight for both of you to Israel, that would be good," Thomas said with a smile. "Do both of you have a passport?"

"Don't you need a visa to go there?" Abraham asked, "but we can easily find out."

"I know for certain you don't need a visa to get into Israel," Thomas said, "just a passport that is good for the next six months."

"I have one, Abraham said.

"So do I. I got it when I went on that cruise two years ago to the Caribbean," Nana said. "That means we can go with you, Tommy." She turned to Abraham. "Let's do it, Abe, it would be good for you to get away for two weeks or so."

Before he could answer, Thomas dialed the airlines on his cell phone and bought two business class tickets to Israel with his Dad's credit card. Abraham insisted he upgrade his own ticket so they could all sit together.

After that he called Leona at the ministry and told her to tell the others that his father and grandmother would be visiting with him for two weeks.

Chapter 35

The first weekend there, Thomas took his father and Nana to Jerusalem. It proved a wonderful, emotional experience for both as Thomas explained not only the modern sites, but also the ancient ones. Especially, since he could shed light on the upper room and other places where Jesus performed His miracles, that were mislabeled by historians. He experienced the same irritations of churches having been built over the areas of real importance as he remembered them from his dream. But the most tragic thing in his mind was the absence of the majestic Temple and the huge Muslim Mosque in its place.

"Our Temple was actually next to where the mosque is now," he told them. "It was the most impressive building I have ever seen, more so for its spiritual significance than anything else. Every time I drove my carriage passed it, I felt such pride in being a Jew."

Nana was overcome with emotion as they walked the streets of Jerusalem and had to hold on to him as she listened to him tell his stories of how things were.

"It is remarkable to think you experienced it all two thousand years ago," she said in wonder.

Abraham followed in silence as they toured the city. It was still hard for him to get his thoughts away from the death of Sylvia. He seemed to have lost interest in much of what was going on around him. Every now and then Thomas would put his arm around his shoulders and hug him with great affection.

"I love you, Dad. I'm glad you're here with me."

On the Sunday of the second week of their stay, Thomas had a large meeting scheduled in Tel Aviv.

"Would you two like to come with me?" he asked Abraham and Nana. "I will have Mikail there to translate for you what's going on. I think you might enjoy experiencing what I do here outside of working in the clinic."

At first Abraham declined, but then relented when Nana scolded him for not wanting to see where his son worked.

"I will go if no one tries to make me do things I don't want to do," he said in a gruff voice. "You know how I feel about all this religious emotionalism," he grumbled.

"I promise, Dad, all you have to do is sit there and watch. No one is going to bother you. There will be many hundreds of people there and you can fade into the crowds if that is all you want to do." Although, Thomas was praying fervently that Yeshua would reach out to this father and save him. He looked at Nana and knew she was thinking the same thing.

It was close quarters in the van on the way there, since most of the team was scheduled to accompany Thomas. It was one the larger meetings since the new Prime Minister had come into office and everyone knew they could be arrested for disobeying the re-instated laws concerning religious gatherings.

An hour into the trip, Thomas' cell phone rang. It was Miriam Berger.

"Thomas, Ibrahim wants to talk to you."

"Mr. Prime Minister," Thomas said, surprised, "what can I do for you?"

"We would like to come to your meeting, Dr. Peterson if that is alright with you."

"That is wonderful, Sir. You do realize it maybe raided and we could all get arrested?" Thomas sounded anxious. "I would hate for this to happen to you, Sir."

"That is alright, I have been through a lot worse lately. All I ask that you do not let the crowd know I am there. Miriam and I will try to disguise ourselves as best we can, but should we be recognized, I want you to be prepared. The main reason we are calling you, we want you and your team to come to my new house afterwards for dinner. It is not too far from where your meeting will be. The meal won't be elaborate, but we would be honored to have you."

"That sounds wonderful, Sir," Thomas said, "my father and my grandmother are with us and if it is alright, they would be delighted to meet you."

"Splendid, bring them and we will all have a good time."

"You do travel in high circles, Tommy," Nana said with a chuckle.

"Well, Ibrahim Berger is no longer in office, but was asked to leave in total disgrace. So I don't know about the high circle, it's not so high anymore."

"How did you get to meet him?" Abraham asked.

"His wife Miriam was dying of a brain tumor and he sent his secretary to have me pray for her. The Lord healed her instantly," he added quietly. "That's when Ibrahim became a Christian."

His father didn't say anything after that.

The crowds were even larger than they had expected by the time the van drove up to the meeting place. It was outside of Tel Aviv in an open field. There were no chairs except for way up front where the podium stood. A sort of golf cart was waiting to pick Thomas and his team up to take them from the parking area to the front. There they were met by a man called Isaak Weinberger.

"Welcome, Dr. Peterson. I am Pastor Weinberger and these are pastors from the surrounding areas. We are so glad you decided to come. We know the Lord is going to do great things, because this is probably the last meeting of this kind we will ever be allowed to have."

"So the authorities are ok with this?" Thomas asked as he shook his hand.

"I don't know about that, but so far they haven't stopped it."

"Pastor, I want you to meet my father and grandmother from America. I wonder if they could sit up front with Mikail, my translator?"

"Of course, Sir. We are honored to have them." He pointed to three chairs. "Would these be alright?"

"They are fine. There is one more thing," Thomas said and waved for the Pastor Weinberger to step aside so the others couldn't hear him. "Prime Minister Berger and his wife will be here in disguise. Should they be discovered, could one of your people whisk them away immediately before it becomes known and causes a problem."

"Oh my goodness, how can we protect him and his wife from the spies in our midst? They may recognize them and arrest him and that in turn would jeopardize this meeting." He sounded frantic.

"Let's hope this does not happen," Thomas said. "We will just have to trust the Lord. The Prime Minister is well aware he might be in danger, but I don't think he thought about the consequences for this meeting." He smiled at the Pastor. "Just relax, the Lord is in control and whatever happens, He will be there for us." Thomas looked out over the vast crowd and they were still streaming in. "There is no way the spies can pick out two people in this," he said as he pointed to the masses in front of him. "It looks like this is the largest meeting we have ever had; the Lord is going to do a mighty thing today," Pastor Weinberger."

It was then Thomas spotted the Media trucks in the distance. There were at least five of them with their satellite dishes and cameras. He didn't say anything for fear of upsetting the pastor even more, but he knew they spelled trouble.

Thomas stood at the microphone and looked over the crowd and then at his father and Nana. *Yeshua, You are the only one who can do this. I am nothing and You love me anyway. Be here today for my father and draw him to You. Protect us today from the enemy and let Your Gory shine. Holy Spirit, fall over this crowd and touch each and every one of those who have come to see You, just like You did two thousand years ago.* He stood in silence as the crowd waited expectantly.

"I want all the people in wheelchairs, on crutches and with lifelong disabilities make your way down here. Yeshua is here and wants to heal you. While you do that, allow me to tell you of my walk in the past and how He loved me in spite of my shortcomings. For it is not how good you are, but how much He loves you that makes the difference. It is not what you have done right or wrong in your life, but that you are willing to give your body, soul and spirit to Him right now so He can use you for His purpose in these perilous times."

Thomas shared his story as hundreds of disabled, sick and dying people made their way up front. The crowd sat in rapt attention while he spoke.

A good half hour later, the sick were lined up in a long row in front of the podium. Some in wheelchairs, some held up by others and still more standing by themselves, their eyes riveted on Thomas with great expectancy.

"I watched Yeshua how He healed people with no great fanfare, shouting or dramatics. Some He touched, some he spoke to and others he never even saw, like the Centurions' servants. The one thing most of them had in common, they expected to be healed. If that is you and you came to be healed, then do not look to me, but to Him. I cannot heal anyone, but He can. All I can do is what He did, speak a simple word to ask Him to touch you."

Thomas stepped around the podium and walked down the long row and said a short prayer and touched each person. As he got further down the line, there was a stir in the crowd as people got out of their wheelchairs, shouting and jumping, while others raised their hands, crying. Thomas continued until he had prayed for every person and then returned to the microphone.

"It is not just our bodies who need healing, Yeshua wants to touch your spirit as well. If you have never given your life over to Him, I am going to ask you to agree with me as I pray for your salvation. He sent me here to preach the Good News to His people Israel before He returns. And that is you. Please, bow your head and repeat this prayer after me,

"Father in heaven. I have come here because I am a sinner and need You. I don't deserve Your love, Your sacrifice on the cross or that You would even be mindful of me. I give You my life and accept You as my Meshiah as You forgive my sins and accept me into Your Kingdom."

The thousands of voices praying sounded like the waves of the ocean reaching the shores. As he looked out over the crowd, he saw many had fallen on their knees with their heads to the ground. He looked over to where his father sat and noticed he was on his knees, praying. *Thank You, Yeshua.*

Out of the corner of his eyes, Thomas suddenly saw a long column of trucks filled with soldiers driving up on the left side of the crowd. *Oh God!*

"Please, remain calm and stay in the spot where you are. If you stay in your place, nothing is going to happen to you. I will talk to the officer in charge and find out why they are here," Thomas said. Trust in Yeshua, He will be with us."

Before the trucks reached the crowd, they stopped abruptly. Then, slowly and without explanation went back where they came from. When they were far away, praise songs broke out here and there as if directed by someone. They were picked up by the crowd and soon the singing sounded like a huge heavenly choir without a director.

Thomas stood riveted to the ground as he watched the holy spectacle. He knew the Lord had saved them somehow from being arrested, but couldn't imagine how. He raised his hands in praise as he joined in the singing. Then he walked up to his father and the two embraced.

"I am so sorry I didn't believe you before, son," Abraham cried. "Yeshua is God and I belong to Him." Suddenly he looked at Thomas with great sadness. "Your mother missed it. What is going to happen to her?"

At the dinner at the Prime Minister's home, no one could explain why the army had come and then turned back so un-expectantly.

"I still have connections in the government," Ibrahim Berger said, "let me call someone and ask them what happened."

He was very thoughtful when he got off the phone.

"This is what my source told me. The new prime minister had planned to arrest as many Christians as he could, that is why he allowed the meeting to proceed. Once everyone gathered, he ordered the troops to arrest as many as possible, but especially those who organized it. That means you, too, Thomas, you and your team. Here is where it gets weird, when the convoy got to the meeting place, they saw hundreds of heavily armed men standing at the edge of the crowd, pointing their weapons at them. Not wanting an all-out shooting war, they were ordered to turn around."

"You are kidding, we didn't have armed men there," Thomas said. And then his face took on a shine as he whispered, "They were angels, the Lord sent angels to protect His people."

Everyone sat in stunned silence, until Ibrahim said in awe, "This is not the first time in modern days this has happened. There is a documentary which tells of two Israeli soldiers who got lost behind enemy lines. Sure that they would be caught and put in a prison camp, they walked through enemy territory back to their unit, when a column of jeeps stopped in front of them. The two raised their arms in surrender and were astounded when the jeeps filled with soldiers turned around and fled. After they returned to their unit and took some of them prisoners, they asked them why they fled when there was only the two of them.

"Didn't you see the hundreds of large soldiers, armed with heavy weapons behind you?" they asked. "We had no chance against them."

(This is a true account from the Six Day war of June 1967 in Israel)

Chapter 36

The next day's headlines told of an astounding event at the meeting near Tel Aviv. UNKNOWN ARMED GUARDS AT CHRISTIAN MEETING. The team sat glued to the TV as they watched what had to have been angels. Yet when they saw the pictures of the meeting, no armed guards were visible anywhere. Rumors circulated that the officer in charge of the detail, who had ordered the convoy to turn back, was in trouble and suspected of being a Christian sympathizer. The reporters who had called in the footage of the guards, were ridiculed and couldn't explain why their presence hadn't showed up on the extensive video they had sent back.

Reports of many hundreds of people being healed made their way to Shalom Outreach, but were ignored by the press. In spite of that, it brought a large influx to the prayer room in the back of the clinic and countless invitations for Thomas to speak all over Israel.

The team was awed and grateful for God's blessings and protection. It gave everyone a boost in their faith that no matter what happened, Yeshua was looking out for the ministry in ways they could never have imagined.

Thomas took Abraham and Nana to several more meetings and it served to confirm their new faith as they watched countless more astounding miracles.

"How I wish Sylvia could have seen what I witnessed," Abraham said with sadness one day on their way back from one of them. "Even she would have believed in Yeshua." There was silence after he spoke. No one wanted to talk about the consequences of her unbelief, it was just too heartbreaking to think about. Thomas choked back tears as he wondered if God had not somehow been merciful and saved her in spite of what he had witnessed. The scripture came to him where it says there will be no tears in heaven. How could he not cry when he got there and not find his mother? Maye he would not remember her, but could anyone not remember their own mother?

It was a sad day when Abraham and Nana had to return to Philadelphia. Everyone somehow knew they would never see each other again until they were united in eternity. The hope of that prospect helped as Thomas said goodbye to his father and Nana at the airport.

"Find a good church, Dad," he said, "and learn more about Yeshua. Tell the people what you saw and heard over here and always be ready to share how you met your Meshiah."

"I will, son, trust me. It has been the most exciting and miraculous time of my life and I will do my best to tell about it wherever I go, even if people ridicule me like they did you."

"Tommy, my dear boy," Nana said, "you are a blessing not just to your father and I, but to our people. May the God of Abraham, Isaak and Jacob be with you in the difficult days ahead. I will be praying for you every day." She tried hard not to cry, but the tears came in abundance as she turned and walked through the gate without looking back.

Thomas stood still as a wave of sorrow washed over him. These two wonderful people were the only family he had left. He walked back to the car in a daze of pain. *Yeshua, it isn't always easy to serve You. It comes with a price. If it wasn't for Your promise of an eternity with You, I don't think I could pay it. Please, tell me if my mother is with You, it would make things easier to bear.* There was only silence in his heart.

As he drove back to Tiberias, the tears flowed freely, but they didn't wash away the pain of not only losing his mother, but Melissa and Helena as well.

The days that followed were filled with meetings and ministering to those who came to the clinic in search of Yeshua. In spite of increased crackdowns on churches and other religious organizations, Shalom Outreach was spared for some reason. Thomas had an inkling Rabbi Shamir was planning another scheme to shut it down, but in spite of putting out feelers among the locals, he couldn't find anything that could shed light on it.

It was on a clear, beautiful day in August, near the city of Jerusalem. Thomas had been invited to speak at a meeting of church leaders from many different churches and ministries. There were about two-hundred people there, mostly pastors, led by the head of the largest evangelical congregation in the area. It was a secret underground training seminar on how to survive persecution by the local religious authorities and was held in the gym of a large school with a Christian principle under the guise of a public teacher's training seminar. Several look-outs had been posted at all exits to alert the attendees to the presence of police or members of a volunteer organization formed to alert the local government to illegal Christian activities.

Thomas had not yet been asked to speak, when from behind the curtain of the stage, three men appeared with heavy weapons and fired into the crowd at will. It was clear, they were not Arabic, but Israelis, shouting in Hebrew, "Christians go home!" Thomas was hit by the first round and fell to the floor, unconscious. He never saw the many go down or heard the screams and cries of the wounded victims as the slaughter continued. He also never saw the many dead and dying all around him when the hail of bullets finally stopped, but laid very still, bleeding from a large wound in his chest.

Through a fog, he suddenly heard a familiar voice. "Take this one, I want him alive. He was vaguely aware he was being carried on a stretcher into an ambulance.

It was days later when he finally woke up in a strange bed inside what looked like a hospital room. He was hooked up to a monitor and tubes were coming out of his stomach. He was struggling to come fully awake. A woman stood by his bed, wrapping a blood pressure cuff around his arm. A burly man was standing by the window, holding a gun.

"He is awake," she said, "you can get the boss."

"Where am I?" Thomas managed to whisper. "What happened?"

The woman did not answer, but continued taking his vitals.

Soon the door opened and a short man with small, cold eyes looking from behind dark, horn-rimmed glasses walked in. He was bald and the many folds of fat made it look as if his head sat on his shoulders without a neck in between. His middle was round and sat on short legs, hidden by a long gray robe.

"Well, here is the preacher man. What do they say, physician, heal thyself?" he said in English with a high-pitched voice filled with sarcasm. I have waited a long time to get you, Thomas Peterson. Now that you belong to me, I will teach you what we do with people who come from America, thinking they can lead our people into pagan worship. You may be a Jew, but you are no Israelite. Since you read the Torah, you know what our God does with people who worship other gods. I am going to make sure you never have the chance to lead anyone else away from the God of Abraham, Isaak and Jacob."

"Who are you?" Thomas asked with difficulty.

"I am Paul Meinfeld, the Rabbi in charge of religious purity in Israel."

"Did you kill all those people at the meeting?"

"I ordered it done. The Christians need to be terminated like rats in order to cleanse our country in preparation for the coming Meshiah. And you are the biggest rat of them all. I will show you what it means to offend the living God with your heresy and make you wish you were never born." He was shaking with anger as he stood over Thomas, looking down on him with hate. "You will be sorry for ever setting foot into our land."

"Does the government in Tel Aviv know what you are doing?"

"Of course not. I thought the new Prime Minister was different, but he is as soft on foreigners as all the others before him. So I took matters in my own hands and eliminated most of the leaders of the churches in the area." He leaned over Thomas with a vicious smile. "Except you, you are different. I couldn't help but show you in a special way what it means to blaspheme the Lord Yehovah."

"I suppose it wouldn't do any good to tell you I am an American citizen?"

"As if that matters anymore. America has become weak and corrupt from within and is no threat to anyone. Besides, no one knows where you are. It was a secret meeting and it shall remain that way, because the bodies have been removed without a trace left behind. They can always tell their people the rapture has occurred and they were left behind by their false god."

"How many died?"

"All of them."

Two weeks went by and Thomas recovered from his injury. He was never allowed to venture outside or see anyone other than the nurse and the guard with the gun. Both were ordered not to speak to him. At night he was left alone in his room until morning when they returned.

The days ran one into another and he lost track of time. His body became stronger, but his mind was traumatized by the scene he had seen before he was shot. The thought that two hundred pastors and leaders had died, haunted him day and night and he felt guilty that he was still alive. *Take me home, Yeshua to be with Melissa and Helena. This feels like 'The Tombs', I am rotting away in this isolation. I still love You, Lord and want to continue to serve You. What good am I sitting in this jail?*

As the days past, he went through despair, and deep feelings of abandonment by Yeshua, the team and anyone else he could think of. The thought of being useless and sick, hidden away in some sort of prison, made him feel frustrated and angry. The thought of all the people who would not hear the Gospel and turn to Yeshua, caused him to question why the Lord would allow this to happen.

How can You let all those pastors die, when they are the ones to hold Your church together? Why would You allow Your enemies to triumph by killing the very people who spread the Gospel? I don't understand Your ways, Yeshua, I never have.

"My ways are not your ways, Thomas, and My thoughts are not your thoughts. (Isaiah 55:8)

I know, Lord, but I would like to understand Your ways, it would make it easier for me to deal with what is happening to me right now. I don't mind dying, Lord, but I do mind this waste of precious time with me doing nothing, when I could be about Your business.

It feels like I am back in 'The Tombs', helpless, angry and wasting away. For some reason, after all that time, my wound is getting infected. You could heal me and get me out of here like you did with the Apostle Paul. Could you maybe spare one angel to do that?

He chuckled in spite of his dire situation, with no expectation the Lord would answer his prayer.

His wound did get infected and he slipped into a high fever, followed by delirium. Days passed until he finally recovered enough to ask for water. The woman gave it to him without a word and then turned to the guard,

"I think he is going to make it. What a shame. We are here to help him to recover just so they can kill him." She spoke Hebrew and Thomas understood, since he had learned to speak it pretty well by now.

The days passed and Thomas gained his strength back slowly. He was too weak to get out of bed, when Paul Meinfeld arrived with two men. They stood and looked down at him with a strange look.

"You think he is ready?" Meinfeld asked the men.

"I am sure he is. Either way, it won't take long to do it."

"Remember, I want him to suffer for a long time, you do know how to do that, right?" The fat little man smiled a satisfied smile as he looked at Thomas. "I finally get to show you how weak and miserable you really are, Preacher."

"What are you going to do?" Thomas asked, fear filling his heart.

"We are going to have some fun with you." He turned to the men. "Tomorrow we start. Be here early in the morning."

With that they left.

Thomas stared out of the window. *Yeshua, help me. They are going to torture me, I know it. I am not strong enough and not really good with pain. I know I will say anything and probably deny You, Lord. Please don't believe me when I do, I won't mean it. I love you and give my life to you right now. Take it by letting them kill me, just don't allow them to torture me.* Thomas was shaking with fear.

As the sun set on the horizon, he knew it would be the last time he saw it and prayed out loud,

"I am ready, Lord to give my life for You. I have served You as faithfully as I know how and submit to Your will. Whatever happens, it is alright; into Your hands I put my body, soul and spirit." He suddenly felt joy rising up within him and he started to sing and worship God. It was so loud, the guard came in and told him to be quiet, but he continued.

"How can you be so happy when you know they are going to torture you tomorrow," he finally asked Thomas.

"Because I believe in the living God who sent His Son Yeshua to die for my sin. You can also believe in him. Come, sit here and I will tell you how I know this."

The man hesitated and then sat down by the bed.

"I have nothing else to do, so go ahead."

Thomas sat up and proceeded to tell him about his journey into the past. When he was finished, he asked," Do you want to accept Yeshua?"

"I do, because I am sickened by what we are doing here. But there is no way this Yeshua will ever forgive me for all the horrible things I have done in this job."

"He came for sinners, and forgave even those who killed Him. And He will forgive you and set you free from this life you lead."

"What must I do?"

Thomas prayed for him and the man fell to his knees and asked Yeshua to come into his life.

"What is your name?"

"I am Saul."

"From this day on you shall be called Paul," Thomas said. "Go in peace, the Lord has a great work for you to do before He returns."

After that, Thomas was exhausted and went sleep almost instantly.

It felt like it had only been a minute, when a Being in brilliant white garments touched him on the shoulder.

"Thomas, get up, put on your clothes and follow me."

Thomas did as he was told and felt no weakness or pain. When he was dressed, the angel raised his hand toward the door and it opened by itself. They walked through a narrow hallway to the front door. It opened silently and they stepped out into a street, lined with houses on both sides. The angel put something in his hand and vanished. Thomas looked down and saw it was his cell phone and smiled. *That's amazing, Lord, You are high tech.*

Chapter 37

"Somehow it's astounding to me the Lord would know about cell phones," Leona said. "I know it's crazy, but I can't imagine angels dealing with technology."

The others laughed.

"That's exactly what I thought when he handed it to me," Thomas said, joining in the fun.

"He should have just beamed you back here like on Star Trek," Caleb laughed. "That would have been so 21st century."

"We are just glad you are back, Thomas," Bob added and reached over to pat him on the shoulder. "That was a close call."

"Was anything ever reported on the massacre in Jerusalem?" Thomas asked.

"We have not heard much about it," Meta said. "There has been talk in the Christian churches, but since no bodies have been found and this incident only involves Christians, the press is not interested. The police are doing their best, but since there is no evidence of foul play other than Thomas' words, they are stuck with the investigation. They checked out the house and the gym, but found nothing to indicate a massacre."

"I have a feeling they have been directed to find nothing," Thomas said. "There is no way Paul Meinfeld could have cleaned the place up enough for forensics not to find evidence of blood on the floor of the gym. Someone is pulling the strings and I have a feeling it is the Rabbi Shamir, who is a good friend."

Thomas had returned three days ago. Bob checked him out thoroughly. His scar was quite visible and poorly stitched up, but other than that, he seemed to be healthy, without any other signs he had ever been wounded.

"You have been through quite an ordeal," he told Thomas and I want you to rest for a few days before picking up your hectic schedule again," he added. "There are dozens of invitations to speak, but I think you should not accept any of them, it is too dangerous."

"Bob, I wasn't just set free by an angel to sit around and play it safe," Thomas said calmly. "I have been healed and feel fine. I will do what the Lord has set out for me to do and that is that. Apparently He has my safety very well under control and won't let anything happen to me before my time."

"You haven't heard the latest on the world front." Bob shifted uneasy in his chair. "The Russians have moved thousands of troops into Syria. They have also sold fighter planes, tanks and weapons to Iran, promising they will stand with their friends against any enemy, be it America or Israel in case of a nuclear attack. What that means is, Israel is alone and extremely vulnerable to be overrun by Syrian and Russian troops using modern weapons. We all know, there is no way this tiny country has the kind of firepower or strength to defend itself in case of an all-out attack by Russia or Syria."

"They don't need a reason to do it either, just Israel being there is enough," Caleb said, fear showing in his voice. "And I have no doubt it is going to happen," he added.

"All the more reason to get on with our work," Thomas said with confidence. "Leona, schedule me for every speaking request that comes in. We have no time to lose."

Weeks went by and Thomas held countless meetings accompanied by miracles, signs and wonders. The churches, in spite of the terrible loss of their Pastors, continued to grow and even flourish, proving to everyone again that God's purpose cannot be stopped or even slowed down. It had become dangerous to profess to be a Christian, not just in Israel, but across many of the countries of the world. Because of the UN leader, Mohamed Abdul Musharak, a professing Muslim, Islam was on the rise everywhere. To the world, theirs was a religion of peace and harmony, which brought order out of the recent chaos. It clearly showed, according to Musharak, how society should be controlled by using Sharia law and tolerating only Allah as god. The new order was recommended by him to be seen as the new world religion to bring peace and security for everyone who embraced it.

While Jesus was not denied, He was relegated to being a historical figure or a minor prophet far below in status of Mohamed. Many church buildings had been converted into mosques all over the world, especially the beautiful cathedrals in Europe.

The fashion industry actually promoted wearing the hajib for women to be worn on especially formal occasions. It soon became all the rage and before anyone noticed, it was expected to be worn to all official UN and other government functions. Not to wear it, gave rise to suspicions of being a Christian.

Israel, while opened to peace plans by Musharak, never tolerated Islam, but remained faithful to the God of Abraham, Isaak and Jacob. Yet out of fear of offending Iran or Syria, it was not, however willing to persecute it like it did Christianity. In Jerusalem, a boiling pot of the three major religions of the world, on the surface, the time of the Christians seemed to have come to an end. With the financial help of Jews from all over the world, the foundation was laid for a new Temple, right next to the Dome of the Rock. It was an uneasy alliance between Jews and Muslims, but with the help of Musharak, the Muslim community tolerated the construction of a Jewish Temple with very little opposition. The many Christian churches, however, were either torn down or turned into synagogues or mosques, with the result, all vestiges of Jesus were eradicated in the city by the religious leaders. The Rabbi Shamir had risen among their rank and was seen as one of the major figures in this effort.

One good thing about that was, the good Rabbi had no time to interfere with Shalom Outreach or the clinic, since he had moved to Jerusalem. In spite of the changing, dangerous environment, the ministry was somehow allowed to continue unhindered. Thomas spent most of his time traveling to the many underground congregations throughout Israel, leading thousands to the Lord in the process. And so it happened, that, while Christianity had vanished on the surface, it was growing and thriving unnoticed in spite of all efforts to eradicate it in the land of Israel.

Thomas was amazed at how Yeshua was fulfilling His words to reach out to His people before His return. Each day, he was overcome with gratitude to have been chosen to play a part in His plan and only wished, Melissa and Helena could have been here with him.

Chapter 38

It was mid-afternoon. The clinic was still filled with patients. Thomas had decided to stay and do several surgeries, since Bob had been overloaded with work and asked him to take a few days to catch up. He enjoyed his work and had just finished his third case, when a horrendous boom shook the walls of the clinic. Several others followed. He could hear screams from the waiting room and rushed out to see what had happened, but there was no damage or any sign the explosions had occurred near Shalom Outreach.

People were running outside in terror and Thomas followed them to see what had happened. Several large fires could be seen coming from the downtown area as heavy, black smoke rose into the sky.

"It's the bomb!" someone screamed. "Iran threw the bomb!" From the way the smoke rose up, it did not look like the mushroom cloud of an atomic bomb, Thomas decided. Palestinians had probably decided to attack the business district of Tiberias with several large rockets and for some reason they had penetrated the tight Israeli defense system. Thomas hurried back inside and instructed everyone to be ready for casualties.

Soon, sirens were heard coming closer and the wounded filled the waiting room to capacity.

"Am I ever glad I stayed here today," Thomas said to Bob as each stood over their seriously wounded patient on the operating table.

"You have no idea how glad I am," Bob answered. "I could not have handled all this."

They worked tirelessly into the evening and were ready to call it a day, when they heard shouting coming from the waiting area.

"You will let me through. I must speak to Dr. Peterson!" The voice sounded familiar, but Thomas couldn't quite place it. He went to where it came from and stood face to face with the Rabbi Shamir. His mind was instantly flooded with thoughts of anger, hate and feelings of such intense fury, it took his breath away. Here was the man who had killed his Melissa and little Helena and probably was involved with ordering the killing of the two hundred pastors, plus many hundreds of believers across Israel.

Thomas had everything he could do not to put his hands around the man's throat and strangle him.

"You have to help him, Doctor, it's my son, he is dying. Please, pray for him." The Rabbi was sobbing and screaming at the same time. "He is my only son, please, ask your Yeshua to heal him. Please!" He had fallen on his knees before Thomas, with his hands grabbing his surgical garb.

Thomas looked at the man with hatred in his eyes and wanted to say, *you murderer, how dare you come to me to help your son. You killed my wife and child in cold blood, just so I will leave. I hope your son dies!* The hatred in his heart choked him as he stared at the pathetic figure on the ground.

At that moment the ambulance attendance brought in a patient on a stretcher. Thomas looked at the young man, a boy of about sixteen, his face covered in blood with a large gash on his head. But it was the chest wound that caught his eyes. It was a huge, open wound with pieces of shrapnel sticking out everywhere. His medical training took over and he waved to the attendance to take the boy into surgery.

"I will try to fix this, but it doesn't look good. He seems to have lost a lot of blood and I will have to see if any vital internal organs are damaged." He looked at Rabbi Shamir and said in an icy tone, "You wait here and think about what it is you are asking me to do in spite of what you have done to me."

It turned out to be a grueling, five-hour surgery. By the time Thomas and Bob were done, the boy barely hung on to life.

"There is no way he is going to survive this," Bob said.

"I have done all I can. It serves the good Rabbi right to know what it feels like to lose your only child." Thomas' voice was cold and hard. "For the life of me, I can't say I feel sorry for him," he added on his way to the waiting room.

Rabbi Shamir was sitting there, his head in his hands, with his shoulders hunched over in abject sorrow. When he saw Thomas walk in, he slid off the chair and fell on his knees.

"I know I have killed your wife and child and many others in my zeal to serve the Lord. I am nothing but a horrible murderer who deserves no mercy. Please forgive me, Dr. Peterson. I beg you to ask Yeshua to heal my son. You have always said He forgives even the worst of sinners and I am one of them. There is nothing I can do or say to change that. Yeshua, forgive me, I am not worthy to even say Your name." He sobbed and his body shook with such intensity, Thomas thought he was going to collapse.

Just as he opened his mouth to tell this terrible man how he hated him and hoped his son should die to make up for what he had done, a vision of his life in 'The Tombs" appeared before his eyes with such clarity, it made him reel. In horror he watched himself brutally kill the man who ruled the Tombs, in agony he saw as he poured poison into the young woman's mouth to abort his own baby; and then, after she died, discard her body like trash. His stomach lurched as he watched himself mistreat the countless sick and dying victims of leprosy, stealing from them and making them pay for every morsel of food.

But that wasn't the worst. He re-lived the moment when, close to death, he made it to Yeshua, saying almost the same words with the same shame as the Rabbi Shamir had just cried out to him, begging to be forgiven and healed. *Oh God!*

In an instant, his anger, hatred and un-forgiveness melted away and a deep sense of shame took their place. *Forgive me, Yeshua, how could I forget even for an instant that I am no better than this poor man, finally facing his sins in Your presence.*

Thomas reached down and lifted Rabbi Shamir up to stand before him and looked at him with eyes filled with compassion and love.

"You and I are one of a kind, Rabbi. I have been where you are and have done the same evil things you have. I have no right to hold a grudge against you, because Yeshua has forgiven me and so shall I. He is the One who will heal your son, not me. He is the One who will save your soul and give you eternal life if you turn your heart over to Him. His sacrifice on the cross two thousand years ago made it possible for you to become His child in spite of your sins, for His love and mercy triumphs over judgment."

Rabbi Shamir stared at Thomas in shock.

"How can you forgive me for what I have done? How can Yeshua forgive me and love me in spite of my sins?"

"There was a man called Saul of Tarsus in Yeshua's time, Thomas said. "He also persecuted the early Christian church like you are and had many of them killed or tortured. Instead of condemning him, Yeshua appeared to him on the way to Damascus, knocked him off a donkey and asked, "Saul, Saul why do you persecute me?"

"Who are you, Lord?" Saul asked.

"I am Yeshua, whom you are persecuting," he replied. "Now get up and go into the city, and you will be told what you must do." (Acts 9:4-6)

"He does not only forgive you, but wants you as His beloved son to be with Him for all eternity. That is why He came to the people of Israel and yet they rejected Him. Do not reject Him today, Rabbi, but accept Him into your heart and become a Christian. And like the man Saul, who became the Apostle Paul and wrote two-thirds of the New Testament, you will also be used greatly in the days to come."

"I am not worthy, Dr. Peterson."

"None of us is, for all have sinned and fallen short of the Glory of God as it says in His Word. (Romans 3:23) The wonderful thing about Yeshua is that He came for the sinners and not the righteous." Thomas smiled at him. "And you will have to admit, both of us fit that category perfectly."

"Tell me what to do to become one of His followers, Dr. Peterson," Yitzhak Shamir said.

"Please, call me Thomas, if we are going to be brothers," he said as he took the Rabbi's hand.

"Then you must call me Yitz, all my friends do."

After they prayed together, Thomas took Yitz by the hand and led him to the recovery room, where his son Jacob rested in a deep sleep from the medication.

"He will wake up soon and be in much pain," Thomas said. "I do not know if he will survive this, but I am doing all I can."

"No, you're not, Thomas."

"What are you saying?"

"I want you to pray for him. If I had wanted him to have surgery, I would have taken him to the hospital in Tiberias. Instead, I knew Yeshua was the only one who could heal him, because I was certain, without it, my Jacob is going to die." Yitz sounded adamant. "We must pray right now, please."

Thomas walked up to the bed and took Jacob's hand and asked Yeshua to touch him. After that the two men sat for a long time as Thomas told his new brother about his journey into the past. Thomas was certain, Yitzhak Shamir, the Rabbi who persecuted the Christians in the same way the Apostle Paul did, would become their greatest ally and protector in the days to come.

The two sat by Jacob's all night, talking about what the Torah says about the Meshiah, until finally, at four in the morning, they both fell asleep, sitting in their chairs.

It was six o'clock when the nurse walked in and woke them up. Jacob was sitting up and smiled at his father.

"I am feeling much better," he said as he started to get out of bed.

"No, no, young man, you just had surgery," the nurse said. "I can't let you get up yet until Dr. Peterson says so."

"I think it is alright, Kelly," Thomas said with a tired smile. "The great Physician has done what I could have never accomplished with my surgery." Thomas got up and checked his wound. It was dry, clean and showed no signs of infection. "How do you feel, Jacob?"

"I feel great. I am sure I can go home soon, can't I?"

"I am sure you can, what do you think, Yitz?"

"I think you are right, Thomas. Yeshua has given me back my son." He was crying.

"Father, what are you saying?"

"You were dying, son, so I brought you here for Dr. Peterson to pray for you."

"But you hate him and all the other Christians who believe in Yeshua. How is it that you did not take me to the hospital in Tiberias?"

"Because you were too sick and would have died without Yeshua healing you," his father said. "I have since given my life over to the Meshiah and will serve Him for the rest of my days."

"Father, you have become a Christian?" Jacob was stunned. "You hate Christians."

"I know, but the Lord has forgiven me and I have turned my heart over to Him. If He will have me, I will serve Him, wherever He wants, even if I lose my position and my life in the process."

Jacob leaned back, trying to understand what he had just heard.

"What does this mean, father?"

"It means, I will no longer be a Rabbi, but a hated Christian, Jacob.

"What is our family going to say?"

"I don't know, I will try to explain it to them as best I can and hope they will understand and not turn me in to the authorities."

Chapter 39

The rocket attacks had destroyed much of downtown Tiberias. The population was scared and looking for someone to blame. And so their anger turned toward the Christians. It became too dangerous for any member of the team to go out, even to get groceries. Petra had to hire a local person to buy food and whatever else was needed. They were literally prisoners inside the mission.

Several days later, it started out as a shouting match outside the front door of the clinic, with a group of teenagers demanding the Americans go home. The crowd grew larger each day, until the first rock was thrown into one of the windows of the clinic. "Yankees, go home!" From then on, gangs of Jewish youths, Palestinians and Muslim young men, bombarded Shalom Outreach with stones and rotten fruit almost daily. It was not long, until no one dared come to the clinic for fear of being killed.

When Caleb called the police, they said they could do nothing since there were too many riots and shootings in the bombed streets of Tiberias. Commerce had come to a halt and many people were unemployed. This added to the volatile situation and promoted criminal gangs to flourish, stealing, breaking into homes and roaming the city.

"We have to leave," Caleb said one morning. "It is too dangerous to go anywhere for any of us." They were sitting around the breakfast table.

"There are no more church gatherings of any kind," Thomas said. "The churches have stopped meeting and are now holding small services in different homes every week for fear of being raided and killed. Yitz called yesterday and confirmed that there are plans of closing down Shalom Outreach any day now. He suggested we get out as soon as possible before all of us get arrested. When I asked him if it was safer in Haifa or Tel Aviv, he said maybe for now, but the government is cracking down on dissidents as they call us now. Christians everywhere are being arrested and put into camps north of Kfar Nahum. The conditions in them are deplorable from what he has heard."

"The Rabbi has been instrumental in helping many escape or go underground since his conversion," Meta said. "I talked to somebody in the church I used to go to and she said, he has organized a network of Christians in towns and cities all over Israel who take in people on the run."

"I always knew the Lord had a big job for him to do," Thomas said as he took a piece of bread. "He will be a powerful witness and lead many to the Lord."

While he was still talking, a knock came from the front door.

"I will go answer it," Caleb said in a shaky voice. "We may be too late."

"Are you in charge of Shalom Outreach?" Caleb looked into the cold eyes of a policeman. Three others stood behind him, weapons drawn.

"Yes, I am. What is wrong, officers?" he asked in a trembling voice.

"You and your team are under arrest for belonging to a group of foreign dissidents. All of you will come with us to the station to be processed and taken to the camp east of here."

"We have done nothing wrong, why are you arresting us?"

"I am not here to argue with you, but to arrest you. Do not give us any trouble, these officers behind me don't mind shooting Christians."

Caleb turned around and looked at the others in a helpless gesture.

"Are we allowed to pack some things" Thomas asked.

"Well, look who we have here, the major troublemaker, Dr. Thomas Peterson himself," the officer said. "No, you may not take anything, just get into the van and don't give us any trouble."

It was a short ride to the police station. Thomas looked at the group. They had been together for several years and they were his family. There was Caleb, Bob, Meta, Karl, Leona, Mikail, Petra and Paul, all of them as dear to him as brothers and sisters.

"What do you think is going to happen to us, Caleb," Petra asked in her heavy Russian accent. I didn't think I would ever have to go through this again when I came to Israel."

"I don't know. Maybe they will let us go."

"Let's remember we belong to the Lord," Bob said. "He knows what's happening and will be with us wherever we are going. Do not give in to fear, there is nothing they can do except kill our bodies, but not our faith. As Christians we have the hope of eternal life and as martyrs we get the crown of glory. What an honor it is to suffer for the Lord's sake."

"Yeshua told the disciples while I was there," Thomas said into the silence, "But they will lay hands on you and persecute you. They will deliver you to the synagogues and prisons, and you will be brought before kings and governors, and all on account of my name." (Luke 21:12)

"I am still scared," Leona whispered.

"So am I," Meta said defiantly, "but I will not ever let them see that. "I came here to Israel, because my family disowned me when I became a Christian. You are my family and you and I will stick together until the end." She looked around at everybody with a brave smile. "We have each other, but what's more, we have Yeshua." She took Petra's hand in hers on one side and Bob's on the other. When everyone had joined the circle, she said, "Let's pray together before we get there."

"Yeshua, we are all scared, but You tell us not to fear. That is easy for You to say, Lord. Unless You give us courage, strength and perseverance to face what is to come, we can't make it. We put our lives into Your hands and ask You to be with us when we get to the camp. Help us to continue the work of helping the poor and minister to those who need You, with the help of Your Holy Spirit. Open the door for us so that we might be a light in the darkness."

It was at that moment the van stopped.

Thomas remembered the area where the camp was from his dream. Yeshua liked to go there when He wanted to be alone and pray. Except then it didn't have a dozen rows of low, grey, unfinished cement block buildings, surrounded by a barbed wire fence.

"What is the difference between this and the camps at Auschwitz?" Meta whispered when they waited for the wide, wooden gate to open for their bus to drive through.

How glad I am Melissa and Helena are with You, Yeshua, he thought. *I don't think I could bear them in here. And yet how upset*

I was when You took them home. Your ways are always good and right.

The bus slowly drove inside the compound and stopped in front of a what seemed to be the main house.

"Everybody out! Women to the left and men to the right."

Thomas looked over to where Meta, Leona and Petra stood as a female guard took them inside the building.

"I sure hope they treat them well," Bob said. "This is insane, how can they treat us like dissidents, we have done nothing but help these people and look at the thanks we get."

"They can't possibly put all the Christians in Israel in concentration camps. There are millions of them," Caleb said. "This really does remind me of what Hitler did to the Jews. How ironic that they haven't learned anything from that horrible time and now committing the same insanity. Will man never learn from past sins?"

"You will follow me," a guard shouted at their group. "No talking."

They were led to a building with the letter C on it. The guard opened the door and waved them to step inside.

"Find a bunk and wait for further instructions."

It was dark inside with only a little bit of daylight coming through the small windows with milky glass on them so they could not see out. Thomas looked at the rows of bunk beds lining both sides of the long room. They each had one blanket and a pillow on them.

"I like to sleep up top," Caleb said and climbed up on top of one of them. "That way I can see what is happening."

"I will take the one under you," Bob said. "I am not one for climbing up and down at my age."

"I think I will take one below, it feels safer somehow," Karl said. "I don't think the flimsy bed could hold my weight anyway."

The guard stood silently as they chose their spot. When everyone sat down on their beds, he stepped closer to where Thomas sat.

"It seems I can't get away from being your guard," Dr. Peterson.

"Paul! Is it you?" Thomas jumped up and they hugged. "This is the guard that kept watch on me when I was shot in Tel Aviv," he said to the others. “His name was Saul until I led him to the Lord, now it is Paul.”

Paul looked around carefully and put his finger on his mouth.

“Please, not so loud, no one knows I am a Christian. I volunteered for this job so I can help those who come here. I was sure, you and your team would end up here.”

“Are they arresting all the Christians?” Thomas asked.

“No, just pastors and other leaders. They figure, if they get rid of the Christian leadership, the churches will cease to exist,” Paul said.

“Who set all this up?” Caleb asked. “I had never heard of this camp. Is this the only one or are there others across Israel?”

“There are three more. All of them were set up by the Rabbi Shamir and his friends. He is the worst of them all from what I hear.”

Thomas looked at the others, hoping they would not say anything about his conversion.

“Does he ever come here to visit?” Thomas asked.

“As a matter of fact he is scheduled for tomorrow. He didn’t say what it is all about, but since he is in charge of this, he doesn’t have to, does he?” Paul said with disdain. “Please, don’t let on that you know me or that I am one of you, especially with the Rabbi coming. They would kill me if they knew. This way I can make it easier on the inmates here. There are many other guards, but none of them are Christians as far as I know. I have to be very careful.”

“We will keep your secret, Paul. It is just good to know we have one person in here who is on our side.” Thomas sat back down on his bunk. “How long are they going to keep us here, Paul, do you know?”

“I don’t have any idea. I am a low ranking guard and nobody tells me anything. Let me show you where the facilities are and give you some of the rules of this place. There is no electricity in here, so lights are out when the sun goes down. You will be allowed to go outside twice a day when I or the other guards let you. Food is brought to the door in the morning and the evening. There is no lunch. For water, there is a faucet in the bathroom, that’s where you get your drinking water. There is one shower for everyone with only cold water. There are no toothbrushes or toothpaste.

You will find a cup, a plate, a fork and a spoon over at the end of this room on a shelf. Please clean them under running water each time you use them. There are prison clothes for you to wear also on that shelf. They will be washed twice a month."

Paul looked apologetically at Thomas.

"I am sorry, it isn't much, but there is nothing I can do to change anything. What I can do is, sneak some food in or maybe get some toothbrushes or anything you might need. I have to be extremely careful about not getting caught. They say the Rabbi has no mercy for anyone who goes against his rules."

"What are we expected to do all day?" Karl asked.

"You will join a work crew to keep the compound clean, haul the trash and do other manual jobs. The women will be expected to do the cooking and wash and such things. It is a self-sustaining camp with very little contact to the outside world."

"Who else is housed here?" Thomas asked.

"They will be here by later this afternoon. I kept them working outside so I could talk to you. Please don't tell them about me, because there might be some who would give me up in order to gain favor. Trust no one in here, talk to no one about your faith unless you are absolutely sure they are believers. If you get caught talking about Yeshua, you will be punished severely."

"How long do you think they will keep us in here, Paul," Bob asked.

"I have no idea. Some people have been here a long time, while others were picked up and taken away after a few days. I have no idea where they went or what happened to them."

After Paul left, the team sat on the side of their beds, trying to make sense what happened.

"This is not exactly what I thought would ever happen to us," Caleb said into the silence. "Does this mean the Lord is done with us and we just sit in this horrible camp for the rest of our lives?"

"Now listen, everyone," Bob stood in front of them as he spoke. "Most of the Apostles ended up in prison and in the end were killed for their faith. Did we really think it wasn't going to happen to us? Remember, we could have all gone home, but chose to stay." He looked at the men and continued. "The Lord has not forgotten us, but has made sure we are in the exact place we are supposed to be. With the countless miracles he has performed during the last few years, we are not going to give in to despair or hopelessness. He is in charge of our lives and we will proclaim His love and mercy, even in this place. There will be many who have lost faith or are depressed and worried about being here or have loved ones left behind. We were sent to Israel for a purpose and that purpose has not ended. As a matter of fact, I am quite certain it has just begun. These are the last days and the time is short for us to gather in the harvest, whether at Shalom Outreach or in this place. Our job is not done until either the Lord returns or we are called home by Him. We are and will be in His service until the end, where those in need can turn to, to find their Meshiah."

Chapter 40

There was frantic activity in the camp. The Rabbi Shamir was coming in the afternoon. All prisoners were put into groups to clean the outside and inside of the buildings. Thomas and his team were told to clean the bathroom, sweep the floors and make sure every bed was made with military precision.

"Nothing like cleaning the toilet to keep you humble," Caleb grumbled while he was scrubbing the shower.

"I am sure this is not the worst thing that can happen to us in this place," Bob said with a chuckle.

"Still, I wonder if Yeshua ever cleaned anything. The Word says He was tempted in every way as we are, but I doubt He ever wanted to do women's work." Caleb sounded disgusted.

"Listen to you, hotshot; too good to do the low jobs, hey?" It was Karl. "I had to help my mother every Saturday with the cleaning since she worked full time. It didn't hurt me then and it doesn't hurt you now. And where is it written that this is women's work? A little male chauvinistic, are we?"

The others laughed when Caleb grumbled something to himself, his head stuck in the shower.

Thomas wondered if the Rabbi had forgotten what happened and gone back to his old ways of persecuting Christians. It sure looked like it. He overheard the guards talking how tough he was and even cruel. On the other hand, they probably had not seen him since the incident with his son happened and could be talking about his behavior before that. It would be interesting. Apparently, he had kept his conversion a secret, if it really happened.

At around one o'clock the big wooden doors to the compound opened and three cars slowly drove up to the main house. Thomas stood just outside his building and watched. The Rabbi slowly got out of the car and looked around for a long time. There was no chance he could have seen Thomas, because he was too far away. Before Thomas could see more, he was told by a guard to get inside and not show his face again. It was two hours later, the door of their barracks opened and Rabbi Shamir entered.

"This is a special prisoner, I want to talk to him in private," he said to the guard in a harsh tone. "Take the others out and leave us until I call you." He waited until the door closed behind the last guard and turned around with a big smile,

"Thomas, my dear friend, how are you?"

"You're kidding right?" Thomas sounded angry. "How do you think I am since you probably put all of us here."

"Please, do not be upset, it was the only way I could protect you and your team from being killed by a group of zealots, who blame you for the large number of Christians in Israel. Since I have accepted the Meshiah, I am no longer one of them in spirit and they realize something changed. They just don't know what. We had planned quite a while ago to have you killed. To prevent that, I had to move mountains to get you put into this camp to save your life. I will do everything I can to allow you to work as a doctor here. Just be careful what you say about Yeshua or your beliefs or they will punish you severely. You are their prize catch and they will watch you carefully. At this point I am limited as to what I can do to help you."

"There is a guard here named Saul. He is a Christian. I know, because I led him to the Lord. Can you protect him if he is found out helping us?" Thomas asked.

"No, I am so closely watched, it would give me away. Just talking to you like this will be reported back; and in spite of my high rank in the religious community, suspicion is running high at my recent behavior." Yitz sighed, "Let's face it, I am the one who designed these camps and the rules they are run by, I cannot undo the monster I have helped to create; and have no doubt that one day I will be in here as one of you."

They hugged and Yitz left, his shoulder hunched over in shame and sadness.

A week later, Thomas was called into the main office by Paul.

"Something is up, Thomas, I don't know what it is, but I don't think it's bad."

"I think I know what it is, they are going to make me the doctor here at the camp. That's great, because then I can talk to many people without it being suspicious." Thomas sounded upbeat.

"You are the famous Dr. Peterson?" The woman was in her forties, her gray hair hanging in over her eyes in ringlets. Her rough, square face was lined with deep wrinkles and her small, blue eyes looked at Thomas with cynicism. "We are going to teach you that being a rich American or a famous Doctor is not going to help you in here. To us you are a despised Christian who polluted our country with your heresies and lies." She leaned over her desk towards him. "I will make sure you pay for what you did in spite of Rabbi Shamir's orders to treat you nice, because you are going to help treat the prisoners. I don't care if they die when they get sick, they deserve it, but I have to follow orders. Just make sure you don't talk about this cursed Yeshua or I will make you sorry." She looked at Paul. "Take him to the infirmary and watch him. For some reason the Rabbi has picked you for the job. I don't understand why, but once again, I have to follow orders."

Paul grabbed Thomas roughly by the arm.

"Let's go, pig."

Once they were outside and out of earshot, he apologized.

"I'm sorry, Thomas, but I have to talk like that in order to be able to stay with you. I will try hard to protect you from getting into trouble, but I can't promise anything. Just don't get offended when I talk bad to you or treat you unkind, it helps to keeps me and you safe."

"Don't worry about it, Paul, I understand."

The infirmary was a small building to the side of the main office, about fifty feet away. An older woman stood in front of a cabinet filled with medications.

"I am Rachel Weiler, Dr. Peterson. I am a nurse and have been ordered to help you."

"Are you a prisoner?" Thomas asked.

"Yes."

"Then you must be a Christian?"

"I am not."

"I see. Well, everybody knows I am one, so let's all relax. We are going to be working together, Rachel, so try to understand that I will do a lot more than treat illnesses, but minister to the soul and the spirit as well."

"Dr. Peterson, I realize who you are, but have no intentions to be killed because you want to play the hero. I left behind a husband, children and grandchildren and will obey the rules, so I can go home. I worked in the hospital and was overheard talking to another nurse about this blasted Yeshua as she tried to convert me. She was one of the leaders of a church and the authorities thought I was with her. It didn't do any good for me to deny it and so they put me in here. I hate Christians and will turn you in in a flash if you go around preaching. Once is enough, I don't want to be blamed for listening to one of you heretics again and be flogged."

"Flogged? Are you telling me they beat people here?" Thomas looked at Paul.

"They do if you don't listen to this good woman and keep your mouth shut about your religious beliefs. There is a pole in the center of the camp with chains to hold your arms up while they beat you. I will not hesitate to string you up and let you know what it means to offend the living God of Israel." Paul turned to Rachel. "I will see to it that someone finds out that you are innocent. Until then, don't make any trouble. The people here need a doctor and you don't need to make anyone mad if they don't believe what you tell them at the main office. Come to me first and I will pass on what you tell me if this guy does anything wrong, understood?"

"That sounds good to me, all I want is to get out of here."

Thomas smiled on the inside. Paul was a lot smarter than he gave him credit for.

"How about letting me check things out what we have in the way of medicines and equipment, nurse."

"There isn't much and what we do have, is old. I know, because it came from one of the hospitals in Haifa and is stuff they replaced several years ago and had it in a storage facility," Rachel said. "There are no surgical supplies, no anesthesia or anything else, but a few outdated medications, bandages and other things for simple injuries or complaints. Anyone getting real sick in here is out of luck or maybe, if they are lucky, will be transferred to a hospital."

"Is it just me or does this whole thing sound familiar? Auschwitz comes to mind," Thomas' voice was dripping with sarcasm. "It boggles the mind to realize that the Jews, who suffered so horribly under Hitler because of their faith, design a similar place in order to do the same thing to others."

Rachel and Paul looked at him with surprise.

"That has never occurred to me," Rachel said. "It is a sobering thought."

The rest of the day was spent in arranging the infirmary. Thomas noticed, she treated him with a little less animosity after his last remark. Paul remained quiet.

When Thomas returned to his building, he was in a confident mood.

"I think I found a way to reach out to those in need," he whispered to the others, careful not to be heard by those who filled the rest of the spaces. "With Paul to watch over me, I will be able to minister in spite of the nurse who hates Christians. The Lord is here; I can sense He is watching over us."

"We worked the grounds detail today," Bob grumbled, "I never thought I would have to do that."

"Now who is complaining," Caleb grinned. "I can't say I like it any better than scrubbing the shower."

"How is your guard treating you?" Thomas asked.

"It is a guy from Tel Aviv, totally occupied by railing against Christians," Paul said in his quiet way. "I'm afraid he is looking for a reason to punish us. From what I heard, his mother and sisters accepted Yeshua and fled to Jerusalem. He hasn't heard from them since." He turned to Thomas. "He blames you, since they became Christians at one of your meeting."

"You are Dr. Peterson," a voice said from behind. "I am John Buchwald, a youth pastor from a church near Haifa. I have heard you many times at your meetings." He was a young, good looking man with thick, dark hair and facial features that looked very Jewish. He wore the lose fitting prison garb like everyone else. "I am so honored to meet you, Doctor. I used to take the young people from my church to hear you and many accepted the Lord. Thank you for what you did for the people of Israel."

"You can get hauled off and beaten if you continue to talk like that, John," another man two bunks over said in a loud voice. "Please, stop talking to him, it will just get us into trouble." The voice sounded angry and fearful. "I have had one beating; I don't want another." He put the flimsy cover over his face as he turned his back on the group.

"That is Hamadi, he is a Palestinian pastor and worked in Jerusalem when they arrested him in a restaurant, talking to another pastor. He left behind a wife and three children across the border and will probably never see them again, because they will not be allowed to come into Israel now." John was whispering.

"Do you know most of the people here in this camp?" Caleb asked.

"I have been here since it was established about a year ago. From what I can see, they take only leaders like pastors, elders and other important people in the churches. This way they hope to disperse the believers and the churches will cease to exist."

"Who started these camps?"

"One of the major players is Rabbi Shamir and some of his friends in the Jewish religious hierarchy. They feel extremely threatened by the number of Christians in Israel since Dr. Peterson has come here." He turned to Thomas. "You and your ministry are the ones they want to eliminate, but for some reason something or someone has prevented that and sent you here instead. There is great excitement in the camp when word got around yesterday that you have come. Now we all have hope."

"There is very little I can do." Thomas said. "I have just been appointed to be the medical doctor of the camp by Rabbi Shamir, but that doesn't mean I can do anything to help anyone other than medically."

"You see, that is the weird part. Why are they not killing you or torturing you in here?" John was getting excited. "Something doesn't make any sense. The Rabbi was your greatest enemy and now he makes you a doctor. What could possibly have happened that would make him do that?"

"I have no idea," Thomas answered. "I just thank Yeshua for allowing me to be here and helping people when they get sick."

Chapter 41

A month had gone by and life had settled into a routine of going to the infirmary every day and coming back to the barracks in the evening. Rachel turned out to be much less difficult than he had expected. She was a crusty soul with a good heart and the two of them managed to get along quite well. But no matter how Thomas tried, she would not allow him to share about Yeshua.

"Don't even go there," she would say when he started. "I am here because I listened once and look where it got me. Besides, the whole thing is a hoax and in any case, I can't say I believe in God or any kind of religion. From what I've seen, it doesn't bring anything but trouble into people's lives."

That day, early in the morning, Meta came into the clinic, accompanied by a guard. Thomas started to greet her and give her a hug, when she stared at him with such an empty look, he backed up.

"Meta, what can I do for you?"

"She is here for an abortion," the female guard said.

"An abortion?" Thomas was aghast. "Meta, sweetheart, what happened? Who hurt you?"

"She is the camp commander's girlfriend," the guard answered for her. "He wants you to take care of her."

"You tell that swine I do not do abortions." Thomas had all he could do to remain calm.

"You do as you are told, Doctor or you will be beaten."

"Then you will have to beat me, but I refuse to kill a baby."

"Thomas, just go ahead and do it, I don't care." Meta's voice was lifeless and her eyes looked at him with such sorrow, it took his breath away."

"Meta, sweetheart, I will not do this. Listen to me, trust in Yeshua, He is with you, no matter what's happened to you. Turn to Him and give your life to Him, even here."

There was a glimmer of life in her eyes as he spoke.

"I will try."

"You tell your commander that I will not do this, no matter what you do to me," Thomas shouted. He shook with anger. "How dare he treat this beautiful girl in such a way!"

The guard shrugged her shoulder and motioned for Meta to leave.

"You will hear more about this, Doctor," she said with a sneer.

That afternoon, two burly guards took Thomas to the infamous pole in the middle of the camp.

"Take your top off," one of them yelled.

When he refused, the other ripped if off of him.

Thomas stood with his head down as fear flooded through him. He remembered when they beat Yeshua and cringed. *Lord, I don't do well with pain. You have been in this place, You know how much it hurts. Please be with me and take the pain away.*

But the Lord did not. Thomas felt the first lash and it was every bit as searing as he imagined it to be. By the time the tenth lash fell on his back, he collapsed, screaming in agony.

When they finally stopped, his back was a bloody mess and he lay on the ground whimpering like a child. Two prisoners helped him get up and walked him to the infirmary, where he was put on a table, where Rachel cleaned his wounds.

He couldn't see it, but he heard her crying as she worked on his back with Paul watching.

"The cruel bastards," she whispered. "I can't believe they would do this; they are no better than the Nazis were." She looked at Paul to see if he was listening.

"I agree with you, Rachel. Please help him, he is a good man and doesn't deserve this."

"Why won't he do an abortion, there is nothing wrong with it?" she asked.

"Because God has made this child, even done in this way and Thomas will not kill it, even if they threaten to kill him."

"How do you know this?"

"I just know, don't ask."

"You are a Christian aren't you?" She looked at him through tears. "I have always suspected, but now I know."

"Are you going to turn me in?" He held his breath.

"I won't. These people are evil and I don't want to have anything to do with them."

"I thought you hated Christians?"

"I guess not, now that I see who the bad guys are. Dr. Peterson is an honest, kind man who has treated everyone with love and respect as far as I have seen. He is truly a good man and doesn't deserve this."

Thomas heard everything she said.

"Rachel," he said in a weak voice, "be careful what you say, they will do the same to you."

"Let them, I am so angry and ashamed that my people will do this kind of thing. They are no better than the Muslim terrorists."

"Rachel, don't hate them. Yeshua says to love your enemies and do good to those who spitefully use you."

"You are kidding, right? You want me to love these horrible monsters? What kind of a wimpy God is this Yeshua?"

"He is a God of mercy and will forgive them if they repent. He died for people just like them so they can turn around and change their ways and accept Him as their Meshiah. That is why He came, to save us and become more like Him."

"Thomas, you must be delirious. Now be quiet so I can bandage you up." It was the first time she called him Thomas.

It took several days for his back to heal to the point, he could stand or walk without pain. After a week, he was told to go back to work. Paul had inquired about Meta and came back with the sad tale of her ordeal.

"They sent her to a doctor on the outside and he performed the abortion," he told Thomas.

That morning she came in for a check-up. Her face was a stony mask and she made no attempt to talk.

"Meta, tell me how you are. I am worried about you. Are you with the others from the team and are they taking care of you?" But no matter how he tried, Thomas could not get her to say anything. It was as if she was in a catatonic state and couldn't hear what he was saying. Finally, in desperation, after he was done with the examination, he laid his hands on her and prayed, "Lord Yeshua, Meta has served You faithfully. Reach down into her mind, her soul and her spirit and touch her with Your love and heal her wounded soul. Please, Lord, do it because You love her."

Rachel watched him as he prayed and started to cry.

Meta got up from the examining table and got dressed in silence. Before she walked out, she put her hand on Thomas' face and said in a whisper,

"I love you, Thomas, don't worry about me. Yeshua has heard you. My faith is intact and I will serve Him, no matter what comes. I will not hate, but forgive and so keep myself from dying on the inside," she said and walked out.

Rachel stood as if mesmerized.

"I cannot believe this. Are you telling me, this woman has forgiven the monster who is doing this to her all because this Yeshua wants her to?"

"Yes, Rachel, that is what it means to be a Christian. It is not just saying you believe, but doing what Yeshua says to do. And He is not just talking either, because I was there in my dream as He forgave those who killed Him."

"Thomas, would you tell me about this dream? Everybody talks about it, but I have never actually heard what happened."

"I will be glad to. Maybe later this afternoon, we have time as we clean up after work."

And so it was, that Thomas told Rachel about the journey he took into the ancient land of Israel; how he met the Meshiah, who told him to preach the Good News to His people before His return. When he was finished, Rachel sat, astonished and awed.

"I wish I had listened to the many people who tried to tell me about their faith. Instead, I had to come to prison to be set free. I want this Yeshua, Thomas. I want to give Him my life the way you did and learn to walk in faith and forgiveness instead of hatred." She sat down in a chair and cried as she prayed to receive her Meshiah.

From that day on, Thomas was free to pray and minister to the many who came to be treated by him since everyone in the infirmary was now a believer. As word spread, there were suddenly a lot of people in the camp who had mysterious illnesses, insisting they had to go see the doctor.

Chapter 42

The conditions in the camp were appalling, lacking adequate sanitation and food. People were beaten for the least offenses and the constant fear of being killed demoralized the inmates to the point they renounced Yeshua just to get on the good side of the guards. The women of the team, except for Meta, who was still bound to the camp commander, worked twelve hours in the kitchen and laundry under harsh conditions. The men had to clean the compound, fix the fences and anything else that required manual labor. In the process they were able to pray and encourage many. Especially Bob proved to be tireless in ministering to everyone he could without getting caught.

One day there was a great commotion in the camp. Thomas found out from Paul that several prisoners had escaped. This happened quite frequently, a sign the Rabbi's underground network was working. He had heard from several prisoners that someone worked tirelessly to smuggle people out of Galilee to Jerusalem, where they could disappear in the big city into safe houses. Thomas wondered if it was Yitz and if so, how long could he keep his Christianity a secret until he would be caught and killed or put into one of the camps.

"It is time for you and your team to leave," Paul said to Thomas as they watched the guards search the camp for the missing prisoners. "There is talk the authorities want to override the Rabbi Shamir and have all of you killed, especially you, Thomas. Apparently, imprisoning the Christian leaders is not working, because the number of underground churches is still growing."

"How can we leave, Paul, I have no way to organize it so my entire team can escape. Besides, I have to take care of the sick in here, not just with medicine, but more so with prayer."

"You won't do anyone any good dead, will you, Thomas?" was all he answered. "I will be the go-between with your team members. It will take a few days to find out how it can be done. I do know there is a group of prisoners who, with the help of someone on the outside, can arrange it. I have no idea who that someone is, but it has to be a higher up leader.

Thomas smiled. He knew, it was Yitz.

Several days later, a man came into the infirmary with a complaint of a stomach ache. When Thomas checked him out, he could find nothing wrong.

"I am here to tell you to get ready to leave, Doctor. Everything is ready," the man whispered under his breath. "All except the girlfriend of the camp commander, we cannot get close to her."

"I won't leave without her."

"Are you willing to let everyone else on your team die?"

"I won't leave without her, she is family."

"Then wait until we can try and notify her. From what we know, both the guard and the nurse in here are Christians. Would they help?"

"Yes, they would. As a matter of fact, can you include Rachel, my nurse in the escape?"

"We don't have room for her in the van."

"We will make room." Thomas looked at the man thoughtfully. "If Meta, that is the woman with the camp commander, if she can complain about some ailment, she can come to the infirmary and I can tell her what's going on. But you have to let me know the exact day and time when this is going down so I can let her know."

"Maybe you can fabricate something serious so she has to stay here over night. It would make it so much easier for everyone."

"What is your name?" Thomas asked.

"I don't have a name, it's safer that way."

"I will ask the Lord to richly bless you for what you are doing."

"That is about all I can expect, because if I get caught, my life is over, but it is what the Lord has for me to do." He looked at Thomas with a smile. "I don't expect to ever get out of here alive."

It was three days later when Meta appeared at the clinic with a female guard.

"She is sick, do something or you will get flogged." The guard sounded bored. "I will go outside for a smoke."

"Meta, I am going to give you some stuff that will make you sick to your stomach and throw up. That way, I can tell the guard you have to stay here tonight."

"I am ready. A guard named Paul told me, we are breaking out of here tonight, is that true?"

"Yes, it is. Here, take this. It will take effect right away, but by tonight you will be fine." Thomas handed her a spoon filled with a brown liquid. "It is harmless, go ahead."

When Thomas told the guard Meta had to stay overnight, she didn't object.

"I will tell the commander. She will be safe here without me. I will pick her up in the morning."

Rachel looked at Thomas.

"I don't know if I want to do this; I'm afraid. They will do terrible things to us if we get caught."

"They will do terrible things to you if they find you here and Meta and I gone."

"I hadn't thought of that. I guess I really don't have a choice, do I?"

"The Lord is not through with me yet, He will protect me and the team just like He has done before." Thomas sounded sure. "Come with us, Rachel, you have been faithful and deserve to go back to your family."

"No I won't, that's the first place they will look for me."

"You can still get in touch with them later until they have stopped looking for you."

The rest of the day went agonizingly slow. Both Thomas and Rachel were nervous and anxiously waiting for someone to come and tell them what was going to happen. Paul had asked for a day off so he would not get blamed for the escape. For some reason, he was not replaced with anyone else.

It was around midnight, when the door to the infirmary slowly opened. A man in black clothing waved to them to follow him. They made their way to a truck standing close to the fence near an entrance at the back of the camp. It was used for delivery vehicles. When they reached the truck, the man motioned for them to get in the back. To their surprise, every one of the team members were there, laying in a row on the truck bed. Thomas, Meta and Rachel silently laid down in the spaces left for them and the truck slowly moved toward the exit.

When the vehicle was outside of the camp, it did not stop, but kept driving on for about fifteen minutes. When it came to a halt on the side of the road, a male voice spoke,

"Dr. Peterson, please come with me."

Thomas got up and jumped off the truck and was led to a waiting car. Before he could ask about the rest of the team, the truck had moved on. He was asked to get in the car and it sped away into the night without delay.

"Who are you?" he asked the two men up front.

"We are under orders to take you to Jerusalem."

"What about my team?"

"Don't worry, they are safe."

"Who are you working for?"

"That we cannot tell you. Just relax, you will be ok."

Thomas leaned back into the seat. He worried about the others. Why had they taken him and not them? Somehow the escape had been too easy, too smooth to be real. There was no way that many people could escape without anyone noticing. He couldn't see the two men in front of him because of the darkness. They were definitely Jewish and sounded educated.

Before long, the lights of Jerusalem came into view on the horizon. He strained to see where they were going, but couldn't make out any landmarks he recognized. Finally, the car drove into a long driveway lined with trees and came to a stop in front of a large villa. The two men took him inside to a nicely furnished room with an adjacent bathroom.

"Try to get some sleep, it will be a long day tomorrow," one of them said and left.

Thomas sat on the edge of the bed, wondering who could have organized his release from the camp. His main concern was the team and he had an uneasy feeling about their wellbeing, but realized there was nothing he could do for them. He laid down on the bed and soon fell asleep.

The bright sunlight woke him up. It took a minute for him to remember where he was. When he went to the bathroom, he marveled at the beautiful shower and soon used a half a bottle of body soap to scrub himself clean for the first time in months. When he finally stepped out, he saw the neatly folded pile of clothes on the side. A toothbrush, toothpaste and an electric razor made him feel like he had arrived at a five-star hotel.

"Bless whoever is making this possible," he said out loud as the razor took away the last vestiges of prison life. He felt great. "All I need now is a good breakfast and life is good," he said with a chuckle. "Whoever abducted me, knows how to spoil a man after months in prison."

"You are to come with me, Dr. Peterson," one of the men from last night said through the door. "Breakfast is waiting."

"That sounds good to me, I haven't had a decent breakfast or any other meal for many months." He turned to look at the man. He was middle-aged with dark hair and an open, clean shaven, friendly face. He was dressed in a business suit and smiled at Thomas.

"Come, the boss is waiting for you."

They walked down a long corridor until they stopped in front of a door.

"This is as far as I go; just go on in."

Thomas stepped through the door, curious to see who his benefactor was, when he saw a man sitting at a table by a large window. He had his back to him. Thomas hesitated and then slowly walked toward him.

"Come and join me, Dr. Peterson. I have a good American breakfast with all the trimmings waiting for you."

Chapter 43

The truck rumbled down narrow, dirt roads for the rest of the night. Without anything but a few thin blankets, their bodies were sore and bruised by the time it finally stopped on the edge of a large air strip. A lone plane stood in the distance in front of a large hanger.

"This is as far as I can take you, I have to turn around and go back before this car is reported missing." The man in the black clothes motioned for them to get off the truck bed.

"Go to where you see the plane, it will take you out of Israel and to safety. May the Lord bless you and be with you. Shalom." He smiled and climbed back into the cab before anyone could thank him.

Caleb looked at the others.

"I think we are safe, but what about Thomas?"

"We can't leave him behind," Bob said, "what are we going to do?"

"There is nothing we can do since we don't know where he is," Karl said. "The Lord still has something for him to do or He would not have allowed them to take him."

"Let's walk to where the plane is, maybe the pilot can tell us where we are going," Caleb looked at the group. "I everybody ok? How about you, Meta, can you walk that far?"

"I am fine, Caleb, I lived better than all the rest of you with that man. He treated me alright, if you can call living like that alright." Her voice was strong. "I have lived through a nightmare, but so have we all."

It took about ten minutes for them to reach the hanger. A man was standing in the doorway, smoking a cigarette.

"It's about time you people showed up. We got to get out of here before the sun is fully up." He pointed to the open door of the plane. "Everybody, get in as fast as you can."

"Where are you taking us?" Caleb asked.

"Cyprus. From there you have to contact your embassy to get you home, wherever that is."

"Some of us are Israeli citizen," Petra said. "Are they going to take us?"

"I don't know. All I am supposed to do is drop you off there."

"Who hired you?" Caleb asked.

"I don't know, some Arab guy, he paid me in cash and didn't give me his name."

Within ten minutes, the plane was in the air. For some strange reason the Israeli defense system did nothing to stop it and after a little over an hour, they landed safely in Cyprus.

Chapter 44

"Yusuf Nabeth!"

Fouad's brother motioned for him to sit.

"You deserve a good meal after all those months in Rabbi Shamir's personal hell."

"How did you get me and my team out so easy?"

"My father's name still carries great weight in spite of his declining health. The strange thing is, he would not let it rest and insisted that I bring you here. Since I couldn't do it without his word in the right places, I had no choice but to separate you from your team."

"Where are they?"

"They should be in Cyprus by now."

Cyprus?"

"Father has connections with some shady characters there and they allowed the plane to land at an isolated air strip. He also made a call to let the plane out of Israel without too many questions."

"So he really is with the Muslim Brotherhood?"

"I don't know and if I did, I wouldn't say. He is an old man now and can't do much damage anymore. He has some good days and bad, but I think his guilt is destroying him from within. It is a sad thing to see."

"Thanks, Yusuf. We all owe you our lives."

"Don't thank me, thank my father. He is the one who wanted to see you set free so he can talk to you."

"Do you know what he wants to talk to me about?"

"I don't know, but it's the least I can do for him."

"There is one thing I can do, Yusuf for saving my life." Thomas looked at the handsome young man with a smile. "I told you about the time I spent with Yeshua so many years ago. He still wants you to be His, just like He wanted your brother. The time is short, because He will return soon. Don't miss His call, but accept Him as your Meshiah."

"I have thought about that often since you spoke to me the last time and have started studying the Koran. There is much good in it, but also much of it I cannot believe or want to do. Allah is a stern god, demanding absolute obedience. But then, Yehovah is the same when you think of the Crusaders and the things they did in the name of their God. So what's the difference?"

"It is always wrong to judge a religion by what people do, Yusuf. To know what Yeshua is like, you have to read and then judge what He did and asks us to do, not by what we actually do. The Lord walked this earth for three years healing the sick, forgiving the sinners and loving those who turned to Him. To forgive your enemies is the purest form of righteousness and that is what He did and asks us to do. Allah on the other hand tells you to kill those who not only are your enemies, but who do not wish to follow him. Unconditional love is what Yeshua preached, unconditional hate is what Allah demanded when he demanded the death of your brother and his wife and child for no other reason, but that they would no longer follow him. It is this difference that shows you which god is the greater. Look at what this demand of hate and the inability of your father to ask for forgiveness for murdering his children and grandchild has done for him. He is condemned in himself if he does not repent and equally condemned if he does, because he would be in disobedience to Allah. The dilemma in his mind and heart is not from the murder he committed alone, but that he is stuck between his heart being sorry and his faith telling him he can't be. It is a prison from which there is no escape. What a terrible place to be in, when he could turn to Yeshua and find not only forgiveness and peace, but eternal life with a loving God who desires for him to live with Him as a beloved son." Thomas looked at Yusuf intently as he went on, "Do not miss your chance like your father does and accept Yeshua into your heart. Turn your life over to Him and you also will find forgiveness, peace and eternal life in His Kingdom. What are seventy-two virgins, but an empty promise and a meaningless promise of carnal pleasures. Your body rots in the grave when you die, it is your spirit that will either go to heaven or hell, it is your choice."

Yusuf Nabeth looked at Thomas for a long time.

"You have a way with words, Thomas. Although, the additional pain it would cause my father if I became a Christian after he sacrificed one son and his family, would be beyond measure.

"Yahweh sacrificed His one and only Son so that you and I may live, have you considered that?"

Yusuf stared at Thomas in astonishment.

"I have never thought about it that way. Would it be alright with Yeshua if I didn't tell my father that I have become a Christian?"

"Yes, Yusuf, it would, because it is not what you do that changes your father's heart, but it is what the Holy Spirit does. Yeshua wants you to continue to be an obedient son to him by loving and honoring him the way you have. Nothing says that you cannot love and obey the Lord at the same time."

"Then I will pray with you and accept this Jewish Meshiah as my God. Maybe He will save my father from this terrible mental prison in time as well."

Yusuf did not tell his father that Thomas was at his house for many days, because he wanted to have some time to learn and read more about Yeshua and his new faith. They spent hours together, studying and reading the New Testament. It was as if a light had been turned on in his heart.

During that time Thomas watched the news for the first time in months and was horrified at the changes in the world. It looked as if Mohamed Abdul Musharak, the Secretary General of the United Nations, was firmly in control of the many member countries. The world over he was heralded as the only one who could bring peace and order into the chaos. Even Thomas was astounded at the brilliant ways he had accomplished what no one else had been able to do before. Countries, who had been bitter enemies, were suddenly able to stand together under his able leadership. Even Israel started to rally behind him at the prospect of peace with Palestine and the other Arabic countries. Rocket attacks had seized and for the first time since anyone could remember, the Jewish people felt safe. There was no doubt in Thomas' mind, this was the anti-Christ and the Lord's return was imminent.

There was one report that filled him with joy. The team had returned safely to the US. Shalom Outreach in Chicago was involved with the State Department, demanding a search for Dr. Thomas Peterson, the famous Philadelphia doctor, who became a

Preacher and healer in Israel. The Israeli government promised co-operation and expressed feelings of concern for his disappearance, but did not do much other than talk.

"Why don't you want to get in touch with your people?" Yusuf asked Thomas.

"Because it would cause the government to send me home and I have not finished my purpose yet. I don't know why I feel that way, I just do. The Lord will let me know when it is time to leave."

"How about your family, could I not call them and let them know you are safe?"

"My father and grandmother are believers, they will trust the Lord and know I am either dead or still doing what the Lord has for me to do."

"As you wish," Yusuf said. "By the way, I heard that the Rabbi Shamir has been arrested and is in the camp where you were. They caught him helping Christians escape. Not only that, so was Ibrahim Berger, the former Prime Minister. He was arrested as he attended a church service in Tel Aviv with his wife. Both of them are at a camp, I don't know which one. The government has not allowed any reports about either one of them to be released, since it might cause riots among the population."

"I knew somehow this was inevitable for both of them; and so did they. They are too prominent to be able to hide their faith in the long run. I am amazed it took this long for the truth to catch up with them. I am almost certain they will be killed in order to silence their whereabouts permanently." Thomas sighed deeply. "I bet the government wishes they had killed me when they had me in the camp. It would be very difficult for them to eliminate me now that the world knows I might still be alive."

The next day, Yusuf told Thomas, his father was having a good day and it was time to take him to see him. Thomas was nervous. He remembered the anger and hatred from the last time they met and couldn't figure out why the old man wanted to talk to him. The words of his command to the young man in the room, 'beat him until he is dead', still rang in his mind. He couldn't imagine he had changed his mind.

"I can't say I am looking forward to this, Yusuf. Your father can get very angry."

"I know, but he didn't sound angry at all when I told him we were coming. Actually, he was unusually calm."

"That makes me even more nervous," Thomas said as they drove up to the iron gate to the villa. "I am having flashbacks of my last visit."

"I will be there with you and won't let anything happen." Yusuf sounded confident.

Mohamed Yusuf Nabeth sat in his favorite big chair as they walked into the spacious living room. He looked considerably older than when Thomas saw him last.

"Here you are, Dr. Peterson, the man who took my son away from me."

"Father, you promised you would be polite to Dr. Peterson," Yusuf said before he could go on. "I will not stand for you to insult this man. He has done nothing wrong and you know it."

"Have a seat, Dr. Peterson," the old man motioned to a chair across from him and then turned to Yusuf, "I want to talk to him alone, please leave us."

Yusuf looked at Thomas. He nodded in agreement.

"I will be ok."

"It is good to see you, Mr. Nabeth. I hope you are well. I want to thank you for getting me and my team out of the camp."

"I did not do it because I am a kind old man who felt sorry for you. I did it so I can tell you what you have done to me and my family." He looked at Thomas with deep sorrow. "I am a broken man, void of any feelings other than sadness, regret, guilt and shame with no other way out but death." He leaned forward with an intense look on his face. "I want you to help me die."

Thomas sat, stunned.

"I cannot take a life, Mr. Nabeth, not for any reason, but I can give you life by offering you salvation through Yeshua. He will forgive you and take you home as His beloved son if you ask Him to."

"I cannot do that, Dr. Peterson. Allah is an unforgiving task master and will never allow me to leave him."

"Allah does not exist, Sir, except in your mind. There is no God but One and He sent His Son to die for you so that you may live with Him in eternity."

"How do you know that?"

"I have seen Him in my dream and He has confirmed it with countless, dramatic miracles over the last three years. He is real and His love and power is also real. Accept Him and He will prove it to you."

"You have a lot of courage to come and preach to me, Doctor. Don't you know I can still kill you in spite of what my son thinks? I am not this tottering, senile old man whose mind is gone and his body is wasting away. Even if he is right, there is just one more thing I need to do before I die and I will not rest until it is done. After that I have no doubt I will rot in hell because of the way I lived my life. There is no God who would ever forgive me, whether it be Allah or this Yeshua. I am lost and that is that." He wiped his forehead in a tired gesture. "I asked you to help me die before I can do what has to be done, but since you refuse, so be it."

"What is it you have to do, Sir?"

"That is none of your concern. You may go."

Chapter 45

Thomas was quiet on the way back to Yusuf's house. He did not want to burden his friend with what his father had asked him to do.

"It was a good, honest talk, Yusuf. Your father is a remarkable man. I am just sorry I could not convince him to accept Yeshua."

"I didn't think so. He is a firm follower of Allah and cannot change."

"It reminds me of my mother. She could not believe in God, any god, even on her deathbed. It broke my heart. I still hope the Lord somehow reached her before she died, that is all I can do to deal with it."

"Why is it God choses some people and not others to reach out to Him?" Yusuf asked. "It doesn't seem fair."

"I don't know. Many scholars have asked that question. The answer is reserved for God to know. All we can do is present the Gospel and leave the choice up for each to make. I know He doesn't reject anyone if they ask for salvation, but I don't know why some won't, no matter how often they hear the truth. I did present this truth to your father and he understood that it was his choice, but somehow could not bring himself to make it. Although, I had the distinct feeling, his faith in Allah was not near as strong as it used to be. I am very sure he understands the cruelty that was asked of him by Allah and the horrible prison of guilt and shame it has put him in to be unable to ask for forgiveness."

"Maybe there is yet time." Yusuf sounded deeply saddened. "I know my father has done terrible things in his life, but he is my father and I love him."

They sat in silence for the rest of the way.

Thomas could not go to sleep that evening. His thoughts were of his father and grandmother. He knew they were terribly worried about him, no matter how much he told himself they were believers and could handle it. He knew he would have to call them, no matter the consequences. Slowly, he picked up the cell phone Yusuf had given him to use and dialed.

His father's sleepy voice answered.

"Dad, its Tommy."

"Oh thank you, Lord. Tommy, how are you? Where are you?" He was yelling. "Please tell me, are you alright?"

"Dad, I am fine. I am staying in a very nice home with friends and I am well. How are you and Nana?"

"We are fine, son, especially now that we know you are alive. We have talked to your team. Nana and I went to Chicago when they returned. We heard all the stories of your experience in the camp and the escape. Do you know who got you guys out?"

"Yes, I do, Dad, but I can't tell you anything, it is too dangerous. I have no idea what is going to happen from here on or if I will ever be able to call you again. Give my love to Nana and tell her I love her. I love you, Dad, keep praying for me, I have a feeling I may need it."

"I love you, too, Tommy. The Lord keep you safe."

Thomas hung up with a heavy heart. He somehow knew it was the last time he would ever talk to his father. There was a feeling of foreboding in him he couldn't shake in spite of everything looking calm on the outside. Israel experienced a time of calm, if not peace. People were optimistic and life was getting back to normal after a long time. He knew it wouldn't last.

The next morning, he found Yusuf up and ready to go back to work.

"I have to go to the office, there are many things I have neglected for so long. I will see you later," he said on the way out. Thomas sat for a long time, not sure what to do alone in the big house with just a few servants. He was not used to inactivity like this and knew he had to find something to do. He turned the TV on.

"We interrupt our regular program with this important USN Headline News Alert. The Secretary of State, Herbert Downy, in a short statement to the press a few moments ago, has confirmed that Iran has declared war on the state of Israel. Due to the volatile and dangerous situation in the Middle East, he has issued a travel advisory for all US citizen for the entire region. All air traffic between the US and the Middle East has been suspended as of now. All non-essential personal in Israel and most of the Middle

Eastern countries have been ordered to leave immediately via special military transportation. All other American citizens are urged to contact the State Department or the American Consulate in order to be evacuated immediately. Secretary Downey emphasized that it is entirely possible that any delay might make it impossible for the State Department to be of any assistance later, due to the possibility of nuclear war in the region.

When asked the question if the White House is seriously considering the possibility of a nuclear confrontation, the Secretary declined to answer and promised more information as soon as it becomes available.

Stay tuned as USN Headline News, as always, will bring you the latest updates as soon as we have them. This is Marsha Kendrick with USN Headline News."

"There goes the peace promised by Musharak," Thomas said out loud. "It didn't last long, did it?" But then he remembered the prophecy of Yeshua in Matthew 24:21 where He says,

"There will be a great distress, unequaled from the beginning of the world until now."

And then the prophetic vision of Daniel 9:24-27 where he says that the Antichrist will confirm a covenant with Israel and many of the nations for a seven-year period, which will be the beginning of his reign. He still didn't understand all that was to know about this time and wished he had paid closer attention to when Melissa tried to get him to listen to the many teachings about the subject. Maybe this declaration of war was only an empty threat by Iran to keep Israel from bombing their nuclear test areas. The current leader was a fervent believer that in order for the Muslim Meshiah to come, he had to find the believers in mortal combat with Israel and other non-believers. This was in contrast to Yeshua, who will not be in conflict with the human race, but with Satan and the Antichrist and finish the enemy of mankind off once and for all and establish His Kingdom on earth. It is the culmination of the battle that began with Adam and Eve in the Garden and will be won by the returning Meshiah Yeshua.

Thomas stared at the TV set. There was still time to share the Gospel and he made up his mind, that is what he would do, but unless, Yeshua opened the door for him, he had no idea how.

It was several days later. Israel breathed a sigh of relief when Musharak announced he had convinced Iran to withdraw its declaration of war. It confirmed his position as leader of the world, who brought peace among the nations, even the Middle East. Even the Jews were ready to follow him when the Israeli government was assured that no one would be allowed to do any harm to their country as soon as the peace treaty was signed.

Thomas was sitting alone in the beautiful courtyard of Yusuf's home. The family had gone to visit relatives in Jerusalem. He enjoyed the peace and quiet and was reading the Bible, when he heard someone ring the front door. The servant answered and then cried out in fear. Four men appeared in the door and stared at Thomas, guns drawn.

"You will come with us, Preacher."

"This is getting old," Thomas said as he rose from his seat. "I wonder who wants me this time."

"Shut up or I will make sure you will never speak again, infidel." He was a burly man with a rough looking beard and unruly hair. He grabbed Thomas and shoved him toward the front door. "You are coming with us." His English was minimal, but Thomas didn't need words to know this was not going to be a pleasant drive into the country.

He was shoved into an expensive limousine and thrown onto the backseat. Before he had time to sit up, they sped off and out of the city of Tel Aviv toward the open country. There was no fear in Thomas as he looked out at the beautiful, green, lush fields on both sides of the road. As always, he thought of the time he drove through these lands in a carriage with Lucius on the way to see patients or listen to Yeshua. The men with him spoke Arabic and he did not understand what they were saying, although he did make out the name Nabeth several times.

That's when it dawned on him what Mohamed Nabeth had been talking about when he said he had one more thing to do before he died. He was going to kill him! *Oh God.*

His heart started pounding. This was it, he was going to die. Fear gripped him like a vice and he suddenly felt cold.

Lord, if this is the day I am going to die, please give me peace and strength to meet You with joy. I give you my life gladly, but I am still afraid to die, I hope you understand. I remember You in the Garden when You cried out to the Father to let that cup pass You by. I now say with you, please do not let this happen. But just like You did, I now tell you that Your will be done. I am ready to meet You and my Melissa and Helena.

The car turned toward a solitary house at the foot of Mt. Tabor. It was surrounded by a cluster of trees. A black car stood in front of it. Thomas was asked to step out and one of the men led him through a simple, wooden door. The inside was dark and smelled dusty. It was more like a barn than a house, with no furniture, just a bare room with old farm equipment and a few chairs around a beat-up table.

Thomas was not surprised when he saw Mohamed Abdul Nabeth sitting there, facing him with a grim expression on his face.

"This is what I have held on for, Preacher. It is the only way I can find peace before I die to make up for the loss of my son and my grandchild. Maybe Allah will accept me into paradise if I kill you. I know it will please him and he may have mercy on me after all."

Thomas knew he spoke Arabic, but he heard only English and knew the Lord was with Him.

"Allah doesn't exist, Mohamed. It is not too late for you to accept Yeshua. Even if you kill me, He will still forgive you if you ask Him." Thomas felt a strange, wonderful calm as he spoke. "I am ready to die. I forgive you, Mohamed and pray that God may have mercy on you. I can truly say that I love you and want for you to be with me in paradise when I meet my Yeshua Meshiah."

"Take him," the old man said in a monotone voice "Take him and make it quick.

"Kneel with your head down, infidel," the burly man said. "And don't move, it will go easier that way."

In the next instant there was a brilliant light. Thomas stood perfectly still, his body feeling light and free of weight. Suddenly, he saw "someone like a son of man, dressed in a robe reaching down to his feet and with a golden sash around his chest. His head and hair were white like wool, as white as snow, and his eyes were like blazing fire. His feet were like bronze glowing in a furnace, and his voice was like the sound of rushing waters. His face was like the sun shining in all its brilliance." (Revelation 1:13-16)

Yet somehow, Thomas did not know how, the Lord looked exactly the same as He had in his dream. He fell to his knees and held up his arms in worship, overwhelmed by joy, peace and awe at the splendor of His Being. And then he heard Him speak with His old familiar voice,

"Well done, My good and faithful servant! You have been faithful with a few things; I will put you in charge of many things. Come and share your master's happiness!" (Matthew 25:21)

Yeshua smiled at him with His wonderful, warm smile and it filled him with such unspeakable joy, he could barely contain it.

When he looked up, he saw Melissa and little Helena walk toward him. She was a little older and looked very much like His Helena from the dream. Right behind them was his friend Lucius, holding out his arms held in welcome. Next to him stood Nicodemus, dressed in the robes of the Sanhedrin, greeting him with a welcoming smile. And finally, he saw all the people he had led to the saving knowledge of their Meshiah. It was a great multitude, dressed in white robes and praising Yeshua.

Not the End, but the Beginning of the Future

If you read this book and do not know Jesus as your Savior and Lord, please join me in this prayer. It is written just for you so that you may also be one of those dressed in white in the presence of the King of Kings, Yeshua.

Dear Lord,

I am a sinner. Just like Thomas, I am a flawed person and not worthy to come to You and ask for forgiveness. But Your word says You came for the sinners and I am one of them. I give You my life and want to serve You, my Meshiah, until You call me home to be with You for all eternity as Your beloved child. Amen.

Dear Reader,

If you have enjoyed the two books, **MORE THAN A DREAM** and this sequel **COUNTDOWN TO THE FUTURE**, please consider writing a review on Amazon to let other potential readers know your opinions and thoughts. Reviews are the lifeline of any writer and will help to spread the "Word" in more ways than one. (Both are available on Kindle and in paperback)

Please go to my website **at www.barbarahmartin.com** to purchase some or all of my other six books. You can also find out how to schedule a **speaking engagement**. I have been a motivational speaker and teacher for many years with my books or any subject suitable for your church, women's organization, seminar or conference.

Here is a description of my other six books which you can find on Amazon or on my website.

WHEN THE EAST WIND BLOWS, a #1 bestseller with a 4.5-star rating on Amazon, is a modern day historical novel and deals with my mother's story during the last six months of WWII in Nazi Germany. It tells of her heroic flight from the incoming Russian front into the carpet bombing of the Allies with her four children and a maid. On the way they meet up with an escaped Jewish concentration camp prisoner who then travels with them dressed as a girl. (available on Kindle. In paperback **only** through my website)

THE LITTLE BOOK OF MIRACLES shares 16 inspirational stories of real, astounding miracles which happened over the many years since I came from atheism to finding the Lord in a dramatic way. (available on Kindle. In paperback **only** through my website)

WALKING IN POWER deals with a deeper walk in the spiritual realm with personal experiences and comparisons between today's Christianity and the early church. It can be used as a study guide for Bible studies, using Scripture as back up. (Available on Kindle. In paperback **only** through my website)

If you like good, clean suspenseful Christian murder mysteries, you will love the **PERFECT CRIME TRILOGY**. (All three are available on Kindle and in paperback)

SILK SHEETS AND OTHER THINGS THAT DON'T WORK
A parody on getting old together with all the changes and pitfalls, wrinkles and quirks that come with being married for a long time. In reading this book, you will find yourself and your spouse with amusing clarity and realize, all things considered, getting old together is not so bad after all. (only available on Kindle)

If you wish to get in touch with me or have any questions, please go to my website at **www.barbarahmartin.com** and click on 'Contact'. I will answer all correspondence promptly if at all possible. May God bless you.

Made in the USA
Columbia, SC
27 November 2017